FILMING JOHN FOWLES

FILMING JOHN FOWLES

Critical Essays on Motion Picture and Television Adaptations

Edited by
JAMES AUBREY

McFarland & Company, Inc., Publishers
Jefferson, North Carolina

LIBRARY OF CONGRESS CATALOGUING-IN-PUBLICATION DATA

Filming John Fowles : critical essays on motion picture and
television adaptations / edited by James Aubrey.

p.   cm.

Includes bibliographical references and index.

ISBN 978-0-7864-9764-5 (softcover : acid free paper) ∞
ISBN 978-1-4766-2230-9 (ebook)

1. Fowles, John, 1926–2005—Film adaptations.   2. English
fiction—20th century—Film adaptations.   3. Film adaptations—
History and criticism.   I. Aubrey, James, 1945– editor.

PR6056.O85Z663 2015
823'.914—dc23   2015019244

BRITISH LIBRARY CATALOGUING DATA ARE AVAILABLE

On the cover: Meryl Streep in the 1981 film *The French
Lieutenant's Woman* (United Artists/Photofest)

Printed in the United States of America

McFarland & Company, Inc., Publishers
Box 611, Jefferson, North Carolina 28640
www.mcfarlandpub.com

In memory of
John Robert Fowles,
1926–2005

Acknowledgments

I was first alerted to John Fowles's interest in film by the late Liz-Anne Bawden, retired professor of cinema at the Slade School of Art in London and 1990s curator of the Lyme Regis Museum.

I trace the idea for this book on film and video adaptations of John's literature to a conversation in Calcutta with his widow, Sarah Fowles, about Satyajit Ray and cinematic art.

For help received during the research process I owe a debt to the staff of the Auraria Library, particularly Alan Vanhoye, Kalia Lo, and Joel Casavant.

For advice about gathering materials in electronic form I am grateful to Mike Erskine's staff in Educational Technology Services, Metropolitan State University of Denver.

For help with the illustrations I am grateful to Jennifer Jones and her staff at Mike's Camera.

For allowing me to photograph a rare document held by the Denver Public Library, I am indebted to Steve Schneck.

I also appreciate the friendly service of Joseph Grannes at Ricoh.

Finally, I owe additional, special thanks to David Tringham, Kirki Kefalea, Bob Goosman, and Russell McDermott for their valuable consultations, and to Lorna Hutchison for her inspiring intelligence.

Table of Contents

Introduction

James Aubrey

From his sudden fame with *The Collector* in 1963 until his death in 2005, John Fowles was one of those rare novelists who manage to be both popular and respected. Fowles was never entirely comfortable with his popularity, for he saw himself foremost as a serious writer, even as a philosopher who happened to be entertaining as he wrote his characters into extreme moral dilemmas. Readers, however, found his stories compelling, and that kind of appeal immediately attracted agents and producers looking for material that might be adapted to film or television.

Adaptation from one artistic medium to another is an art form in itself. Audiences often evaluate a film adaptation of a literary classic in terms of whether it is "faithful," that is, equivalent to its original, a criterion that can lead them to overlook differences between media that make perfect fidelity impossible and expectations of close fidelity misguided. Sophisticated readers and literary critics usually acknowledge the problem but are often more familiar with verbal than with visual art, and thus tend to critique particular films or videos more as literature than as cinema. Film critics sometimes discount faithful adaptations of literature to film or video for lacking originality or, as prominent film theorist Dudley Andrew does, relegate them to "the most narrow and provincial area of film theory," where the original is treated as a signified rather than as a referent.[1] However, even Andrew acknowledges that all films derive in some way from a prior text, most often from a written narrative, and that particular adaptations are discursive events to be examined in their social and historical contexts. James Naremore goes even further, to argue that "adaptation will become part of a general theory of repetition," part of "the study of recycling, remaking, and every other form of retelling in the age of mechanical reproduction and electronic communication."[2] Although critical expertise in both literature and cinema studies is difficult to attain, the writers of the essays that follow are working across that media divide in the laboratory of social history as they examine the various screen adaptations of literature by John Fowles.

Fowles is a particularly interesting case for adaptation study because he was unusually knowledgeable about both cinema and literature, and conscious of the differences between the media on a theoretical level. Fowles was fluent in French and, as is evident from chapter 13 of *The French Lieutenant's Woman*, he was aware of French critical theory in the 1960s; in 1969 he reviewed a book on deconstruction for the *New York Times*; and in 1999 he engaged in an interview about whether he was a postmodern writer (he said, "Yes").[3] In a 1971 essay about looking at nature, and in another written in 1985 to accompany a book of photographs, Fowles discussed theoretical limits of visual and verbal media, particularly the difficulty of representing thoughts with pictures, or images with words.[4] In the intervening years Fowles produced works that combined words and photographs in graphic essays that have come to be seen as pioneering works of postmodern hybridity.[5] The etymology of the word *cinema* privileges movement, but the cinematic medium is inherently a hybridization of the kinetic with the visual and the verbal and the aural. Fowles consciously engaged with this multi-faceted medium of cinema throughout his career. At age 42 he insightfully observed that his having watched more than 2,500 films over the years must have profoundly influenced his thinking and writing, even his way of seeing the world.[6] Several years later Fowles would more probingly examine this aspect of himself as he wrote *Daniel Martin*, his longest and most autobiographical novel, whose title character is an aspiring screenwriter who discovers, along with the theories of Antonio Gramsci, that he is temperamentally better suited to writing novels than screenplays.[7] Fowles's insights and knowledge of cinema were not merely abstract and intuitive, however. Across his career, off and on from 1962 to 1998, Fowles was actively engaged with the film and television industries as a consultant for all but one of the adaptations of his written work to the screen: *The Collector* (1965), *The Magus* (1968), and *The French Lieutenant's Woman* (1981) as full-length feature films; *The Last Chapter* (1974) as a short film to accompany a feature in theaters; and *The Enigma* (1980) and *The Ebony Tower* (1984) as programs for British television. In the late 1990s two more films were released that contain elements adapted from *The Magus*: *The Game* was a feature film released in 1997 that creatively updated the novel, and *The Return of the Magus* was a documentary made for Greek television in 1998 that dramatizes scenes from the novel. Typically, Fowles was involved as an unpaid creative consultant. As will become evident in the essays that follow, Fowles liked to involve himself as more than just the author on location as a guest, preferring to weigh in on various filmmaking issues such as casting, costume design, site selection, and set design. Fowles himself wrote the screenplay adapting *The Magus* for the 1968 feature film with that title, for which he received sole screenwriting credit.[8] During that time Fowles even considered becoming a film director himself, so he evidently felt the limitations of his consulting role.[9] The producers who had optioned the rights to adapt probably wanted Fowles's prestigious name associated with their projects more than they wanted his advice, but they got his advice nevertheless, and it led to distinctive expressions of his artistic aims in a different, cinematic form. Indeed, Fowles deserves a new label in addition to novelist and writer, for he was also a creative cinema consultant.

"I really want to teach morally with my novels," Fowles candidly told an interviewer in 1998.[10] In practice, however, Fowles was neither didactic nor moralistic. Behind his simplistic-sounding declaration was a socialist who didn't trust social institutions, an intellectual who didn't trust professors, and a pessimist who nonetheless hoped to foster mutually respectful relations between men and women. Fowles attracted wide reading audiences, particularly in the 1960s when *The Collector* was a Book-of-the-Month Club selection, *The Magus* became a cult novel, and *The French Lieutenant's Woman* was on the *New York Times* bestseller list for more than a year—for six months at number one.[11] However popular he was, Fowles was attracted to the possibility of appealing to an even larger audience through visual media such as film and television.[12] When consulted about adaptations, he probably felt the typical artist's wish to protect the integrity of his previous work, for his judgments tended to favor form and content over audience. As teacher-philosopher Fowles particularly wanted to see the central ideas embedded in his stories preserved: class division in *The Collector*, atheism in *The Magus*, creative writing in *The Last Chapter*, conventional thinking in *The Enigma*, modern art in *The Ebony Tower*, and postmodern art in *The French Lieutenant's Woman*. In many instances, despite his advocacy, Fowles's version of an idea often would end up effaced in the final, screened adaptation. But even so, Fowles's contributions were often significant and warrant the critical attention afforded here.

John Fowles kept a journal for most of his life, and its entries reveal insights into his thinking about cinema and document his involvement with the film and video industries. In 1962, even before publication of his first novel, *The Collector*, Fowles and his agent found themselves involved in competitive negotiations for the film rights. Although Fowles was dismayed by later reviews of the novel as crime fiction rather than as a parable of class difference, he hoped that a planned black-and-white film adaptation would correct some of the misunderstandings. Sale of film rights to *The Collector* enabled Fowles to quit his teaching position in London in order to write full time; it also freed him to become involved with the film production itself as it evolved into a Technicolor, Hollywood project. The draft screenplay by producers Jud Kinberg and John Kohn and screenwriter Stanley Mann must have had problems, for Fowles wrote that his agent convinced the writing trio that they "must have me in to clean things up."[13] A series of contentious meetings subsequently took place in a London hotel room. Fowles was initially horrified by the shooting script he was shown, particularly by changes to his novel's characters and ideas. The other three writers, Fowles observed, "are geniuses for finding melodramatic gimmicks" that he would then try to argue them out of. One newly invented scene that Fowles did not persuade them to eliminate from the film involved a bound-and-gagged Miranda, a nosy neighbor, and an overflowing bathtub. Fowles lamented, "I have to wear them down, line after line, into some sort of sense—or realism."[14] His efforts to keep the film realistic weren't limited to revising dialogue. Although most of *The Collector* was filmed in Hollywood, Fowles scouted locations in London where an abduction might realistically be carried out; and the kidnapping of Miranda by Clegg did end up being filmed near the Fowles flat in central Hampstead. A few months later, Fowles flew to the United States for two weeks as a consultant on the film set, where he persuaded director William Wyler to film a scene with Miranda dressed in a realistic-looking cardigan and faded trousers instead of the feminizing dress preferred by the costume designer.[15] Fowles similarly advised the set designer that the furniture was not realistic, was not sufficiently distressed, that it should appear more used in order to look authentically lower class. Fowles even tried to help lead actress Samantha Eggar by coaching her for an hour one evening, to help her deliver what he thought would be a more convincing performance.[16]

An important change that Fowles succeeded in persuading the director to impose on the script was rejection of a proposed happy ending, in which the novel's doomed kidnap victim was to survive, after all. According to Fowles's journal, screenwriter Mann was mostly on his side, producer Kohn against, and Kinberg "on the fence."[17] Initially, director Wyler seems to have been favoring the conventional, happy ending, for he gave Fowles a gratuitous lecture about what dictated the choice: "My art is working in the limits of what the public will pay to see.... That audience is just going to say, 'What happened, why'd she die?'"[18] Ultimately, however, Fowles's view prevailed: in the final cut of the film, Miranda dies and her abductor sets off to find another victim, as in the novel. Thus *The Collector* deserves to be called the first modern horror movie—four years before *Rosemary's Baby* would attain that supposed status.[19] And that generic label would not apply to *The Collector* if Fowles as consultant had not persuaded the filmmakers to change the happy ending of the shooting script to the dark ending of the completed film, with its disturbing, final absence of justice.

Overall, however, Fowles's experiences with *The Collector* left him disillusioned, and he determined to see that his long novel *The Magus* did not end up mangled by producers and screenwriters. He insisted on writing the screenplay himself, even as he complained about the preliminary stage in his journal for 27 November 1965: "I plod on wearily through the film treatment of *The Magus*, a job that both bores and disgusts me."[20] He declared the abstract treatment finished two weeks later and started on the screenplay itself the next month: "Much more enjoyable than the treatment; and I think a good discipline—to be so forced to prune to essentials."[21] Twentieth Century–Fox optioned *The Magus* in August 1966, and chose Guy Green to direct. Fowles was pleased that a "good craftsman" rather than a visionary had been selected, perhaps in hope that his screenplay would not be changed much.[22] In pre-production Fowles participated in casting the part of Julie, the seductive protégé of the story's master manipulator, Maurice Conchis. Fowles made clear his preference for Jean Shrimpton, a model and popular cover girl, who Fowles admitted could not act but who had "cool looks" that he believed would work on screen.[23] No one else agreed, and the part eventually went to Candice Bergen. Given the industry wisdom that casting is the most important element of a film's prospective success, Fowles's advice to cast on the basis of looks alone is a reminder of his limitations as a cinema consultant.

As shooting for *The Magus* got under way on the island of Majorca in 1967, Fowles was enlisted to deliver the opening line of the film, as a crew member on a ferry boat. Having performed this speaking role, Fowles remarked about acting: "So I am an authority now."[24] He was not entirely serious, but his experience did encourage him to express his views, including his admiration for the performance of lead actress Anna Karina as Alison, and his disdain for lead actor Michael Caine's performance as Nicholas, which Fowles found "wooden and hopelessly without depth."[25]

Even as the sole-credited screenwriter, Fowles had to justify his treatment and script to the producers of *The Magus*, John Kohn and Jud Kinberg, who also had produced *The Collector*. Again, Fowles found himself arguing with them over how the film should end. Kohn wanted a happy ending, one that would reunite Nicholas with his girlfriend, Alison; Fowles wanted the film to end with Nicholas alone, looking sadder but wiser, and Alison's whereabouts unknown. By February 1967, evidently having settled for a reuniting of the characters, Fowles was again at odds with Kohn and Kinberg, who now wanted the ending to be made melodramatic, whereas Fowles and Green wanted it "quiet and emotional."[26] In December Fowles sounded resigned to letting others decide: "They've changed the ending again; but at least they have gone for simplicity."[27] So Fowles was pleased later to learn that Daryl Zanuck and some other Fox moguls had watched the nearly finished rough cut "and asked for the last scene (the happy ending in London) to be cut, as I've always wanted."[28] Fowles's "unhappy" ending had been rejected but was now being restored. Although Fowles had not been so persuasive during the making of *The Magus* as he had been with *The Collector*, both films ended his way.

The various disagreements reinforced Fowles's skepticism about the collaborative nature of film making: "You cannot make good art like this. I know the film is doomed already at this level—never mind about the mess being made at lower ones." Fowles later would say that he liked his producer but that "my sense of reality fights John Kohn's sense of showmanship.... He ruins all the details. Yet he is good on that mysterious film god, Structure."[29] Fowles likewise found himself admiring director Guy Green's ability to "take the script to bits and put it together in a simpler way, and it's nice (healthily humiliating) to help him do it."[30] Perhaps if their views had prevailed and the film had ended more conventionally, *The Magus* might have been more successful commercially. In any case, the film was a failure, most famously condemned by Woody Allen, who wished that he could live his life over again just so that he could avoid seeing that movie.[31]

During the making of the film, Fowles found himself thinking that he could probably direct as well as Green because "the technical knowledge needed doesn't seem very great."[32] Fowles's fantasy was not far fetched, for his ambitious script was already driving the project. As sole credited screenwriter for a film with a temperamentally weak director who was eventually overruled on how the film should end, Fowles bore significant responsibility for the final product. He admitted, "I am partly to blame— completely where the script is just bad, and unconsciously where I didn't foresee the danger of overwriting with someone like Guy Green.... All the dialogue is spoken at a snail's pace and every meaningful line is atrociously overstressed, both in delivery and in the killing pause that precedes it."[33] In a sense Fowles deserves to be called this film's *auteur*, not quite as the term is used in film circles to describe certain directors but, in this case, as the effectual director whose authorship, or personal vision, is discernible in the final product.[34] For better or worse, the movie version of *The Magus*, like the novel it is based on, is "by" John Fowles.

In 1970 Fowles sold an unwritten screenplay for $5,000, based on his unpublished story "Zip," about a failed writer who bombs a New York cinema in frustration.[35] That screenplay was never produced, but in 1971 "The Final Chapter," another unpublished story by Fowles, was adapted and produced by Blazer Films as *The Last Chapter*. The director and screenwriter, David Tringham, had formerly been the assistant director of *The Magus*; when he asked Fowles for other material with cinematic possibilities, Fowles offered him this story of a successful author of spy thrillers who gets a comeuppance when visited by one of the Classical muses, in disguise as a teenage fan. Fowles joined lead actor Denholm Elliott for a read-through of his part, and he watched Elliott and Susan Penhaligon walk through their scenes at Shepperton Studios. As with the previous two films, Fowles again had disputes with Tringham over his proposed changes to the ending of the story. The disagreements ended in compromise,[36] but Fowles evidently was content with the outcome; when he saw the final cut, he described it as "not too bad."[37]

From 1972 to 1975 Fowles wrote his novel *Daniel Martin*, whose protagonist is a failing screenwriter who, among other things, finds his calling as a novelist.[38] Among the lessons Daniel learns is that skill in novel writing does not easily transfer into skill in screenwriting, and in 1981 Fowles indicated that he had come to the same conclusion. In his foreword to Harold Pinter's published screenplay for *The French Lieutenant's Woman*,

Fowles disavowed any lingering aspiration to adapt his own works: "I am no longer in the least interested in scripting my own fiction.... True scriptwriters are a race apart in a craft apart. It is only vanity that makes other writers believe that anyone at all can turn a hand to it. I believed so myself once." This is not just an apology for *The Magus*, and not just deference to Pinter. Fowles elaborates on the problem: "both media are essentially narrative ... yet there are ... visual things the word can never capture (think for instance, of the appalling paucity of vocabulary to define the endless nuances of facial expression), and word things the camera will never photograph nor actors ever speak."[39] Despite this awareness, Fowles did not abstain from some uncredited script-doctoring. Fowles wrote in his journal that Pinter had trouble writing emotion into scenes, that "he didn't argue at all when I re-wrote the scene [near the end between Charles and Sarah] to put some of that back and read it to [director] Karel [Reisz] and him."[40] How much Fowles contributed to that scene is impossible to determine, but it seems from his description to have been significant.

Another intervention by Fowles into the filming of *The French Lieutenant's Woman* involved the selection of location for an early scene in the forested Undercliff, as Charles wields his geologist's hammer on a vertical piece of white cliff while, below him, Sarah walks by.[41] The actual outcropping of limestone, about two miles west of Lyme Regis, was known in the seventeenth century as Whitechapel Rock, a meeting place for Dissenters. Today the formation is in the Undercliff Nature Reserve, but access is considered dangerous and is forbidden without a guide. This particular place was of deep personal interest to Fowles, part of a pattern of attractions he had long felt to geographical irruptions to landscape or seascape, perhaps for their symbolic value as representations of individualistic behavior.[42] In 1979 Fowles was finishing a non-fiction book titled *The Tree*, in which he mentions thinking about this Whitechapel Rock location when he was writing his Lyme Regis novel back in 1967–68: "I used this wood, and even this one particular dell, in *The French Lieutenant's Woman*, for scenes that it seemed to me, in a story of self-liberation, could have no other setting."[43] The place was probably on his mind again in May 1980, when filming began and locations would have been discussed.[44] No professional location scout for a film could have found this site, nor would he or she have chosen such a place, whose remoteness necessitated having stairs built and pulleys brought in for maneuvering the camera and heavy equipment. It is little wonder that the film crew displayed its unhappiness with the location by having tee shirts made that read, "I HATE THE UNDERCLIFF"—which Fowles still remembered eight years later when he was writing an introduction to a book on the area.[45] In 1980 Fowles probably insisted on the Whitechapel Rock location for its personal importance to him, and his consultation appears to have left its mark on filmmakers as well as on the film itself.

In 1980 the British Broadcasting Corporation presented an adaptation of Fowles's short story "The Enigma" on its *Playhouse* television series. The screenplay was written by Malcolm Bradbury, fellow novelist and friend. Although he "retained script oversight and consulted with Bradbury before production," according to biographer Eileen Warburton, the resulting video adaptation departed from the original detective story in providing a closed ending, a solution to the mystery that is left unresolved in the anti-formula detective story Fowles had written.[46] The traditional closure of the adaptation accommodated the expectations of BBC viewers, and Fowles probably did not oppose Bradbury's decision to change the ending for the different medium, consistent with his vow later that year not to try to write movie scripts.

Despite his ongoing belief that novelists and screenwriters are a breed apart, Fowles continued to serve as an informal film consultant. In 1983, during pre-production for his story "The Ebony Tower" for Granada television in the United Kingdom, Fowles met at his London flat with director Robert Knights and adapting writer John Mortimer. They all "discussed script problems" and tried to figure out "how to placate Laurence Olivier, who felt that he didn't have a good enough last scene." Fowles found this objection "slightly absurd," but the old artist-character's last speech was expanded.[47] In 1984 Fowles's 114-page novella became *The Ebony Tower*, an 80-minute movie made for television. The following year Fowles published his last novel, *A Maggot*, so one may fairly say that he remained a cinema consultant until the end of his career as a fiction writer.

John Fowles's role in the making of film and video adaptations of his own works is interesting enough, but the adaptations themselves are remarkable works in their own right, as the eight essays in this volume attest. In "Bluebeard's Basement," Eileen Warburton examines the production of *The Collector* in its biographical and social contexts, and how the project evolved from a small art film about class to a horror film about a monster and his victim. *The Collector* went on to win both the male and the female Best Actor awards at the Cannes film festival and to receive an

Oscar nomination for Best Picture of 1965. In "Cinematic Godgames," James Aubrey examines *The Magus* as adapted by Fowles himself in 1968, reduced in dramatic and historical scope but not in its intellectual ambitions. In "Undercover Hero," Michelle Buchberger examines *The Last Chapter*, adapted from an unpublished short story by Fowles, filmed in 1972 and distributed in 1974 by Twentieth Century–Fox as a 29-minute drama about an Ian Fleming–like writer of spy thrillers. In "Safe Dreams," Buchberger examines the adaptation of "The Enigma," one of Fowles's published short stories, about a detective trying to solve the mysterious disappearance of a British Member of Parliament. Broadcast in 1980 as part of a television playhouse series on BBC2, *The Enigma* is entertaining, Buchberger observes, but lacks the complexity and nuance of the original story. In "Situating Sarah," Carol Samson examines the 1981 United Artists release of *The French Lieutenant's Woman*, a major production that would win the Golden Globe award for Best Picture and two Academy Awards including Best Screenplay, by Harold Pinter, who later would win the Nobel Prize for Literature in part for this work. Samson focuses on the implications of setting, particularly the decision to end the film at a middle-class architect's house in the picturesque Lake District, rather than in the urban environment of the novel's final chapters in London, at the Chelsea residence of the Rossettis and their fellow artists and models. One consequence is a dulling of the novel's feminist edge. In "Rhizome and Romance," Dianne Vipond examines *The Ebony Tower* as a television drama starring Laurence Olivier as a famous British painter living in exile in Brittany with two young women, and the art critic who ventures to interview him. Vipond analyzes the structural differences between the verbal and the visual texts and locates them both squarely in their postmodern era. In "*The Magus* as Thriller," James Aubrey examines *The Game*, a 1997 Universal Studios film starring A-list actors Michael Douglas and Sean Penn, and Deborah Kara Unger, lead actress in David Cronenberg's *Crash*. Although its ontological relationship to *The Magus* is unacknowledged, Aubrey argues that *The Game* is a brilliant adaptation of Fowles's philosophical novel in a different medium to a different genre: the cinematic thriller. In "Postmodern Documentary," Craig Svonkin examines an extraordinary form of cinematic play with the same novel in a 1999 Greek television documentary, *The Return of the Magus*. The eponymous magus is Fowles himself, who is shown returning to the Aegean island of Spetses for the first time since he taught school there as a young man, where he later would set his novel *The Magus*. Svonkin pays particular attention to the documentary's adaptation of scenes from the novel with Fowles himself at age 72 acting the part of his novel's protagonist. Fowles was heavily involved in conceiving, advising and shaping *Return of the Magus*, as he had been with other film and video adaptations of his fictions, so this creative documentary provides an elegant, circular closure to his artistic career.

Notes

1. Dudley Andrew, "Adaptation," *Concepts in Film Theory* (New York: Oxford University Press, 1984), p. 96.

2. James Naremore, "Introduction: Film and the Reign of Adaptation," *Film Adaptation* (New Brunswick: Rutgers University Press, 2000), p. 15.

3. John Fowles, *The French Lieutenant's Woman* (Boston: Little, Brown, 1969), p. 95; "The Most Secretive of Victorian Writers, a Kind of Great Mouse," review of *Thomas Hardy: Distance and Desire*, by J. Hillis Miller, *New York Times Book Review* 21 June 1970, p. 4; *"Do you consider yourself a postmodern author? Interviews with Contemporary English Writers*, ed. Rudolph Freiburg and Jan Schnitker, *Erlanger Studien zur Anglistik and Amerikanistik* (Münster: Lit Verlag; rpt., Piscataway, NJ: Transaction, 1999), p. 129.

4. John Fowles, "The Blinded Eye," *Animals* 13.9 (1971): 388–92; "Essay by John Fowles," in *Land*, by Fay Godwin (Boston: Little, Brown, 1985), pp. x–xi.

5. James R. Aubrey, "John Fowles and Creative Non-fiction," in *John Fowles*, ed. James Acheson (London: Palgrave MacMillan, 2013), pp. 34–35.

6. John Fowles, "Notes on Writing a Novel," *Harper's* July 1968, p. 92.

7. John Fowles, *Daniel Martin* (Boston: Little, Brown, 1977).

8. *The Magus*, screenwriter John Fowles, dir, Guy Green, perf. Michael Caine, Candice Bergen, Anthony Quinn, Anna Karina, Twentieth Century–Fox, 1968.

9. John Fowles, *The Journals: Volume Two [1966–1990]*, ed. Charles Drazin (London: Jonathan Cape, 2006), p. 26.

10. Interview with Kirki Kefalea, in *The Return of the Magus*, Inkas Film and T.V. Productions, 1999–2000.

11. Raman K. Singh, "An Encounter with John Fowles," *Journal of Modern Literature* 8 (1980): 186.

12. Eileen Warburton, *John Fowles: A Life in Two Worlds* (New York: Viking Penguin, 2004), p. 244.

13. John Fowles, *The Journals: Volume One [1949–1965]*, ed. Charles Drazin (London: Jonathan Cape, 2003), p. 560.

14. Fowles, *The Journals: Volume One*, p. 598.

15. *Ibid.*, p. 594.

16. *Ibid.*, p. 602.

17. *Ibid.*, p. 562.

18. *Ibid.*, p. 586.

19. Jason Zinoman, *Shock Value: How a Few Eccentric Outsiders Gave Us Nightmares, Conquered Hollywood, and Invented Modern Horror* (New York: Penguin, 2011), pp. 8–9. By "modern horror" Zinoman means realistic, terrifying cinema—not, for example, Jack the Ripper or *Dracula*.

20. Fowles, *The Journals: Volume One*, p. 648.
21. Fowles, *The Journals: Volume Two*, p. 10.
22. *Ibid.*, p. 21.
23. *Ibid.*, p. 27.
24. *Ibid.*, p. 31.
25. *Ibid.*, p. 43.
26. *Ibid.*, p. 26.
27. *Ibid.*, p. 33.
28. *Ibid.*, p. 39.
29. *Ibid.*, p. 26.
30. *Ibid.*, p. 28.
31. Woody Allen, letter to James Aubrey, 10 June 1988, confirming that Allen once said that if he had his life to live over again, he would want everything exactly the same with the exception of seeing the film version of *The Magus*. Allen says that he liked the book.
32. Fowles, *The Journals: Volume Two*, pp. 26–27.
33. *Ibid.*, 43–44.
34. François Truffaut advanced the theory of the *auteur* versus the *scenarist* in an essay that launched the French New Wave, "Une certaine tendance du cinéma français" ("A Certain Tendency in French Cinema") in *Cahiers du Cinéma*, 1954.
35. Fowles, *The Journals: Volume Two*, p. 95.
36. David Tringham, letter to Michelle Buchberger, 13 March 2013. The Fowles-Tringham collaboration is described in Buchberger, "Undercover Hero," this collection.
37. Fowles, *The Journals: Volume Two*, p. 126.
38. *Ibid.*, p. 200.
39. John Fowles, Foreword, *The French Lieutenant's Woman: A Screenplay*, by Harold Pinter (Boston: Little, Brown, 1981), pp. ix–x.
40. Fowles, *The Journals: Volume*, p. 252.
41. *The French Lieutenant's Woman*, dir. Karel Reisz, screenplay Harold Pinter, perf. Jeremy Irons and Meryl Streep, United Artists, 1981.
42. James R. Aubrey, Introduction, *John Fowles and Nature: Fourteen Perspectives on Landscape* (Cranbury, NJ: Associated University Presses), p. 24.
43. John Fowles and Frank Horvat, *The Tree* (London: Aurum Press, 1979; rpt., New York: Ecco Press, 1983), p. 75.
44. Fowles, Foreword to Pinter, p. ix.
45. John Fowles, Foreword, *The Undercliff*, by Elaine Franks (Boston: Little, Brown, 1989), p. 9.
46. Warburton, p. 402.
47. Fowles, *The Journals: Volume Two*, p. 272.

Bluebeard's Basement:
The Collector on Film

EILEEN WARBURTON

Terry Stamp was feeling anxious. Summoned to an early 1964 meeting with the legendary William Wyler, one of the "all-time great film directors," Stamp had been told that Wyler wanted to cast him as Freddie Clegg in the film of John Fowles's best-selling novel *The Collector*.[1]

Stamp had vaulted to movie celebrity with the 1962 release of *Billy Budd*, in which he played the innocent, stuttering, doomed handsome sailor, the essence of pure good and beauty. He had appeared in only one other film. Stamp wanted desperately to work with Wyler and was dying to play the role of Clegg. He had eagerly read the script proofs while riding home on the top of the #73 London bus and was so engrossed that he missed his stop. But, as he told his agent, it was "physically impossible to fold myself into the part ... the boy was small, grey and nondescript, symbolic of the anonymous mass who lived their lives unnoticed by others. He was spotty, his nose ran ... the further I read the more miserable I became."[2]

When Stamp met with Wyler, he stammered out his insecurities. Wyler assured the young actor that he wanted no one else. "But the, in the book ..." Wyler shushed him, draped an arm around Terry's tall shoulders and whispered conspiratorially, "I'm not making the book.... I'm going to make a love story. A modern love story.... And you're going to be ... just purrfect."[3]

From the moment he signed on to direct *The Collector*, William Wyler was set on a very different vision of the narrative than the one conceived by John Fowles. While the film version is a fairly faithful re-telling of the plotline of *The Collector*, the manner of the telling works mighty changes in the experience and the meaning of Fowles's novel.

The Collector was John Fowles's first published—and first publishable—novel. Begun in 1960, written between 1961 and 1962, and published in 1963, *The Collector* also was Fowles's first novel to be turned into a movie. It was sold in 1962 before publication, shot in 1964 and released in 1965. As with the novel, which vaulted Fowles from complete obscurity and poverty to being a celebrated and wealthy public figure, the film of *The Collector* went from being a modest black and white film of ideas to a Hollywood spectacle, a Technicolor horror story spun from a character study of erotic obsession.

The novel's story concerns young Freddie Clegg, a shy, socially awkward clerk in an English town records office whose passion in life is butterfly collecting. He is a proud stalker and killer of butterflies and his settings have won awards. His other passion is a lovely art student, Miranda Grey, with whom he falls in love at a distance. He watches her remotely, certain that she wouldn't give him the time of day. Unless, of course, they had time alone together—then she would "get to know" him. Then she would fall in love with him. This is his romantic fantasy. Clegg has an astounding capacity for self-justification. It is one of the scariest things about him.

Clegg's life changes abruptly when he wins the football pools. Given money and independence, he elects to make his fantasy real. He quits his job and buys a remote country cottage with a secure cellar. He fits out the cellar for a "guest," drives to Miranda's London neighborhood, assaults her with chloroform, kidnaps her, and imprisons her in the cellar. He treats Miranda with what he believes is courtesy and respect and showers her with gifts. But Miranda—predictably—is frightened by the situation and repelled by Clegg, whose behavior alternates unstably between morose adoration and the violence of a sadistic gaoler. Clegg himself—a narrow, meagerly educated, sexually repressed petit bourgeois—discovers that Miranda isn't the demure, easily led, adoring girl of his dreams, but an opinionated, uncooperative person with advanced arty ideas, who despises his values and schemes for her freedom.

Not surprisingly, this all ends badly. After two months of attempts to educate or reason with her captor, failed escapes, and intense interior reflection, Miranda comes down with pneumonia. Too alarmed to seek help, Clegg convinces himself that she is faking illness to try to escape. So Miranda dies—locked in an underground cellar, far from friends and family, buried in an unmarked grave. Clegg, grandiloquently heartbroken for a week or two, finally decides that he needs another guest and goes stalking a local girl.

The Collector owes much of its dramatic situation to classic animal groom tales like "Beauty and the Beast," "The Frog Prince," "Cupid and Psyche"—stories in which an imprisoned heroine actually does come to understand and love her monster husband, thereby transforming him into a handsome human lover.[4] But the tale that most influenced Fowles in writing the novel was "Bluebeard," a disturbing story in which the imprisoned wife grows too curious and unlocks a forbidden room with an enchanted key, only to find it filled with the bloody corpses of her husband's former wives.[5] After such knowledge, either the bride or Bluebeard has to die, depending on which variant of the tale one reads.[6] Bruno Bettleheim's observation could be applied to *The Collector*: "That which happens in 'Bluebeard' has nothing whatsoever to do with love. Bluebeard, bent on having his will and possessing his partner, cannot love anybody, but neither can anyone love him."[7] *Bluebeard's Castle*, Béla Bartók's operatic version of the tale, was a major inspiration for Fowles. Attending a performance of the opera in the late 1950s, he was "struck" by "the symbolism of the man imprisoning women underground."[8] This melodramatic situation echoed John Fowles's own primary sexual fantasy. He admitted in his diaries how "from puberty until recently I frequently had conscious fantasies, or nocturnal day-dreams, about imprisoning women underground," imaginings not stopped by his "very happy marriage." The "girl kidnapped" was never a mature woman, but always a young female about twenty years old. She always fell in love with her captor, and the imprisoning was always "a forcing of my personality as well as my penis on the girl concerned."[9] Fowles cataloged many variations of this fantasy, including a scenario with Princess Margaret, four years his junior. Universally, his variations were about upper class girls, indicating Fowles' own class sensitivities that would be reflected in the character of Clegg. Fowles, however, believed what they all had in common and aroused him was "the dramatic psycho-sexual implications of isolating extreme situations."[10] Then, too, his profession at the time of writing as a teacher at a business and finishing school for international girls heightened the frequency of his fantasy. "Once," he wrote in his diaries, "I used to 'kidnap and imprison' generalized girls—archetypes. But for many years it has had to be someone I know—students."[11]

There is, frankly, a lot of John Fowles in his characterization of Freddie Clegg and his obsessions. Fowles himself was a fanatical collector—of butterflies, of hunted birds, of vintage china, of orchids, of exotic plants, of obscure words, of all manner of historical detritus. For all his gentlemanly charm, he was dogged and ruthlessly competitive in his pursuits. In other ways, *The Collector* reflects the period of Fowles' life in which it was written. By the late 1950s when he began, he had produced a handful of novels that remained rejected or simply unpublished. After a failed operation, his wife Elizabeth had been declared unable to conceive children and the couple was struggling emotionally with the implications of their childlessness. Fowles felt stuck and stale in his teaching job, poorly paid and without a future. He wrote in his diaries of a feeling of entrapment.[12]

These personal diaries influenced the form of this novel. As a dedicated diarist since his youth, Fowles had used the diary, real or fictitious, as a supple, revealing form of exploration for at least fifteen years. Writing in diary format, Fowles was able to present the immediate experience of *The Collector* directly to the reader. Each of the participants sets out their point of view and version of events in diary fashion, making an intimate, unmediated appeal to our comprehension and sympathies in a uniquely rendered voice. Clegg's voice is flat, direct, and filled with self-serving justifications of his imprisonment of the woman he supposedly loves. Miranda's voice has the quality of an intelligent, but still immature undergraduate feeling her way. The dominant butterfly metaphor of the novel presents her in this intimate diary as a chrysalis, trapped and immobile, but undergoing dramatic mental and moral change that should allow her to emerge, liberated, as a magnificent butterfly (the emblem of the soul, a *psyche*). On the savvy advice of Tom Maschler, Fowles's editor at Jonathan Cape, Clegg's diary was cut into Miranda's just at the point she becomes ill. So the reader comes to know Miranda familiarly before learning her ultimate fate from the resumption of Clegg's narrative. This choice considerably deepens the suspense of the plot and the punch of the ending.

While many reviewers, particularly in England, hailed the novel as a suspenseful, erotic thriller, Fowles was dismayed to find his book reviewed in the crime columns.[13] He had originally conceived *The Collector* as the long-sought vehicle for the theme of his social philosophy, the predicament identified by the Greek philosopher, Heraclitus: "the intelligent trapped in the world of the stupid."[14]

Fowles's Heraclitean philosophy was set out in numbered aphorisms in *The Aristos,* a manifesto that the writer was editing and reediting while simultaneously composing *The Collector. The Aristos* was published in 1964, the year after the novel appeared. Introducing that book, Fowles references the theme of *The Collector:*

> History—not least in the twentieth century—shows that society has persistently seen life in terms of a struggle between the Few and the Many, between "Them" and "Us." My purpose in *The Collector* was to attempt to analyse, through a parable, some of the results of this confrontation.[15]

Planning the novel in his diaries, Fowles focused on this confrontation between The Few (the *aristoi*), the best people for our society, and the Many (the *hoi polloi*), the thoughtless who need to be led. The collector himself, Fowles wrote, "is to symbolize the mediocrity of our present society; the girl he kidnaps stands for its hope and its vitality, pointlessly and maliciously crushed." Clegg was to be one of what Fowles called "the New People," given money and social power in post-war England, but not the education or motivating morality to do anything but destroy the best of an older tradition. Miranda represents what the values of that older tradition could become when educated and self-dedicated to the creation of a better world.[16]

In addition, although he shared much of their rage against post-war British society, Fowles scorned the Angry Young Man/working class writers then in vogue, so he wrote his editor that Clegg would be "inarticulate and nasty, as opposed to the 'good' inarticulate hero." Miranda would be "articulate and intelligent ... clearly a better person because she has a better education." The story would "attack the money-minus-morality society (the affluent, the acquisitive) we have lived in since 1951."[17]

Class remains the pervasive social divider in British society, and was more so in the late 1950s and early '60s than today. Fowles himself was extremely class conscious, a product of upper middle class expectations, elite public school, military service in the Royal Marines, and studies at Oxford University. He had come to be ashamed of these establishment legacies and struggled to throw off the marks of his upbringing. Matters of social class assumed a powerful sexual dimension for him as well. He was always very attracted to upper-class girls who were socially superior to him. However, he had married and was wildly in love with a very working class woman, Elizabeth Whitton Christy Fowles, who was smarter, sexier, more politically committed, and more complicated than any woman he had ever met. Class was an issue with them throughout their lives and she flung his bourgeois limitations at Fowles in every argument. Class-infused lovemaking was his daily life.

The major theme of *The Aristos* was not that there should be an entirely classless society, but that class distinctions should be based on merit, on wisdom, sensitivity, education, moral courage, and personal growth rather than on inherited title, land, or wealth. "When Miranda talks about the Few, in *The Collector*," Fowles wrote in 1964, "this is the kind of people I meant her to mean: preeminently creators, not simply highly intelligent or well-informed people, not people who are simply skilled with words."[18]

Class was less an emphatic theme for the American filmmakers shooting *The Collector*, however. While social distinctions like money, race, ethnicity, and religion remain hot buttons for Americans, they still tend to believe that "class" is fluid and social mobility is always possible. Director William Wyler and his associates recognized social class as an issue between Clegg and Miranda, but it would become far less important to them than depicting Freddie's increasing sadism, Miranda's mounting terror, and the erotic tension between the two. A diminished focus on social class became a key difference between the film of *The Collector* and the original novel.

In addition to the class parable about the meritorious Few (Miranda) trapped and destroyed by the envious Many (Clegg), Fowles's *The Collector* is also partly a *Bildungsroman* about a young woman evolving into existential authenticity and creating the self she wishes to be by becoming morally responsible for her own thoughts and actions. Fowles frequently uses the metaphor of imprisonment in *The Aristos* to express his existentialist belief that we have only this physical world and our own limited mortal lives in which to find moral engagement and happiness, and that we are solely responsible for creating it for ourselves and our society. Speaking of the problem of free will, he writes, 'We are in a prison cell, but it is, or can be made to become, a comparatively spacious one; and inside it we can become relatively free." Further, he continues: "My freedom is the choice of action and the power of enactment I have within the rules and situation of the game."[19]

Adapting this metaphor to *The Collector*, Fowles shows Miranda learning to find freedom within her imprisoned situation by making self-defining choices. She comes to renounce violence. She finds the courage to reach out to Clegg sexually, with tenderness. She begins to recognize what is false in her own art and her own behavior, and to reject it. She realizes that she loves and wants to be with her mentor, George Paston. In short, Miranda in the novel grows and changes. She is a dynamic character within a static situation. Ironically, much of her evolution occurs because she must recognize her imprisonment and come to terms with it. "A strange thought," the kidnapped girl writes in her diary, "I would not want this not to have happened. Because if I escape I shall be a completely different and I think better person. Because if I don't escape, if something dreadful happened, I shall still know that the person I was and would have stayed if this hadn't happened was not the person I now want to be."[20]

Fowles, in short, constructed the novel *The Collector* around a message, and there should be no ambivalence about his meaning. In 1964 Fowles confessed to classing "all writers as either entertainers or preachers." He was honest enough to admit to being a "preacher" himself.[21] His books were intended to teach. According to producer Jud Kinberg, he and his producing partner, John Kohn, also approached their newly purchased property as "a tightly made 'little black and white film,' both a thriller and a story with philosophical substance."[22] On the other hand, director William Wyler had little interest in the philosophical dimension of Fowles' narrative. He was glad to include existential philosophy, discussions of art, and issues of social class as long as they didn't get in the way of his dark tale of erotic obsession and terror. When such topics slowed the pace or impeded the tension of his narrative, he jettisoned them without hesitation. Wyler's film is not a morality tale and it has no social message. His intention was to capture two unique characterizations and mesmerize his audience with them. As Wyler told the *Los Angeles Examiner*: "Almost every young man has met a girl whom he'd like to kidnap and just keep her locked up … own her. Ordinarily, nobody does anything about it. This man does. I think this picture is going to enable me to portray two characters whom I have never seen on the screen before."[23]

Fowles himself was a great cinema fan. In their Hampstead days, he and Elizabeth were weekly regulars at the Everyman, where he analyzed the immediacy of the film experience, the need for realism, and the range and mobility of the camera eye.[24] By 1968 he judged he had already seen at least 2,500 films in his lifetime and asked, "How can so frequently repeated an experience not have indelibly stamped itself on the *mode* of imagination? … panning shots, close shots, tracking, jump cuts, and the rest …

this mode of imagining is far too deep in me to eradicate."[25] This broad, self-conscious experience as a critical viewer, however, left Fowles believing that he was quite as capable of writing a film script and creating a film product as the professionals. He insisted on participating in the making of *The Collector*, trying to shape the finished film to his view.

Fowles forged an immediate bond with Jud Kinberg and John Kohn, the talented young American producers who had purchased the film rights. They set off together scouring London and the English countryside for locations. Within months, however, the small art film they planned had become a major Hollywood project. The acclaimed director William Wyler read Fowles's novel and gladly gave up *The Sound of Music* to direct the film. Michael Frankovich, the new head of Columbia Pictures, moved the shooting location to Columbia Studios in California, conceding only a few exterior locations to be shot in England. The established scriptwriter Stanley Mann was brought in to write it with John Kohn.

The first script they produced completely altered the book. The characters were "totally changed," Fowles thundered, "motivations changed, most of all my ideas changed." The English dialogue was "distorted with Americanisms." Worst, the ending was changed so that Miranda's life was saved at the last minute. She escapes and turns the tables on Clegg. Fowles fought back, against the advice of his editor, his agents, the producers, and everyone except his wife Elizabeth, insisting on working directly with Kinberg, Kohn, and Mann on script rewrite. It was a frustrating, painful process that Fowles called "watching the rape of one's daughter."[26] However, Fowles did not seem aware of the most important change embodied in the script, that—with occasional exceptions in voice-overs by Clegg—the story was not narrated in diary fashion, but was told from outside as if in the third person. The result is that, in contrast to the interior diaries of the novel, the audience is seldom privy to the intimate thoughts, motivations, and transformations of Clegg and Miranda.

In March 1964 Wyler flew Fowles to Hollywood to consult on the script for two weeks. Fowles documented this adventure in his diaries, in copies of opinionated formal complaints directed to William Wyler, and in a long, unpublished article, "Illusionsville: A Fortnight in Hollywood," that he ultimately suppressed as too damning.[27] Fowles rather naively regarded Wyler's courteous invitation as a *carte blanche* to meddle in all aspects of making the film. While working daily on the script with Kinberg and Kohn, he was also arguing about sets, costumes, dialogue, and casting, haranguing carpenters and wardrobe mistresses, and turning up at rehearsals to object to something or offer his opinion.

Whether Clegg's suits had shoulder pads, whether the finish on furniture was sufficiently distressed, whether there was ugly plush carpet in a Tudor cottage and the right kind of bourgeois knick-knacks in sight, and what the toilet in the underground cellar looked like were extremely important details to Fowles because they were markers or symbols for the dialogue about class that was supposed to go on between Clegg and Miranda. The details were not particularly important to the filmmakers, however, because for them the class issue had become so secondary to the sexual tension between the kidnapper and his victim. Wyler reacted soothingly to the respected novelist, but he left props and costuming to his professionals.

Fowles also believed he should have the final word on casting. He was delighted when Terence Stamp was cast as Clegg. Kinberg called his performance "chilling ... you couldn't take your eyes off him ... letter-perfect, always prepared, and always in absolute control of his voice." The 24-year-old Stamp, a flamboyant swaggering Cockney, completely enchanted the reticent 39-year-old writer who became "Terry's" fascinated and complicit audience for the two weeks—and a friend for years afterwards.

Wyler, Kinberg and Kohn, Fowles himself—they all thought and spoke about Clegg as "the monster." The monster is at the heart of the labyrinth in any fable or tale and, for Wyler at least, this film was about Clegg, the collector. Miranda is simply the beauty with whom he is obsessed. Jason Zinoman points out that in horror movies "the monster has traditionally been a stand-in for some anxiety, political, social, or cultural."[28] This symbolic quality was certainly important to Fowles, who originally created "the monstrous and pitiable Clegg" to deliver the book's social criticism.[29]

> Clegg, the kidnapper, committed the evil; but I tried to show that his evil was largely, perhaps wholly, the result of a bad education, a mean environment, being orphaned; all factors over which he had no control. In short, I tried to establish the virtual *innocence* of the Many. Miranda, the girl he imprisoned, had very little more control than Clegg over what she was; she had well-to-do parents, good educational opportunity, inherited aptitude and intelligence. That does not mean that she was perfect. Far from it—she was arrogant in her ideas, a prig, a liberal-humanist snob, like so many university students. Yet if she had not died she might have

become something better, the kind of being humanity so desperately needs.[30]

For Fowles, observing the monstrous Clegg destroy Miranda was intended to make the reader aware of society's *"state of responsibility"* in order to "arrive at a more just and happier world."[31] Wyler's film, however, presents us with a largely inexplicable monster, one who acts out of selfish desire and "because I can." Although Wyler gives us a bit of an establishing back-story through the early black and white flashback of Freddie mocked by his co-workers before he wins the football pools, there is really no adequate, rational cause for Freddie's sadistic behavior in the film. He is simply bad and, throughout the course of Miranda's imprisonment, he gets worse. Unlike Fowles's monster, Wyler's is not supposed to implicate us, but simply to horrify us.

It is difficult today, when horror films are gory, outrageously violent, and culminate in multiple horrific deaths, to realize how cutting edge Wyler's *Collector* actually was. In 1965, the year of the film's release, the Motion Picture Production and Distribution Code of 1930 (also known as the Hays Code) was still in force, though rapidly eroding. Strictly speaking, *The Collector* violated the Code by focusing on the forbidden theme of sexual perversion and including brief nudity, violence, and the implication of desired rape. Most important, the ending in which kidnap victim Miranda dies and Freddie is not brought to any kind of justice or punishment was a shocking climax by Code standards, a condoning of criminal behavior. By 1968 the Code *would be* abandoned in favor of the Motion Picture Association of America (MPAA) rating system. So *The Collector* is one of those films made during the time of Code erosion and scofflaw movie making (other examples are *Some Like It Hot*, 1959; *Suddenly Last Summer*, 1959; *The Dark at the Top of the Stairs*, 1961; and *The Pawnbroker*, 1964). It was only possible to film *The Collector* according to Wyler's concept of a psychological character study of Freddie's twisted sexuality and Miranda's vulnerability because rigorous censorship was crumbling. The *Village Voice* called the newly released film "the most erotic movie ever to come out past the Production Code."[32]

In characterizing "the monster," *The Collector* also anticipated the wave of frightening, confrontational films that appeared with the eclipse of the Production Code and its replacement with the ratings system. During the decades of the Code and earlier, cinematic evil was clearly something extraordinary and invasive—a creature of supernatural horror like Dracula, a twisted gangster like Scarface. However, from the 1960s on, evil was present in the ordinary. Cosmic evil awaits a young married couple who move into a Manhattan apartment (*Rosemary's Baby*, 1968), or randomly annexes a preteen (*The Exorcist*, 1973), or lurks in the sunlit waters of a beach in New England (*Jaws*, 1975). Jason Zinoman explores films like these in his catalog of "New Horror," scary movies all made since the demise of the Production Code. "What the New Horror movies share," Zinoman argues, "is a sense that the most frightening thing in the world is the unknown, the inability to understand the monster right in front of your face. These movies communicate confusion, disorientation, and the sense that the true source of anxiety is located in between categories: fact and fantasy, art and commerce, the living and the dead." "The central message of New Horror," Zinoman continues, "is that there is no message. The world does not make sense. Evil exists, and there is nothing you can do about it."[33]

The very banality of Clegg's personality, his boy-next-door quality, made him more immediately threatening than any traditional monster. Clegg could be anybody. Kohn and Kinberg pursued Terence Stamp for the part *because* he was pleasant and handsome, not in spite of it. "They didn't want someone who looked like Bela Lugosi, they told everyone. Freddie would be more frightening if he looked gentle and innocent."[34]

Wyler was not a director who depended on experimental shots and camera angles, as did the New Wave directors of the '60s whom Wyler scorned.[35] Most of *The Collector* varies between long to medium shots, mostly from an eye-level angle, as though the audience were watching the action unfold between the two characters in a room or on a stage. For emotional intensity, the camera moves in for close-ups, even occasional extreme close-ups focusing on Stamp's chilling blue eyes or Eggar's terrified green ones. However, Clegg gets emphatic camera treatment several times. The first time he foils an escape attempt, he appears suddenly from above his victim, the low angle of the camera making the normally unassuming clerk appear frighteningly dominant. At the beginning and end of the film, in that thriller-movie convention of a man secretly stalking a beautiful woman, the audience observes the action from Clegg's point of view, watching from over the shoulder as he drives his van through the streets of Hampstead, and keeping track of the potential victim as Clegg does, through the rear view mirror.

Stamp's unnerving ability to morph from shy, socially awkward Freddie into a sadistic monster was key to his outstanding performance. From a loose-limbed, boyish man, hunching his shoulders and gazing downward, he tightens his frame and his eyes seem to glow as if lighted from within. These transformative moments are stressed by Maurice Jarre's score, which turns jarring as Clegg turns monster. Yet the score is perhaps one of the least successful elements of the film. Fowles considered the music "too loud" and even "too whimsical," suggesting to Wyler that at Miranda's abduction "surely silence would be better."[36] Wyler made some adjustments. However, as his biographer opines, "Jarre's sound track is egregiously intrusive. It telegraphs rather than evokes, hyping mood and atmosphere with hammy melodrama."[37]

The film's Miranda was also shaped by casting. Wyler asked for screen tests from several young actresses and, after considerable pressure from Columbia Studio chief Michael Frankovich, Wyler went with Samantha Eggar. Fowles objected. Eggar was nothing like the Miranda of his imagination, for she had none of the vitality and intelligence of his character— or so he thought. He was probably the only man on the set who didn't find Eggar attractive. She was considered so beautiful that Wyler was persuaded to switch filming from black and white to Technicolor (although in subdued tones) to capture her creamy skin tones and rich red hair color. In testing her for make-up, cameraman Robert Surtees was excited by Eggar's luminous skin texture, green eyes, and rich coloring. Film editor Robert Swink remembered comparing her to "a ripe peach." Ultimately, Wyler and Surtees decided to film Eggar's close-ups without gauze, revealing her freckles and occasionally shiny nose. Stamp, ironically, was filmed through a gauzed lens.[38] The actress's shining auburn hair was also used as a sexual trigger in several scenes in the finished film, when Stamp as Clegg begins to stroke Miranda's hair, then gradually loses control of himself as he roughly wraps his hands in her long tresses and almost crushes the girl's head.

Wyler's major reason for casting Samantha Eggar was that he believed he could "get a performance out of her." Wyler had wrung great performances out of his actresses, as producer Jud Kinberg cautiously phrased it in an October 1999 interview, by "putting pressure on them." After a pause, Kinberg amended his remarks and said to me, "he bullied them." Kinberg acknowledged that Eggar didn't have the training for the part.[39] However, Wyler needed Samantha Eggar's performance as Miranda to convey the girl's extreme, terrifying isolation and sexual vulnerability. The director used an armory of strategies to achieve this performance.

First, in keeping with his approach to the novel as a psychological study of perverse sexuality, Wyler decided to film the scenes of Miranda's captivity in chronological sequence. This built pressure and tension among the cast and crew and created the illusion for Eggar of actually living Miranda's experience. It was Wyler's intention that the actress would inhabit the role. He completely isolated Eggar, forbidding her to leave the set during the day nor allowing her to eat with the rest of the cast and crew. She was rehearsed on Sundays until late in the evening.[40]

Wyler further isolated her socially, without explanation, by recruiting Terence Stamp to cooperate, playing on Stamp's insecure ego and sense of conspiracy. In the first week of rehearsal, Wyler drew Stamp aside.

"You were at acting school with Sam?" he asked.

"Yeah, I had a crush on her, as it happens."

"Don't get too friendly now."

"Why?"

"I want a real tension on film. O.K?" he said tersely.

"O.K, if you say so."[41]

Indeed, Stamp and Eggar had been fellow-students and eventually good friends at London's Webber Douglas Academy of Dramatic Art in the late '50s. In his memoirs, Stamp waxes lyrical over Eggar "the queen in this hive ... and the girl most of the boys had a crush on," as a "gamine with green eyes and a mop of hair Titian would have flipped over."[42] They were never an item but, knowing he was very sweet on her, Sam Eggar made the thoughtful gesture of sneaking into Terry's dressing room before his most important student performance (as Iago) before critics and potential agents, to wish him well and leave him her precious lucky piece, her Zippo lighter.[43] A few years later, he was proud to escort her as his date to the glittering premier of *Billy Budd* with his parents and the Peter Ustinovs.[44]

Despite their friendship, Stamp complied when Wyler warned him to stay in character during the shooting, to withdraw any friendship or kindness from Eggar and treat her coldly. With the admiring John Fowles as his audience during the rehearsal period, Stamp took this bad boy treatment to extremes. Stamp ignored his co-star even while rehearsing with her, treated her with icy contempt, made fun of her, played mean jokes, and was in general nasty—an attitude which spread through the company.

Fowles observed that "the favorite sport on the Columbia lot is making fun of her behind her back."[45] In a rare moment of pity, he likened Sam to "a Renaissance princess among all the courtiers who know she's going to be poisoned for state reasons at dinner that night."[46] While this mean-spirited charade continued, neither Stamp nor anyone else informed John Fowles that this was all merely an actor cooperating with a director's strategy. Fowles was drawn in. Together, like naughty schoolboys, Stamp and Fowles tormented Eggar, undermining her confidence and even advocating for her replacement.[47]

"I guess I was supposed to feel trapped, and I did," Samantha Eggar would recall.[48] She lost ten pounds and grew thin and gaunt. She stumbled and blew her lines. Three weeks into rehearsal, she was fired. As she later recalled, "Terry Stamp's nasty attitude toward me undermined me so much that I just became a sort of squashed balloon and, rightly, I got fired."[49] Frankovich hid her away in Palm Springs for two weeks while other actresses were publicly vetted. There, Eggar felt more trapped and confused. Fowles, to the end of his days, believed himself responsible for Eggar's downfall, when it was clearly all part of Wyler's strategy.

Wyler rehired her only a few days after Fowles returned to England, loading Eggar with still more restrictions. He also assigned Eggar an "acting coach," Kathleen Freeman, who was actually a character actress. Eggar was allowed to speak only with Freeman on the set. All instructions came through her, as did hair-raising anecdotes Freeman told her about a schizophrenic paranoid relative.[50]

To assist Eggar's performance as a sexually vulnerable girl, Wyler shot the love scene between Clegg and Miranda with Samantha entirely nude in front of her fully dressed co-star (still treating her scornfully), their director, and the crew. As Eggar recalled, "we shot that love scene for what seemed like weeks. I kept wondering why I had to stand there with no clothes on when they were only shooting me from the shoulders up. Willy always used to sit, and it was a strange level where his eyes were."[51]

Wyler's wiles were legion. The terrible dénouement of the film, when Miranda hits Clegg over the head with a shovel and then tries to escape, was to be filmed in torrential rain. Each time Eggar opened the door to enter the scene, Wyler signaled the prop man to throw a bucket of cold water right in her face.[52] In the resulting scene as Eggar, clad in a soaking, nearly transparent garment, struggles shrieking in the wet mud with Stamp dragging her savagely back to her cell, her terror is palpable. Eggar had moved beyond acting and was truly in a terrorized state.

She never forgave Terence Stamp for the way he treated her on the set of *The Collector*.

While Wyler's treatment of Samantha Eggar has been documented and written about over the years, little has been mentioned about how this role-playing strategy of Wyler's transformed Terence Stamp from the warm-spirited, tender, somewhat insecure young man he actually was into a person capable of treating a friend sadistically. Working class, 24-year-old Stamp was lonely and homesick during the shooting of *The Collector*, missing his mother's cooking and his family.[53] Wyler spoke about making Sam live the part of Miranda, but he never spoke about turning Terry into

In *The Collector* Miranda Grey (Samantha Eggar) and Frederick Clegg (Terence Stamp) sit in the dungeon he has prepared for her in his country house. Although Clegg thinks of his captive as a guest, Miranda is a victim, like one of the butterflies in his collection—or one of Bluebeard's wives (Getty Images).

Clegg, about "getting a performance out of him," as well. Yet one suspects that this was part of Wyler's agenda when he asked Stamp to isolate Eggar. Cooperatively, Stamp began by being indifferent and chilly towards his co-star. But, as Fowles's diaries tell us, Stamp's contemptuous behavior and mean jokes became more elaborate, his speeches about her incompetence more over-the-top and rehearsed. Wyler rewarded this behavior. While Eggar was being isolated and ill used, Stamp was invited into Wyler's inner sanctum. Wyler invited prominent directors to the set to watch Terry's work and arranged introductions. Stamp glowed, feeling "like [Wyler] was laying out a career for me, introducing me around. He was very generous to me."[54] He wanted to please Wyler. At the shooting of the final scene in the Columbia studios, before the English exteriors were shot, Wyler privately said to Stamp, "She's dead. Staying faithful to your performance, now what do you do?" Proud of being so trusted, Stamp replied, "Now is my chance to fuck her .... He can't get a hard-on. Now that she's dead, it's my chance." Wyler's mentoring had led Stamp to think like Freddie Clegg as well as to act like him. Weeks after they returned to England, Wyler summoned Stamp to a London studio where they actually shot a piece of this imagined scene of necrophilia. "Just enough for a close-up," urged Wyler. "Do you think you can give me that look? *Now's my chance to do the thing*?" Wyler never used it.[55]

However questionable his methods, Wyler's direction was successful. At the May 1965 Cannes Film Festival both Terence Stamp and Samantha Eggar won Best in their acting categories. Eggar also won Best Actress at the Golden Globes, at the Sant Sordi Awards in Barcelona, and was nominated for an Academy Award. Yet the politicking at Cannes revealed that Wyler's ruthless direction created grudges that never healed. Not only had both the principal actors been nominated for Best Actor and Best Actress, but *The Collector* itself was nominated for Best Film. Reception for *The Collector* was very positive and the buzz was strong that the movie would receive the award. Wyler felt confident of the outcome. Olivia de Havilland, serving as the first female president of the Festival that year, had been directed by Wyler in *The Heiress* in 1949. With his bullying methods, the director "got a performance out of" de Havilland that won her the 1950 Oscar, the Golden Globe, and the New York Film Critics Award, all for Best Actress. As the board began meeting for the 1965 Cannes awards, Wyler assured Jud Kinberg, "Don't worry. Olivia owes me." Kinberg was with Wyler when the bombshell was dropped: "Olivia de Havilland told the board that she would *die* before she would give that son-of-a-bitch Best Picture. And Willy was *stunned!*"[56] The Palme d'Or went to *The Knack ... and How to Get It*, directed by Richard Lester.

In the novel of *The Collector*, Miranda's evolution into an *aristo*, a more mature artist and a more creative, open-minded person is measured through diary entries about her mentor, artist George Paston. A large part of her mental and emotional journey is stimulated by her memories of him. Paston or, as he is designated, G.P., is on the faculty at the Slade School of Art in London where Miranda studies. He is an established artist with a bohemian lifestyle and a reputation for sexual promiscuity that virginal Miranda, in 1960, finds a little shocking. Physically rough-hewn and even ugly, he is old enough to be her father and is something of a Prospero-figure to innocent, "'tis-new-to-thee" Miranda. G.P. encourages her talent, but brutally criticizes her conventional efforts, no matter how clever and accomplished. He is tough on her, mocking her student poses, middle-class background, and sense of entitlement. But he also falls in love with her. Miranda, young and conventional, is afraid. Unlike Clegg, who collects Miranda to own and objectify her, the more ethical G.P. sadly insists that Miranda leave him, releasing her—ironically—into the clutches of the man who will imprison her.

This erotically charged relationship between older male teacher and young, innocent, upper-class female student is one that Fowles had personally experienced several times during his teaching career to that point. In 1953–54 while a teacher at the Ashridge College of Citizenship in Hertsfordshire, he became romantically obsessed with two 20-year-old sophisticates from South Africa, first Sally Simpson and then Sanchia Humphries. These girls were the prototypes and inspiration behind the characters Rose and Lily in *The Magus*.[57] From 1954 to 1963, as a teacher at a glorified secretarial school for well-to-do international girls, he was an admired, favorite master, which indicates some mutual attraction.[58] There is no evidence that any of these friendships were sexually consummated, but the flirtatious attention stroked his ego and haunted his imagination. "I used to 'kidnap and imprison' generalized girls—archetypes. But for many years it has had to be someone I know—students."[59] G.P. is a spokesperson for Fowles himself and often sounds like he's quoting from *The Aristos*, which was being composed alongside *The Collector* in the early 1960s.

Through Miranda's diary, G.P. is present as the third full character in a novel documenting a triangular relationship. Trapped in the cellar, condemned to silence, the girl spends long hours of her underground imprisonment mentally revisiting her relationship with G.P., writing out the memories and dialogue and annotating the narrative with her reflections. She summons him up and, through her writing, makes him a real character. This narrative technique allows Fowles to incorporate discussions of art and ethics into the immediate drama of the struggle between Clegg and Miranda. The Miranda/G.P. philosophical arguments take place in her head and on the page. She ponders G.P.'s opinionated teachings, his demonstrations of "good" art. She pursues his recommendations of recorded music, of paintings, of books. She wistfully recalls his declaration of feeling for her and wrestles with his sexual challenge to her conventional morality. In this way, Miranda grows and changes. At the moment of her death Miranda, like a butterfly emerging from a chrysalis, is ready to embrace her potential as a person, an artist, and as G.P.'s peer and lover. Although she is trapped by Clegg in a completely static situation, the presence of G.P., actively imagined and recalled through her writing, makes Miranda a dynamic character.

The film of *The Collector* is quite different, however. By the time of its completion, the triangular rhythm among Clegg, Miranda, and G.P. had become a tense duet. George Paston had begun as a character written into the script. Kinberg, Kohn, and Fowles used black and white flashbacks to incorporate into the filming both the philosophical discussions of mentor and student and the memories of a budding sexual relationship. The entire script, including the G.P. flashbacks, was filmed with respected English actor Kenneth More in the Paston role, although the conventionally handsome More, the typecast essence of cheerful middle-class normalcy, seems an odd choice for the worn, bohemian, iconoclastic G.P.

The rough cut of the film ran over three hours. Wyler and editor Robert Swink both thought it too long and too slow. They pulled out the first of the Paston flashbacks and felt the speed improved. One by one they eliminated the flashbacks, until none remained. G.P.'s presence in *The Collector* was reduced to a single shot of the back of Kenneth More's head in a Hampstead pub and several jealous, menacing references from Clegg to Miranda about "that chap," that "lah-di-dah painter" that she was in love with. Wyler personally conveyed the bad news to More as the entire Paston episode disappeared.[60]

Length and pacing were the only motivations that Wyler ever admitted to for this massive cut. However, the complete elimination of G.P. and Miranda's flashbacks had the consequence of reinforcing Wyler's vision of *The Collector* as an erotically twisted psychodrama rather than an allegory about the conflict of philosophies and social class. In one fell swoop of editing, Miranda was changed from a dynamic character evolving into an *aristo* to simply a vulnerable victim locked in a struggle to the death with the maniac who keeps her prisoner. She remains static, a kind of proverbial deer in the headlights. The audience hears no arguments about existentialism, good art, or the moral life. While a few class references remain, class is relegated to a subtext of Clegg's psychosis. Without the visual flashbacks into artist's studio and open city streets, the atmosphere of the film also becomes much more claustrophobic. There is no escape from the unrelenting experience of Bluebeard's basement.

The result of Wyler's cutting and his emphasis on the psychosexual horror story was that the Heraclitean philosophy that Fowles had hoped would be presented to the world simply vanished from the movie. Few viewers understood that Miranda represented the *aristoi* (the best possible for a situation) and Clegg the *hoi polloi*, the many. Even fewer understood, because it was never seen on screen, that Miranda changes during the period of her imprisonment, how—like a chrysalis transforming into a butterfly—she is about to emerge as "the kind of being humanity so desperately needs." In the film, Miranda remains—compellingly, simply—a vulnerable, terrified young woman at the mercy of a demented, obsessed young man who becomes more powerful and monstrous as he realizes that he has no restraints. This is exactly what Wyler wanted to achieve and he nailed it.

Fowles himself was publicly flattering to Wyler when he viewed the film for the first time. To his diary he confided that it was "no better, and not much worse than I expected; technicolored and glossied and blunted out of all contact with the book... fatally soft at the edges artistically." He was, however, very surprised by the power of the performance Wyler had "got out of" Samantha Eggar.[61]

Less diplomatically, Elizabeth Fowles's verdict was "I think it stinks. I was bored into the ground the second time around."[62]

The filming of *The Collector* was where a naïve John Fowles was first bloodied by Hollywood. His extensive diary notes of his disillusionment were so scathing that he suppressed the article based on them, "Illusionsville: A Fortnight in Hollywood," that he had hoped to publish. The experience led him to resolve to write his own (disastrous) script for *The Magus* a year later and made him very wary about the sale and filming of *The French Lieutenant's Woman*. Yet he remained fascinated by the movies and continued to dabble, always hopeful that—with his help—filmmakers would get it right. Ultimately, the most enduring legacy to come out of the experience may have been the somewhat autobiographical character and career of the protagonist of *Daniel Martin,* the successful 1970s Hollywood scriptwriter who leaves the film industry and comes home to his true wife, his true country, and his true calling in writing novels.

Notes

1. John Fowles, *The Collector* (New York: Little, Brown, 1963).

2. Terence Stamp, *Double Feature* (London: Bloomsbury Press, 1989), p. 97.

3. Stamp, p. 111.

4. Edna Eileen Hand Warburton, *John Fowles and the Dead Woman: The Theme of Carnal Knowledge and the Technique of Source Inversion in John Fowles's Fiction*, University of Pennsylvania, doctoral dissertation, 1980 (Ann Arbor: University of Michigan, 1980), pp. 172–218. Microfiche.

5. The scene in *The Collector* in which Clegg shows Miranda his butterfly room and she recognizes all her beautiful predecessors in death is an echo of the Bluebeard tale in both the novel and the film.

6. "The Blue Beard," *The Classic Fairy Tales*, ed. Iona and Peter Opie (London: Oxford University Press, 1974), pp. 103–109. The Opies cite several variants. Other variants may be found in *The Grimm's German Folk Tales*, trans. Francis P. Magoun, Jr., and Alexander H. Krappe (Carbondale: Southern Illinois University Press, 1960).

7. Bruno Bettelheim, *The Uses of Enchantment: The Meaning and Importance of Fairy Tales* (New York: Alfred Knopf, 1976), p. 303.

8. "John Fowles," in *Counterpoint*, ed. Roy Newquist (Chicago: Rand, McNally, 1964), p. 219.

9. John Fowles Diaries, vol. 8, 3 Feb. 1963. The full diaries are archived among the "John Fowles Papers" in the Harry Ransom Center for the Humanities (HRC) at the University of Texas, Austin. Subsequent references to these diaries will be abbreviated JFD, followed by the volume number and the date designated by John Fowles.

10. JFD, "THE COLLECTOR: Some Notes," 18 Apr. 1963, HRC 19/5, written in "diary" form, 2 December 1960–18 April 1963. The first draft of "I Write, Therefore I Am" (1964) is in the HRC; the final version is rpt., in *Wormholes*, pp. 5–12.

11. JFD 8, 16 Apr. 1963.

12. JFD 7, 19 Nov. 1960.

13. JFD 8, 7 May 1963.

14. JFD 8, 2 Dec. 1960.

15. John Fowles, *The Aristos*, rev. ed. (New York: New American Library, 1970), p. 10.

16. JFD 8, 2 Dec. 1960.

17. John Fowles, letter to Tom Maschler, 8 July 1963, pasted into JFD 7, 8 July 63.

18. John Fowles, "I Write, Therefore I Am," *Evergreen Review* August–September 1965, pp. 16–17 and 89–91; rpt., *Wormholes*, p. 12.

19. Fowles, *The Aristos*, Chapter 5, # 4, 6, pp. 68–69.

20. Fowles, *The Collector*, p. 228.

21. Fowles, "I Write, Therefore I Am," p. 9.

22. Jud Kinberg, interview with author, 29 Oct. 1999, New York. Quoted in *John Fowles: A Life in Two Worlds*, by Eileen Warburton (New York: Viking Penguin, 2004), p. 229.

23. *Los Angeles Examiner* 31 May 64; quoted in Axel Madsen, *William Wyler: The Authorized Biography* (New York: Thomas Cromwell, 1973), p. 375.

24. JFD V, 9 Sept. 1955 (cited in Warburton, *John Fowles*, p. 192).

25. John Fowles, "Notes on an Unfinished Novel," *Harper's Magazine*, July 1968; rpt., *Wormholes*, p. 29.

26. JFD 8, 18 Nov. 1963.

27. JFD, "Hollywood, March 1964," X, no date, 16–29 March 1964. Contains JFD 10, pp. 1–32; "Illusionsville: A Fortnight in Hollywood" (unpublished article), pp. 1–17; and "For Mr. Wyler—Comments from John Fowles," pp. 1–4.

28. Jason Zinoman, *Shock Value: How a Few Eccentric Outsiders Gave Us Nightmares, Conquered Hollywood and Invented Modern Horror* (New York: Penguin Press, 2011), p. 181.

29. John Fowles, "Hardy and the Hag," in *Thomas Hardy After Fifty Years*, ed. Lance St. John Butler (London: Macmillan, 1977); rpt., *Wormholes*, p. 148.

30. Fowles, *The Aristos*, p. 10.

31. *Ibid.*

32. Andrew Sarris, "Review of 'The Collector,'" *The Village Voice* 24 June 1965. Quoted in Jan Herman, *A Talent for Trouble: The Life of Hollywood's Most Acclaimed Director, William Wyler* (New York: G.P. Putnam, 1995), p. 429.

33. Zinoman, *Shock Value*, p. 9.

34. Ian Herman, *A Talent for Trouble: The Life of Hollywood's Most Acclaimed Director, William Wyler* (New York: G.P. Putnam, 1995), p. 208.

35. Axel Madsen, *William Wyler: The Authorized Biography* (New York: Thomas Cromwell, 1973), p. 372.

36. Herman, pp. 429–30.

37. *Ibid.*, p. 428.

38. *Ibid.*, p. 425.

39. Kinberg, 29 Oct. 1999.

40. Herman, p. 424.

41. Stamp, *Double Feature*, p. 113.

42. Terence Stamp, *Coming Attractions* (London: Grafton Books, 1989), p. 100.

43. Stamp, *Double Feature*, pp. 142–43.

44. *Ibid.*, p. 63.

45. JFD "Hollywood" 10, p. 14.

46. *Ibid.*, 10, p. 17.

47. Also "For Mr. Wyler—Comments from John Fowles."

48. Madsen, p. 374.

49. *Ibid.*, p. 374.

50. Herman, p. 423.

51. *Ibid.*, p. 425.

52. *Ibid.*, p. 424.

53. Stamp, *Double Feature*, p. 116.

54. Herman, p. 426.

55. *Ibid.*, p. 427.

56. Kinberg, quoted in Warburton, *John Fowles*, p. 260.

57. Warburton, *John Fowles*, pp. 156–76 and 199–200, 233.

58. *Ibid.*, p. 204.

59. JFD 8, 16 Apr. 1963.

60. Herman, pp. 427–28.

61. JFD 8, 25 Feb. 1965 and 19 May 1965.

62. Letter from Elizabeth Fowles to Denys and Monica Sharrocks, 1 May 1965, in John Fowles Papers, Sharrocks Collection, Harry Ransom Center for the Humanities, Austin, TX.

Cinematic Godgames:
The Magus on Film

James Aubrey

"The film world stinks," John Fowles wrote in his diary on December 3, 1963, after spending an evening with several visitors from Hollywood.[1] This kind of mistrust was reinforced by his disappointment with the 1967 adaptation of his novel *The Collector*, and made Fowles determined to write the screenplay himself for the 1968 film of his 1965 novel *The Magus*.[2] The outcome was not happy.

It is widely agreed in the film industry that authors of books are often not capable of adapting their own work to the screen.[3] Fowles was more sophisticated about film than most novelists, but even he came to agree that the art of screenwriting requires different talents from novel writing.[4] Writing a screenplay for an encyclopedic novel such as *The Magus* would have posed a challenge to any screenwriter. When would-be producer Jud Kinberg first read the novel, his reaction was "We can't make a movie from this!" but much of the material did seem to have cinematic potential.[5] It was partly the 656-page length that made its adaptation to film seem impossible, as well as its scope spanning the first half of the twentieth century, its several shifts of supposed reality, and its featuring an extravagant title character who seems to have unlimited, perhaps even supernatural resources. This was not the most favorable material to be made into a feature-length film with a screen time of less than two hours.

Another challenge faced by a would-be adapter of *The Magus* is the complexity of the plot, with its multiple layers of supposed reality. The protagonist of the story is Nicholas Urfe, who has exiled himself from responsibilities, including commitment to his girlfriend, Alison, by taking a teaching job in a boys' school on a Greek island. He meets a wealthy eccentric named Maurice Conchis, who invites Nicholas to visit his villa regularly, during which visits he stages various events to unsettle Nicholas. With the assistance of twins named Rose and Lily, Conchis leads Nicholas by turns to believe that Conchis is a deserter from World War I and Lily the ghost of his former girlfriend; that he is a psychiatrist and Lily his schizophrenic patient undergoing an experimental form of therapy; that he is a playwright and Lily an actress in an experimental form of theater. Ultimately, she seems to be an employee hired to manipulate Nicholas into understanding that there is no god, nor can any belief system relieve him of individual responsibility for his decisions in life. At the end of the story, a newly-enlightened Nicholas confronts Alison in London, after which they may part or may remain together: the ending is open.

In late 1965 Fowles wrote a treatment for the film, a description of the concept and approach that would be the basis for "pitching" the project to a studio. He did not enjoy this task, begun in early November 1965 and finished on 10 December, calling it "a job that both bores and disgusts me." He expressed relief in his journal when he could begin writing the actual screenplay, with its dialogue and detail.[6] Fowles's screenplay was fairly faithful to the novel, and the film mostly adhered to the screenplay; however, compressing any long novel into a 100-page script of mostly dialogue posed difficulties. Asking the novelist himself to take on that task added a challenge, for Fowles had no experience with screenwriting. Fowles was probably unwise to preserve the underlying premise, that some eccentric millionaire would devote his resources to reforming a sequence of selfish nobodies. Audiences are often willing to suspend disbelief in an unrealistic premise, but doing so can make a story feel less compelling. Fowles may also have underestimated the difficulty of establishing a sequence of four different "realities"; each scenario had to be made convincing, or at least believable, for spectators to feel a shock of disillusion when the metaphorical rug is pulled out from under them. The disillusioning of Nicholas bewilders him at first, but he and the reader come to accept each successive explanation. In the film, the successive realities tend to bewilder spectators rather than leave them feeling newly enlightened. Fowles probably overestimated the capacity of most moviegoers to understand not only how Nicholas has been changed but that they, like Nicholas, also must change. The new Nicholas may deserve Anne near the end of the film, but no one is sensing his new worthiness when, supposedly dead, Anne suddenly reappears with Conchis in a motorboat and then, just as inexplicably, disappears again. As the film ends, Nicholas muses philosophically, but audience members tend to scratch their heads. The film, like the novel, attempts to teach the audience to take charge of their lives instead of transferring responsibility to some magus figure or false deity. In one of his last interviews Fowles declared, "The one thing I wanted to be clear about in *The Magus* is that there is no god."[7] Alas that lesson, clear enough in the novel, is lost on a viewer of the film adaptation who is having difficulty following the plot.

On the first page of Fowles's screenplay is typed what appears to have been his preferred title for the film, "the god game," above the actual title, in parentheses: "(THE MAGUS)."[8] *The Godgame* had also been his working title for the novel over the decade he was writing it, so Fowles may have been harboring regret over having published the book as *The Magus*, Latin for "the wise man," or "the magician," whose film adaptation would inevitably retain the same title. In any case, the presence of the word *godgame* on the title page indicates the importance to Fowles of the atheistic idea that religion is a psychological trick we play on ourselves. The film does not explain this line of thinking, however, and one of the screenplay's most atheistic lines was omitted from the film: "This life is not a waiting for another world," as Conchis points out to Nicholas.[9] Partly because the film's ideological underpinnings are obscure, many spectators left the theater wondering, "What was that about?"

Fowles's idea for beginning the film was to use "cinematic conjuring tricks" under the opening credits—images such as a modern goatherd turning suddenly into a faun, or three nannygoats among rocks turning into three goddesses, and then back to goats again. Director Guy Green proceeded instead with realism. In another scene, however, where Fowles had suggested realism, Green went for the fantastic. It is during an early scenario, after a dinner when Julie has pretended to be a ghost, that Nicholas and the film audience see her suddenly costumed as Artemis, protecting a girl being pursued through the air and seeming to emerge from a dark tunnel over the empty space above the sea beyond the villa. The spectator is as astonished as Nicholas, for this is evidently a supernatural occurrence, not just some elaborate staging by Conchis. In the screenplay, Fowles had proposed a surprising but not a fantastic event: "Torches suddenly illuminate a path in the trees. A GIRL is running. She wears a classical white chiton and high-laced sandals. Dishevelled hair. CAMERA HOLDS on her terrified face as she casts a look over her shoulder."[10] She is pursued by a male made up to look like a Greek satyr. Suddenly the fig-

In *The Magus* Julie (Candice Bergen), costumed as the Greek goddess Artemis, seems to shoot and kill a satyr during one of the staged events at the villa of Maurice Conchis, where Nicholas Urfe is having mysterious experiences intended to make him a better person (Getty Images).

ure of Artemis appears on a ledge above and shoots a pursuing satyr with her bow and arrow. The scene could have been staged with actors and lighting; however, Green evidently decided to go for a fantastic scene, more like the later, hallucinatory dream sequence than the realistic style of most of the rest of the film. Yet even in that fantasy-dream sequence, a realistic incident occurs when Conchis kicks a machine that is malfunctioning—a comic moment in an otherwise intensely dramatic episode. Such inconsistencies of style could be another reason that audiences watching *The Magus* had some difficulty following the movie.

Fowles's inexperience as a screenwriter can be seen as early as the second page of the script, where Nicholas responds to the first spoken dialogue of the film, as a boat crewman (played by Fowles) points to their island destination and announces, "Phraxos." In the script Fowles writes, "NICHOLAS nods. CAMERA CLOSES ON PROFILE of NICHOLAS's grimly expressionless face. It shows both SENSITIVITY and SELF-ABSORPTION: THE TWO KEYS TO HIS CHARACTER."[11] No performance by an actor could convey all these characteristics through a silent facial non-expression, but Fowles must have imagined it was possible—as it would be in a novel.

The film's open ending further contributed to audience confusion. The original screenplay ends differently, with a reunion between Nicholas and Alison that was cut from the film as it was eventually released. Originally a voiceover quoting T.S. Eliot was to provide a transition between the last two scenes, as the location shifts from Conchis' Greek villa to Anne's London flat. Nicholas stares out the window as Anne arrives in her flight attendant's uniform. She says, "I wasn't sure you'd be here," so they have evidently reached some sort of tentative arrangement to meet subsequent to an earlier scene when she had climbed into Conchis's speedboat and left Nicholas standing, bewildered, back in Greece. Anne sees her paperweight on the table, which Nicholas has evidently brought with him from the villa, where he found it beside a smiling, Archaic Greek statue at the mysteriously abandoned villa. Anne asks Nicholas, "What would you advise me to do with it?" Nicholas replies, "In a world full of bastards like me ... keep it." The next line of the screenplay is the last, as Nicholas asks Anne, "Bring any cigarettes?"[12] They are evidently reverting to their previous, intimate behavior in a renewed relationship. His self-deprecating remark cues the viewer that Nicholas has grown in self-awareness as well as matured morally, and the scene overall provides the viewer with a nearly conventional ending to their relationship and closure to the story. Fowles may have written this scene under pressure from the producers to provide a happy ending, for he later wrote in his journal that he was pleased that the studio had cut it from the released film. But in commercial terms, even though the open ending of the film made it more artful and rhetorically playful and more closely aligned with the novel, the decision to omit the reunion of Nicholas and Alison was probably a mistake.

Other changes Fowles made to compress *The Magus* into a two-hour film were good ones. It was probably an easy decision for him to conflate the novel's twins, Lily and Julie (also known as Rose and June), into one character, Julie, even though doing so required her to explain that someone else wearing a mask enabled her occasionally to seem to be in two places at once. Also well advised was Fowles's decision to make the experience of Conchis in World War II into the moral centerpiece of the story, a flashback in which Conchis, as mayor, makes a choice not to execute three partisans even though doing so would have saved the lives of thirty villagers. Nicholas' later, similar choice not to flog the sexually "unfaithful" Julie is thus made comprehensible as an analogous acceptance of personal responsibility for an ethical decision in the absence of any higher moral authority.

The names of the characters in *The Magus* are symbolic, so it is worth noting that Fowles changed some names but not others in the screenplay. The magus or magician character is named Maurice Conchis, which the novel points out is pronounced with a soft *ch* so that his last name is a homonym for the word *conscious*—a state of mind that he, unlike his protégés, might be said to have fully attained.[13] Conchis' manipulative assistants in the novel are twins named Lily and Rose, apparently named after the flowers that appear on the Tarot card representing him as The Magician, described in the epigraph to the 1965 version of the novel as a "mountebank in the world of vulgar trickery," a quotation from A.E. Waite's 1912 *Key to the Tarot*. On the Waite illustration of the card, the magician stands behind an array of flowers identified as "roses and lilies, the *flos campi* and *lilium convallium*, changed into garden flowers, to show the culture of aspiration."[14] Although Fowles deleted this epigraph from the revised edition of *The Magus* some twelve years later, he evidently knew Waite's Rider deck of Tarot cards well and ascribed important resonance to the quotation when the book came out. In the screenplay, probably to simplify the narrative, the twins are conflated into one, keeping the name Lily perhaps because the lily is the identifiable flower on the Tarot card and also, again perhaps, because the name is privileged later in the novel by its attachment to the mother of the twins and former lover of Conchis, Mrs. Lily De Seitas, a trickster figure whose name when pronounced contains the word *deceit*. In the novel the characters Nicholas and Alison happen to bear the names of the two lovers in Chaucer's "The Miller's Tale," but that is probably coincidental; their names were more likely chosen for their associations with the world of wild nature that Fowles valued so highly. *Nicolas* is the name of the title character in the French autobiography of Restif de la Bretonne, whose childhood discovery of a wonderful, secret valley Fowles quotes from at length in an essay where he remarks that he borrowed from *Monsieur Nicolas* the phrase *sacred combe* for his autobiographical novel, *Daniel Martin*.[15] The name Alison, as Fowles explains in the novel, derives from the flower "sweet Alyssum," whose association with sweetness helps to characterize her, at least in Fowles's mind; so it is surprising that Fowles changed her name in the screenplay to Anne. Perhaps for the film he wanted a more common name to help establish her ordinariness and lack of pretension, to balance her association with the fertility goddess Demeter.[16] Or Fowles may have anticipated that producers would want her character to have a shorter name, one more familiar to American audiences. Likewise the decision to omit the screenplay's reference to Conchis as "Prospero," an allusion to *The Tempest*, was probably made with audiences in mind.[17] As auditors, filmgoers are less likely than novel readers to recognize the significance of devices such as symbolism and allusion.

Objects in the film are obviously meant to serve as symbols, as well. At the end of the film, Nicholas discovers an archaic Greek statue behind a door in a niche at Conchis' villa, which seems to have been abandoned. The camera holds a shot of this mysterious object as Nicholas gazes at it, signaling its symbolic importance. The spectator hears the voice of Conchis start to recite a passage from T.S. Eliot's *Four Quartets*, the same passage that Nicholas has earlier had called to his attention in a book left for him to find on the beach: "We shall not cease from exploration, and the end of our exploring will be to arrive where we began and to know the place for the first time." In the middle of the passage, however, the voice of the reader changes from that of Conchis to that of Nicholas, as if to signal that the pupil has internalized the lesson of the master, whose human face has been the magus but whose underlying truth is more deeply represented by the statue with the enigmatic smile. The novel makes clearer than the film does that the smile represents a kind of truth that lies behind the "vulgar trickery" of Conchis' and the world's illusions. In terms of plot, Nicholas recognizes that Conchis has been playing games with him in order to help him recognize that the human systems are artificial constructs that he must regard with amused, ironic detachment—with a smile. The film provides a spectator insufficient help in arriving at this interpretation, however, so it is small wonder that audiences seeing *The Magus* for the first time felt bafflement more often than enlightenment.

Another symbolic object used in the film but not in the novel is Anne's paperweight, a hemispherical piece of glass that contains a single flower almost as large as its circumference, a daisy with white petals and a yellow center. Anne explains that she never travels without it, that this object has deeply symbolic meaning for her as a representation of what is at the heart of everything, at "the core," as she asks Nicholas in her French accent to confirm is the right word in English. The paperweight is also to be associated with personal integrity. In a flashback to the time of Nicholas' impending departure to Greece, Anne gives the paperweight to Nicholas "impulsively" when he tells her that he will take her with him. She then declares, "I don't need it any more," believing that he has committed himself to their relationship. As soon as she leaves the room, however, he rebooks his flight to leave the next day, without her, demonstrating his lack of integrity and unworthiness to possess the paperweight.[18] When the flashback ends, Nicholas is sitting in his room in Greece with the paperweight on the desk in front of him. He gives it a spin, and as the camera closes in on it, the spinning paperweight becomes a spinning parasol, held by Lily, the ghostly character acted by Julie, for whom Nicholas is ready to betray the memory of Anne.[19] The paperweight is thus a symbol of Anne's love for Nicholas, and a reminder to him that personal commitment to others should supersede more superficial impulses, including beliefs in ideological systems such as the "godgame" that Conchis is playing with him.

The physical paperweight described in Fowles's screenplay is different from the one actually used in the film. Fowles's script calls for a glass paperweight with *millefiore* inside, that is, with a multitude of tiny, variously-colored flowers in the style of Venetian art glass. Someone may have pointed out that tiny flowers would be less easily recognized as such on a movie screen than one large flower would be. In any case, a daisy paperweight would have been easier for a prop manager to obtain. Fowles's primary concern was probably that the paperweight contain a floral image for its association with outdoor nature, Fowles's lifelong preoccupation; so he probably had no strong objection to the change, but he probably considered the daisy a trite symbol of happy feelings—an object of taste that he would have considered to be less artfully resonant than his *mille-fiore.*

A less obviously symbolic device in *The Magus*, but an important one, is the image of a hanged man, first featured on a Tarot card and later as a significant part of the *mise en scène* during the "trial" of Nicholas. The scene with the card takes place during one of Nicholas' early visits to the villa, when Conchis shows him card number twelve, The Hanged Man, and then tries to get Nicholas to take a cyanide pill in order to force him to confront the existential fact of death. The climactic trial scene depicts

In *The Magus* Nicholas Urfe (Michael Caine) undergoes a ritualistic trial in judgment of his previous behavior. The hangman's noose symbolizes the death of his old character, as his new one emerges (Photofest).

Nicholas tied to a throne with a hangman's noose around his neck. The scene has hallucinatory aspects but seems actually to be happening to him in the film, as it happens to Nicholas in the novel. The trial takes the form of a ritualistic ceremony before a panel of supposed experts and, in the film, a huge group of onlookers, all of whom listen to the presiding Conchis review Nicholas' character flaws. Nicholas is forced to watch his beloved Julie perform in a pornographic movie, after which he is given the opportunity to flog her in revenge for her having lied to him about everything. When Nicholas instead throws down the cat o' nine tails and forgives her, or at least declines to inflict painful punishment on her, he seems to have passed some kind of moral test. The scene then changes to an unfamiliar location where Nicholas wakes up amid some architectural ruins, perhaps meant to symbolize the selfish past life he is leaving behind.

The most interesting and significant symbolic object in the trial scene is the hangman's noose around Nicholas' neck as he sits, bound to a throne-like chair, waiting to be judged. This item is not mentioned in the equivalent scene in the novel, so its presence in the screenplay indicates an attempt by Fowles to convey meaning in the film medium by means of a visual referent. The set-up in the screenplay includes a brief lecture by Conchis that does not occur in final cut of the film:

[shot] 233. INT[ERIOR].   A VAST SPACE   THE TRIAL SCENE 233

Start with a series of swift close shots of MASKS. They come swirling in, springing psychedelically out of the darkness at DIFFERENT ANGLES AND DISTANCES. ON TO MORE AND MORE MACABRE MASKS: GOAT ... VAMPIRE ... SKELETON ... WITCH ... DEMON ... GORGON ... FINALLY THE FAMILIAR ANUBIS FIGURE and then-

FULL FIGURE OF CONCHIS FLASHES BRILLIANTLY OUT OF THE DARKNESS. He is dressed as the SORCERER-MAGUS of the TAROT pack. He bows to CAMERA, gestures.

LIGHTS CATCH AND HOLD CONCHIS AND THE SEVEN MASKED FIGURES, NOW STANDING CHORUS-LIKE BEHIND HIM.

CONCHIS (gesturing to the masked figures behind him)

All gods. Ancient gods.

(a beat)

They look different now. Like ordinary human beings with ordinary human names. Freud. Marx. Sartre.

(a beat)

But old or new, they all want the same thing.

(he kneels)

Total obedience.
CAMERA HOLDS him as he kneels, then PANS RIGHT ROUND, and we
see:
NICHOLAS: he is strapped into a coffin-like throne on a dais, and
gagged. He wears the same clothes as in SHOT 224, but he has been got
up in a parody of Masonic ritual—left trouser-leg garter-leg above knee,
left shoulder bare, etc. A hangman's noose round his neck. His eyes search
the darkness for a meaning.[20]

Why did Fowles invent this "hangman's noose" for the movie? Whether
it succeeds in conveying the meaning Fowles intended, what he imagined
that meaning to be can be discerned from evidence external to the film.
The idea of Nicholas being hanged resonates with the Tarot card that Conchis has shown to Nicholas earlier, The Hanged Man, which Conchis
explains, "stands for selfishness."[21] Selfishness is indeed the defining character trait that Nicholas must overcome in the film, but the image of a
hanged man has more subtle implications that Fowles has knowingly
played with elsewhere in his writings and probably intended here. Foremost is the meaning of the card as presented by Waite in his *Key to the
Tarot*, which Fowles evidently knew well, for he quotes from Waite's interpretation of card one, The Magician, in the epigraph to the first edition
of the novel *The Magus*. Of The Hanged Man card, Waite writes, "He who
can understand that the story of his higher nature is imbedded in this
symbolism will receive intimations concerning a great awakening that is
possible, and will know that after the sacred Mystery of Death there is a
glorious Mystery of Resurrection."[22] The phrasing sounds religious, but it
is from the early years of psychoanalysis and could just as easily have been
described as Jungian. Indeed, C.G. Jung identified the hanged man as an
archetypal image, one of the "symbols of transformation" in his collected
works, where he, like Waite, saw the image of the hanged man not as negative but as positive, as an invitation to change by execution of one's previous self in order to give birth to a new self.[23] In his 1977 introduction
to his revised version of *The Magus*, Fowles remarked that Jung's "theories
deeply interested [him] at the time" he was writing the novel, in the mid-
to late 1950s and early '60s.[24] Although Jung's theory, like Tarot cards—
or like Freud, Marx, and Sartre—ultimately is one of the systematic, mentally controlling systems of godgames that Nicholas is supposed to reject.
The potential for change in the image of the hanged man is what Conchis
evidently wants to stimulate in his protégés, and the ruins among which

Nicholas wakes up from his trial probably are a conventional Jungian symbol of his now dead, previous self.

However Fowles developed his interest in the image of the hanged man, the image recurs so persistently in Fowles's works that its importance to him is undeniable. In Chapter 57 of his novel *The Magus*, Nicholas encounters a doll and a skull suspended from the branch of a pine tree.[25] The wooden doll, painted black with bits of white cloth around its ankles, hanging from a noose around its neck, Nicholas immediately interprets to be a representation of his new love interest, Julie. As he examines the similarly suspended skull, he thinks about the disemboweled corpses of two women whom Conchis has described earlier in the novel, hanged by the Germans during World War II.[26] Then Nicholas thinks of something he has read in *The Golden Bough*: "I tried to remember, What was it? Hanging dolls in sacred woods." He may be remembering Frazer's description of Artemis, "annually hanged in effigy in her secret grove," the goddess whom Julie impersonated in the earlier episode with her "striding huntress walk, her silver bow held in one hand by her side."[27] The image of a hanged figure is also used in *The French Lieutenant's Woman*, in a scene where protagonist Charles Smithson goes into a church and imagines Jesus becoming human: "To uncrucify! In a sudden flash of illumination Charles saw the right purpose of Christianity ... was not to celebrate this barbarous image ... but to bring about a world in which the hanging man could be descended."[28] Charles is about to reject religion at the end of that scene, an intellectual decision that Fowles has stated he hoped to inspire with *The Magus*, also.[29] And literally hanged men figure in Fowles's last novel, *A Maggot*, which contains references to a body that is discovered hanging in the woods, and to a historical figure named Captain Porteus, who was hanged by a mob.[30] Even Fowles's first novel, *The Collector*, employs metaphorical hanging as Clegg treats the kidnapped Miranda like one of the pinned butterflies hanging on display in his collection. Thus Fowles's addition of a hangman's noose to the story in his screenplay for *The Magus* is understandable in both formal and biographical terms.

Late in the screenplay Fowles includes critiques of Conchis that would have rounded his character slightly, but they don't appear in the film. Nicholas accuses Conchis of playing his godgames in order to assuage his own feelings of responsibility for the deaths of thirty villagers: "You are mad! A deserter in one war and a collaborationist in the next. You're not punishing me. It's yourself. Your guilt. You play God with other people's lives, hoping we'll fail as miserably as you failed. Because every time we run away or commit suicide it makes it easier for you to excuse what you did at the execution."[31] This diatribe was probably not included in the final cut of the film because it might have led many in the audience to misunderstand the benevolent intentions of Conchis. Instead, his motives seem merely obscure.

Fowles dated the typescript of his screenplay August 8, 1967, a scant month before he would fly to the Spanish island of Majorca to join the film crew.[32] Fowles records in his journal that the time was filled with "the boredom of location shooting," but others recall that he and his wife, Elizabeth, seemed to enjoy their two weeks there.[33] The screenplay contains forty-five pages that were revisions of the earlier, August draft, thirty-nine of them dated 12 September and six of them dated 27 November 1967. Fowles may have brought with him the changes that needed to be typed up, or else he did considerable rewriting during the first two days after he had arrived. Fowles had already changed the nationality of Lily/Julie from English to American and wrote a bit of dialogue that would account for the accent of actress Candice Bergen, who delivers these new lines: "My father works for *The Times*. Until two years ago he was their American correspondent. I was brought up there." In a similar move, Fowles changed the nationality of Anne from Australian to French in order to accommodate the accent of French New Wave actress Anna Karina, who had been cast for the part. When he met the cast on Majorca, Fowles noted that Karina's vivacity and seductiveness made it "hard to imagine her not stealing any scene she's in."[34] On one of the first days of shooting, Fowles wrote that he liked Michael Caine: "He brings a nice presence; a matter-of-factness the amateur always lacks."[35] Fowles added, "They made me play a little scene with him," which would be the arrival of the boat, when Fowles playing a sailor points to the island and speaks the first word of the film, "Phraxos," the fictional name of the supposedly Greek island. Fowles's recorded impression of the English director, Guy Green, was that he seemed a man of technical experience rather than of artistic vision.[36]

On the changed pages of the screenplay occurs dialogue about the paperweight, in which Anne says that she could not part with it, so that her later sending it to Nicholas would have more impact as it indicates that she is growing stronger while he is not. Anne also pays a one-hour, unannounced visit to the island; she misses Nicholas, but the film thus sets up the opportunity for her to be recruited to participate in the game by Conchis and his people. Julie shows Nicholas one of their tricks by hiding in a tree, which in the film becomes a hidden trapdoor, evidently devised after Fowles had revised the screenplay. Likewise, the scene where Julie as Artemis shoots the satyr with her bow is described in Fowles's script as set up with lights in the woods—not requiring the pursued woman to arrive as she does in the film, by air.

During the filming Fowles thought that Anna Karina was "brilliant," Anthony Quinn "wonderful," and the movie "great." The actors themselves were more apprehensive. Candice Bergen worried that the "convoluted script" was "something she felt her looks were not enough to carry her through," given her limited experience as an actress at that time. Bergen recalls a lack of adequate direction when Guy Green "realized that they needed a close-up of an orgasm for a love scene in a dream sequence shot earlier that week." Without a co-actor present, Green asked her, "'Can you just come to climax for us quickly, dear? We're racing the clock.' They had set up a makeshift bed to match the original; swathed in red satin. It was too tight a shot to include an over-the-shoulder with my partner, a German in a cat-burglar suit wearing a mask (a dream sequence, remember: by the time they were finished, no one watching it could make heads or tails of the film), and so I writhed alone."[37] Michael Caine's recollections are even more scathing, as he describes feeling baffled by the script and receiving little clarification: "I read it and I still could not make head nor tail of the plot but when I confessed this to the producers…, they said not to worry as they were going to rewrite the script themselves. This they did, turning the simply incomprehensible into the deeply unfathomable. They also worked on me an old movie trick, which was to say that they would 'fix it in the editing.' I eventually saw the finished film and the editing had made it even murkier."[38] If these motivated readers found the script a challenge to understand, the film itself promised to be an even greater challenge for unprepared audiences. Fowles's impressions had also turned more negative by the time the film was finished, when he lamented, "it had all gone wrong somehow."[39] Fowles was now calling it "vulgar," even a "disaster" attributable to Guy Green's "non-direction," to Michael Caine's "wooden" acting, to a "banal" musical score, and to the "overstressed" delivery of lines and the unedited pauses that precede them.[40]

The publicity campaign for the movie may have contributed to its limited success at the box office. The press kit pointed out that "*The Magus* was a book that intrigued hundreds of thousands of readers. Now it is a motion picture that will entrance theatre audiences. And it has four of the hottest stars in the industry—Anthony Quinn, Michael Caine, Candice Bergen and Anna Karina." All that may be accurate enough, but the posters advertising the movie made it sound as if it would be full of sex and the supernatural, many of them with illustrations of Bergen in a camisole or standing in an embrace with a jackal-headed figure of the Egyptian god Anubis. "The Magus just might show you the difference between love and sex" was one tag line. Even more misleading was a poster showing Bergen tied to a wooden frame and about to be whipped, with a titillating caption: "Man perfected love. THE MAGUS perverted it." Another tag line reversed the meaning of the film by making the earnest Conchis, who is trying to help Nicholas grow into a decent human being, sound like an evil demon: "What is the vicious game THE MAGUS plays?" Thus a would-be art film was sold to movie goers seeking cheap thrills. There must have been considerable disappointment.

Published reviews of the film have been described by Eileen Warburton as "mixed, but mostly poor."[41] Even though there are still viewers who remember watching the film as an unforgettable, life-changing experience for "any thoughtful person," the more typical view is that of *New York Times* critic Rex Reed, who has referred to *The Magus* as "notoriously forgettable." *New York* magazine film critic Judith Crist called *The Magus* one of the ten worst films of the Sixties, and Fowles himself in a later interview called it one of the two worst, the other being the film adaptation of Laurence Durrell's novel *Justine*.[42] What could have gone so wrong?

Despite its shortcomings, the film has not been forgotten. In 2006 *The Magus* was released on DVD with an "extra" that includes interviews, photographs, and excerpted scenes from the 1968 film. Titled "John Fowles: The Literary Magus," the twenty-three minute documentary features testimonials from Eileen Warburton, identified as "The Biographer"; Bob Goosman, "The Admirer"; Dianne Vipond, "The Professor"; Ray Roberts, "The Editor" (at Little, Brown); David Tringham, "The Collaborator" (on *The Last Chapter*); and Anna Christy, daughter of Elizabeth Fowles by a previous marriage.[43] The novel, likewise, continues to attract readers. In 1998 the Modern Library issued a new edition of *The Magus* with a newly-revised introduction by Fowles, and the following year Greek television produced an hour-long documentary about the novel and

Fowles's relationship with Greece, called *The Return of the Magus* (discussed in Svonkin, "Postmodern Documentary," this collection).[44]

Perhaps the strongest evidence that *The Magus* is a compelling story is its having been adapted in 1997, without attribution, as the highly successful film *The Game*, directed by David Fincher. In addition to its similar plot, the characters' names echo those in *The Magus*: Michael Douglas plays the Nicholas character, again named Nicholas; and Sean Penn plays the Conchis character, re-named Conrad.[45] The paratextual relationship with *The Magus* is such that *The Game* should be considered a creative adaptation (see Aubrey, "*The Magus* as Thriller," this collection).

The Magus continues to provide a point of reference for personal identification. Woody Allen once remarked that if he had his whole life to live over again, he would do everything the same except that he wouldn't see the movie version of *The Magus*.[46] During the mass demonstrations in 2011 in Cairo's Tahrir Square, one of the leaders, Ahmed Shahawi, adopted the Facebook alias of "Nicholas Urfe" because, as *Time* magazine reported at the time, when Shahawi learned about the possibility of change from the revolution in Tunisia, he felt much like Nicholas, who "thought he knew everything but didn't."[47] *The Magus* has always appealed particularly to readers on the cusp of adulthood, but it is not the kind of novel that is only of interest to the young. *The Magus* remains a serious coming-of-age story, a late–twentieth century portrait of the young man as an artist. The art is that of living, and despite its limitations, the movie version of *The Magus* offers thoughtful viewers insights into life and its choices.

Notes

1. John Fowles, *The Journals: Volume One*, ed. Charles Drazin (London: Jonathan Cape, 2003), p. 583. The evening was spent in London, and the visitors were editor Robert Parrish and his wife, screenwriter Neil Paterson, actress Sarah Miles, and a "mogul" named Goldstein.

2. Email from David Tringham to Michelle Buchberger, 21 Mar. 2013. The first edition of *The Magus* was published in the U.S. in 1965; Fowles published a revised version of the novel in 1977.

3. Gina McIntyre and Nicole Sperling, "'One Day' Author Part of Exclusive Club," *The Denver Post* 21 Aug. 2011, p. 14E. The *Los Angeles Times* reviewers assert that "conventional movie-industry wisdom held has that novelists could never maintain sufficient critical distance to effectively judge what might work best on screen."

4. John Fowles, Foreword, The French Lieutenant's Woman: *A Screenplay*, by Harold Pinter (Boston: Little, Brown, 1981), p. x.

5. Eileen Warburton, *John Fowles* (New York: Viking Penguin 2004), p. 277.

6. Fowles, *The Journals: Volume One*, p. 648.

7. *The Return of the Magus*, directed by Mike Pearce, Inkas Film and T.V. Productions, 1999–2000, contains various recorded interviews with Fowles—and some performances by him—while he was in Greece in 1998. *Dios fingido*, or "false god," is the Spanish language title of *The Magus*, whose translator evidently understood the novel's atheism.

8. John Fowles, *The Magus: The God Game*, in the John Fowles Collection, Harry Ransom Center for the Humanities, Austin, TX, n.p. The cover page of the screenplay uses all lower case letters in the foretitle and all upper-case letters in the main title on the typewritten cover page, as follows: "the god game" (*THE MAGUS*).

9. *Ibid.*, p. 15.

10. *Ibid.*, p. 45.

11. *Ibid.*, p. 2.

12. *Ibid.*, p. 118.

13. John Fowles, *The Magus: A Revised Version* (Boston: Little, Brown, 1977), p. 80.

14. John Fowles, *The Magus* (Boston: Little, Brown, 1965), n.p. (epigraph to the novel).

15. John Fowles, "Essay by John Fowles," in *Land*, by Fay Godwin (Boston: Little, Brown, 1985), p. x; *Daniel Martin*, pp. 272–73.

16. John Fowles, *The Magus: A Revised Version*, p. 650.

17. Fowles, *The Magus: The God Game*, p. 14. Conchis tells Nicholas that "Later Prospero will show you his domain." Nicholas points out that "Prospero had a daughter," to which Conchis replies, "Prospero had many things. And not all young and beautiful, Mr. Urfe."

18. Fowles, *The Magus: The God Game*, p. 49C.

19. *Ibid.*, p. 50.

20. *Ibid.*, pp. 106–07.

21. *Ibid.*, p. 67.

22. A.E. Waite, *The Pictorial Key to the Tarot* (1911; rpt., Mineola, NY: Dover, 2005), p. 58.

23. C.G. Jung, *Symbols of Transformation*, trans. R.F.C. Hull, *The Collected Works of C.G. Jung*, vol. 5 (New York: Pantheon, 1956), pp. 233, 247, 255, 271, 323.

24. John Fowles, Foreword, *The Magus: A Revised Version* (Boston: Little, Brown, 1977), p. 6.

25. Fowles, *The Magus: A Revised Version*, p. 459.

26. *Ibid.*, p. 430.

27. *Ibid.*, pp. 183, 459–60.

28. John Fowles, *The French Lieutenant's Woman* (Boston: Little, Brown, 1969), p. 363.

29. *Return of the Magus*.

30. John Fowles, *A Maggot* (Boston: Little, Brown, 1985), pp. 67, 178, 191.

31. Fowles, *The Magus: The God Game*, p. 112.

32. Fowles, *The Journals: Volume Two*, pp. 30–31.

33. Warburton, *John Fowles*, p. 299.

34. Fowles, *The Journals: Volume Two*, p. 31. The entry is from September, when he seems to have just met Karina for the first time.

35. *Ibid.*, p. 31.

36. *Ibid.*, p. 31.

37. Candice Bergen, *Knock Wood* (New York: Simon & Schuster, 1984), p. 187.

38. Michael Caine, *What's It All About?* (New York: Random House, 1992), p. 280.

39. Warburton, p. 299.

40. Fowles, *The Journals: Volume Two*, pp. 39, 43.

41. Warburton, p. 309.

42. James Flynn, IMDb posting, 7 Aug. 2006; Rex Reed, *Travolta to Keaton* (New York: William Morrow, 1979), p. 135.

43. "John Fowles: The Literary Magus," dir. John Cork, prod. Corkland as an extra feature to accompany *The Magus* on DVD, dist. Twentieth Century–Fox Home Entertainment, 2006. This 23-minute documentary includes interviews with Eileen Warburton ("The Biographer"), Bob Goosman ("The Admirer"), Dianne Vipond ("The Professor"), Ray Roberts ("The Editor"), David Tringham ("The Collaborator"), and Anna Christy, daughter to Elizabeth Fowles by a previous marriage.

44. John Fowles, *The Magus* (New York: Scribner's 1998); *The Return of the Magus*, dir. Mike Pearce, perf. John Fowles, Inkas Film and T.V. Productions, 1999–2000.

45. *The Game*, dir. David Fincher, perf. Michael Douglas, Sean Penn, and Deborah Kara Unger, screenplay John D. Brancato and Michael Ferris, prod. and dist. Polygram Filmed Entertainment, 1997.

46. Letter to James Aubrey, 10 June 1988.

47. *Return of the Magus*, dir. Mike Pearce, screenplay Kirki Kefalea, interview and perf. John Fowles, prod. Inkas Film and T.V. for Greek television, 1999–2000.

48. Bobby Ghosh, "The Revolutionaries," *Time* 14 February 2011, p. 40.

Undercover Hero:
The Last Chapter on Film

MICHELLE BUCHBERGER

When David Tringham approached John Fowles in May 1970 to investigate the possibility of adapting one of his works for the screen, few could have predicted that the finished short film would eventually enjoy that rarest of accolades: the approval of John Fowles himself.[1] Looking back at the creative careers of both Fowles and Tringham, several inauspicious events that occurred around the time of this project's conception, certainly indicated a less successful outcome. Tringham approached Fowles immediately after completing his work as assistant director on another Fowles adaptation: *The Magus*.[2] That production had been troubled, but obviously not sufficiently so to dissuade Tringham from approaching the author and asking Fowles whether he might have a work "collecting dust in your bottom drawer, some short treatment or long manuscript."[3] Fowles offered an unpublished short story with the title "The Final Chapter," about a writer of spy thrillers who is experiencing writer's block. As Tringham explains, there were reasons other than the opportunity to work with Fowles again which also fueled his interest. In a 2013 email, Tringham describes the appeal of working on a second Fowles adaptation, and it appears that this had as much to do with his own creative goals as with the lure of Fowles's fiction: "I imagine by now that it is apparent that the real attraction of John's story was that it would enable me to step into the director's shoes."[4] For Fowles, expectations for further adaptations of his work could not have been lower after his recent fraught experiences, including those associated with the filming of *The Magus*. In this project, Fowles had assumed complete control of the screenplay, a condition he insisted upon after his experience with *The Collector*.[5] However, the responsibility and pressure associated with a big budget production took an emotional toll. Referring to that time, Fowles remarked in a letter to Tringham, "[C]arrying two-million-and-up dollar projects around is a way of life I begin to find too exhausting"; perhaps, therefore, by 1970 the smaller scale of the proposed project appealed to Fowles, seemed an opportunity for the author to "enjoy being in some modest project for fun."[6] With this surprising alignment of interests, the film adaptation of "The Final Chapter" began.

Eventually re-titled *The Last Chapter*, Tringham's adaptation is an interesting recombination of some of Fowles's familiar themes along with some fascinating new ones; specifically, for the first time Fowles addresses the notion that writers who have "sold out" to the comfortable life of commercial success, rejecting the aesthetic and imaginative in favor of the formulaic, should be condemned. In another letter to Tringham, Fowles explains that the "germ of this story came when I once heard Ian Fleming spitting on the idea of the Muses: on divine inspiration and all that."[7] The importance of the muse is a central theme of *The Last Chapter*, but this protective stance towards the nine mythological Greek goddesses was not a new attitude for Fowles, who had always displayed a great respect for and interest in the mysterious process of creative inspiration. In his essay "Notes on an Unfinished Novel," for example, Fowles describes his own creative process, beginning with the appearance of "mythopoeic 'stills'" that can first suggest the possibility of a "door into a new world."[8] The essay goes on to stress the mysterious nature of creative inspiration, describing the American "strangely pragmatic view of what books are" which, Fowles posits, could be due to the "miserable heresy that creative writing can be taught."[9] The unfinished novel from which these 'Notes' are derived would become *The French Lieutenant's Woman*, and Fowles's reference in the essay to the "mysterious" and "romantic" nature of imaginative writing, together with his rejection of Robbe-Grillet's position in *Pour un Nouveau Roman* and the kind of criticism that reduces the composition of a novel to the assembly of a clever mind game, characterizes the respectful attitude towards the creative process that Fowles retained throughout his writing career.[10] Indeed, Fowles's interest in and respect for the writing process itself could explain the increasing metafictionality of his work, which is particularly evident in later novels such as the highly autobiographical *Daniel Martin* and *Mantissa*, which both depict protagonists actively engaged in the challenging art of writing prose fiction.[11] Like *The Last Chapter*, *Mantissa* also relates the story of a muse's revolt against the author; ersatz author Miles Green's arrogant assumption that he can write a book without the influence of anything but the pragmatic drive to continue a logical, literary, critical discourse with academic readers provokes the ire of his muse, Erato, who condemns him to creative silence at the end of that novel. However, in "The Final Chapter," the written story of *The Last Chapter*, the author suffers a far worse fate.

An examination of "The Final Chapter" is interesting for several reasons, not least because it provides insight into Fowles's attitudes towards what differentiates "serious" writing from the kind of low-brow, formulaic pulp fiction produced by his protagonist, Robert Murray. Additionally, by examining the adaptation of the work by screenwriter and director David Tringham alongside the numerous documented exchanges that occurred between the two men as the screenplay evolved, it is possible to discern something of Fowles's own creative process and how his vision made such an effective (in his mind) transition to the screen. "The Final Chapter" is also interesting for its exploration of a dilemma that was clearly of interest to Fowles: an author's Faustian pact with commercialism and its effect on the act of writing.

Fowles's journal entries and letters illustrate that he was neither a stranger to this balancing act between financial security and creative independence, nor was he immune to some of the other dubious characteristics with which he imbues and then implicitly critiques his protagonist. Fowles's story relates the demise of Robert Murray, a highly successful writer of pulp, spy-thriller fiction, who is confronted in his writing studio by a young girl who, it turns out, is one of the nine Muses. After first pretending to be an adoring fan, the young girl, Penny, reveals herself to be a harsh critic of his vapid and misogynistic work and exposes Murray's own self-disgust in the process. At the end of the confrontation, Murray burns this final chapter and is left effectively "word-less." Unable and unwilling to continue to produce, he commits suicide.

Robert Murray is, like Ian Fleming, a prolific and wealthy writer of pulp spy fiction, but Murray is not only condemned for his denial of the muse and his rejection of the business of serious writing but also for his shameless pandering to the adolescent male sexual fantasies of his page-turning readers. In a communication with David Tringham, also cited in his authorized biography, Fowles describes and vehemently attacks his protagonist as having "made an enormous success out of writing for the eternal adolescent in man and [… he] needs to be reminded that that is not what serious writing is about. He's grown blind to the extent to which he's sold out; and tries to hide his fundamental artistic and spiritual bankruptcy under the mask of the machine-like efficiency with which he churns out his oeuvre."[12] This is a revealing comment since some of the faults Fowles critiques in Murray might equally be directed at himself. Most obviously, and by his own admission, Fowles's own adolescent sexual fantasies permeated his writing in the decade that preceded his writing of "The Final Chapter." For example, in his 1963 novel *The Collector*, Miranda is stalked, kidnapped, and imprisoned in a cellar, during which time she is photographed in pornographic poses before being left to die from pneumonia. In the 1965 novel *The Magus* there are several incidents involving sexual violence against women, including a flagellation fantasy. Nor did Fowles attempt to conceal the presence of his own adolescent male fantasies in his early fiction. In a remarkably frank journal entry dated February 3, 1963, Fowles acknowledges that the imprisonment of Miranda was inspired in part by his own "lifelong fantasy of imprisoning a girl underground.... Of course there was a main sexual motive ... a forcing of my personality as well as my penis on the girl concerned."[13] On one level, it seems, "The Final Chapter" and *The Last Chapter* would be two more such explorations of sexual fantasies, this time by a fictionalized male writer, but this time, the female object of the male fantasy is given the opportunity to strike back.

Fowles's condemnation of Murray's complicity with commercialism is also significant since Fowles himself became financially secure enough to pursue writing full time only after the enormous commercial success of *The Collector*, which included a lucrative film deal that preceded its publication.[14] It is interesting to contrast the production of *The Collector* with *The Magus*, which was ten years in the making.[15] Even then, unsatisfied with its completed state, Fowles revised it a decade later; so *The Magus* is Fowles's *magnum opus*, and not a work written for easy success. This contrasts starkly with *The Collector*, which was completed in a little over three months.[16] A masterpiece in its own right, *The Collector* can hardly be compared with one of the works of pulp fiction churned out with mechanical precision by Robert Murray, but it does suggest that Fowles was aware of the tenuous position held by writers as they navigate the hazardous and unpredictable tightrope between serious writing and commercial success. It may also suggest that Fowles experienced to some degree the same internal conflict experienced by his protagonist. In Murray, this conflict manifests itself physically in the rituals he employs to accompany his writing, which subordinate the influences of imagination and beauty to his mechanistic mode of production. Unlike Murray, the success of *The Collector* freed Fowles to pursue experimentation and innovation. Murray's "crime" is his adoption of a proven popular formula to perpetuate his wealth while impoverishing his art.

Also, for a writer who purported to ignore the vicissitudes of the reading public, Fowles was extremely interested in the sales of his books. He made a point of knowing how his works were selling compared to other writers, among them—and ironically given the inspiration for "The Final Chapter"—how they were selling compared to the works of Ian Fleming. As we read in his journal entry for October 2, 1968, he reflects with what appears to be equal measures of modesty, embarrassment, and disbelief, on the large advance offered by Tom Maschler at Jonathan Cape for the manuscript of *The French Lieutenant's Woman*: "He has offered an advance of £8,000, which he says is the highest Cape have ever given outside the Len Deighton and Ian Fleming thriller class.... I can't really believe the book is that good; or will ever earn, in this country, that kind of money back. I've told my parents and Charlie Greenberg, but with a distinct embarrassment."[17] So despite his apparent contempt for thriller writers and his specific contempt for Fleming's rejection of the sacrosanct inspiration of the muses, Fowles seemed pleased enough to be counted among their number when it came to league tables of financial remuneration.

Also revealing in Fowles's comment to Tringham is his implicit criticism not only of Murray's pandering to adolescent male sexual fantasies and the changing whims of the reading public, but also of Murray's lowbrow genre of choice: the spy thriller. From his journals and manuscripts, however, it is evident that Fowles himself was not immune to the lure of the spy thriller genre. The author completed at least one unpublished, full-length spy thriller novel called *The Device*. Indeed, on February 15, 1971, only a month after meeting with Tringham to discuss the possibility of adapting "The Final Chapter," he wrote that he had "finished revising the thriller—now called *The Device* instead of *Somebody's Got to Do It*."[18] *The Device* was received coolly by Tom Maschler at Jonathan Cape on April 13 of that year, and Fowles was increasingly inclined to "kill the thing" as his journal entry of April 20 indicates.[19] However, his reluctance to give up on the work is surely indicative of the author's engagement with the genre. Given all this evidence, Fowles's outraged denunciation of Fleming's flagrant commercialism and his criticism of writers who pander to immature male sexual fantasies begin to sound like too much protestation—an interesting reflection on Fowles's own obviously complex and conflicting attitudes on such topics.

I suggest that what redeems Fowles's somewhat hypocritical attack on his Fleming-like protagonist, Robert Murray, however, is the degree to which he imbues Murray with so many of his own characteristics that the story might indicate a degree of self-awareness and, perhaps, even of self-critique. As Eileen Warburton points out, there are several places in the narrative where Murray is depicted in ways that remind the reader of Fowles himself—his "looks, age, and many work habits"—so that the story might be read as a critique of many male writers of popular fiction in post–1950s England, including Fowles.[20] Collectively, they display what Bruce Woodcock has characterized as an "appalling crust of masculinity," which might be attributed to Fowles's public school upbringing and to the sociological climate of the United Kingdom in 1945–60, following as it did the Second World War when both England and her male inhabitants were reappraising their respective roles in a now very changed sociopolitical landscape.[21]

The most compelling feature of "The Final Chapter," however, is its focus on the complex relationship between the male writer and his female muse. In Fowles's original, completed manuscript of his short story, Robert Murray, a man in his mid-fifties, is described in a voyeuristic third person, present tense narrative, immersed in the writing process.[22] The narrative depicts Murray at work, where we witness the creation of the last chapter of a book as it coalesces on the pages of typewritten prose. Murray escapes from the banality and comfortable domesticity of his life into the vicarious adventures of Maxon, a handsome, James Bond–type with a penchant for violent sex, often with under-age girls.

As Murray confidently types "Chapter 16" at his typewriter, he is suddenly interrupted by Penny, a 16-year-old girl, the niece of one of Murray's acquaintances in the village. Penny first adopts the persona of a silly, starstruck groupie, begging Murray to grant an impromptu interview for a school magazine. The conversation takes a dramatic turn, however, when Penny appears to attempt a clumsy seduction of the author. Before there can be any kind of sexual encounter, however, Murray orders her to leave. In the dramatic dénouement, Penny reveals herself to be the complete opposite of the sycophantic, gauche nymphet she has been mimicking.

Rather, she reveals herself to be an accomplished actress and writer herself, poised to enter Cambridge University later that year to study English. Penny has assumed the role of nymphet to expose Murray's own desire for young, vulnerable girls. She hurls abuse at Murray, condemning his misogynistic and loveless books, as well as casting doubt on Murray's heterosexuality, before escaping from the writing retreat and Murray's furious clutches. Severely shaken by the encounter, Murray attempts to resume writing, beginning again with a revised version of "Chapter 16," which is now infused with a new tone: nostalgic and pensive. Unlike the film adaptation, in the written story Murray finds himself unable to complete the chapter and shoots himself. In a trial scene reminiscent of *The Magus*, where onlookers render their harsh judgment on Nicholas for his ultimate benefit, Penny joins eight stern-looking female companions—an homage to the nine Classical muses—to take revenge on the writer who has rejected their inspirational presence.[23] Murray is chastened, to the point of suicide.

The importance of the muses in both "The Final Chapter" and *The Last Chapter* is unmistakable. In an early draft of the short story the work was preceded by the following epigraph from Lemprière's dictionary definition of *Musae*: "They were generally represented as young, beautiful, modest virgins and commonly appeared in differing attire according to the arts and sciences over which they presided."[24] Despite the fact that Fowles removed this epigraph from his final typed version of the story, its importance to the writer is evident from its later inclusion, verbatim, in the opening pages of the similarly metafictional, later novel *Mantissa*, where writer Miles Green does have sex with his muse—who subsequently gives birth to the text itself.

Tringham's film adaptation of Fowles's story offers three interesting areas of exploration. First, Tringham's treatment departs from Fowles's manuscript to imbue Murray with more humanity. Second, Penny resembles the confrontational muse, a recurrent figure in Fowles's fiction, which often examines the relationship between a "collector" male and a "magus-muse" female. Third is Tringham's skill in rendering a work that is almost completely a work of dialog into the visual medium.

As the protagonist of both "The Final Chapter" and *The Last Chapter*, Robert Murray joins the class of characters in Fowles's fiction that I call collector males, that is, male characters who are seriously flawed because of their reductive tendency to rely too heavily on the lenses of science, logic, and rationalism. In contrast with the these males, Fowles's muse-like female characters use the lenses of the intuitive, imaginative, mytho-poetic and holistic ways of interpreting the world, an approach that Fowles privileges over the collector-male mentality. This bifurcation of character traits along gender lines is controversial, but it is characteristic of Fowles's thinking and writing throughout his oeuvre and is illustrative of Fowles's own self-professed feminism.[25] Fowles stresses throughout his novels that women are distinctly different from men, and the author differentiates and elevates women from and above men in numerous ways. For one, he casts women repeatedly in the role of catalyst in the "becoming" process of male protagonists (usually towards existential authenticity). According to Fowles's 1963 work *The Aristos*, the ability of women to act as catalysts is attributed to their association with "kinesis, or progress.... Eve societies are those in which the woman and the mother, female gods, encourage innovation and experiment, and fresh definitions, aims, modes of feel-ing."[26] In his novels since that time, Fowles has increasingly associated women with the mythic (usually in contrast to the scientifically oriented male protagonist). Therefore, Fowles's "feminism," if it is to be so defined, is essentialist in nature and, as such, obviously cannot be aligned with Second Wave feminism. Fowles praises and elevates female values in a way that can be more accurately aligned with feminist writers like Mary Daly, whose work *Gyn/Ecology* celebrates the immanence of the feminine and connects this immanence to nature and the body.

Robert Murray bears many similarities with other collector males such as Nicholas Urfe in *The Magus*. Urfe, at the beginning of the novel, believes he has a talent for poetry but undergoes an epiphany when "the scales dropped from my eyes" and he realizes, in horror, that he is "not a poet."[27] In a similar, but much delayed epiphany, Murray, who has enjoyed great commercial success, becomes aware during Penny's interrogation of the formulaic and trivial nature of his work. Murray also anticipates three other collector-male, would-be artists who suppress talent and cre-ativity in favor of commercial gain: David Williams in "The Ebony Tower" neglects his own artistic talent in favor of the far more lucrative world of art criticism; Daniel Martin, eponymous hero and ersatz author of Fowles's 1977 novel, ultimately rejects the comfortable lifestyle afforded by film making, returning instead to the novel; and finally, Miles Green, who writes for academic readers because they are "the only ones who count nowadays."[28]

Robert Murray differs from these other artists in one significant way, however: until the appearance of Penny, he has lacked a female magus/ muse figure who could act as a catalyst in his own redemption, a muse to inspire insight into his overreliance on restrictive, collector thinking and to confront him with the inauthenticity of his existence. He is, in this regard, far more similar to Frederick Clegg than to any of Fowles's other male collector characters. Like Clegg, Murray cannot communicate with the female he confronts, even as he delights in fixing her as the object of his male gaze; whereas Clegg literally imprisons Miranda in his cellar, pinned as a specimen alongside his unfortunate butterflies, Murray is unsuccessful in his pursuit of Penny, semi-nude, into the woods. In his spy novels, Murray has used his fictional alter-ego, Maxon, to pursue vicariously his sexual fantasy-women—one of whom is a mere "fifteen year-old" in his novel titled *Too Hot to Hold*. Unlike Clegg in *The Collector*, who is immune to the attempts of his would-be magus/muse, Miranda, to enlighten him before she dies, Murray, has had no such magus/muse figure in his life. As Penny points out to him, "the only person you've ever made love to is yourself." As a result, Murray's fictional characters are two-dimensional, and his female characters appeal only to adolescent males' fantasies of power and domination; the story refers to his need to "rape and rape again," and several video enactments of spy-novel scenes from Maxon's imagination depict him aggressively fighting with a partially-clad female until, in the last such scene in *The Last Chapter*, Maxon is killed by Kresnick, the enemy spy-master.[29]

Murray's collector-style behavior can be further differentiated from Clegg's as a rather uncomfortable mask he has chosen to wear in order to perpetuate his commercial success, rather than an innate personality flaw. We can infer from Fowles's manuscript that Murray constantly battles to keep beauty and imagination from distracting him from his proven, lucrative writing formula because, occasionally, Murray's guard slips and allows his propensity for poetry and beauty to intrude, albeit temporarily, interfering with his carefully choreographed writing process. For example, walking to his writing hut, Murray witnesses the beautiful spectacle of the English countryside with its blooming vegetation, and he makes a note in his writing diary: "Green fuses. Exploding. Ref. Dy. Tho. Too lit. for Max.?"[30] It seems from Murray's shorthand notes that he is considering a reference to Dylan Thomas' "The force that through the green fuse drives the flower" to be too literary for Maxon's character and, perhaps, for his readers as well. Murray is aware enough of the surrounding beauty of his environment that he must shut it out with a "green eyeshield" as part of a very specific, ritual that accompanies his writing, a ritual that helps to purge all aspects of the creative and, instead, focuses his thoughts on the physical, the logical, and the empirical. For example, a contemplation of his hands, the instruments of his work, allow him to regain control of his thoughts when they stray dangerously close to acknowledging his lack of artistic integrity and creativity. This is particularly evident after his confrontation with Penny. Clearly shaken by the implicit criticism of his work that lies beneath the surface of her questions, weaknesses that he is clearly aware of but must ignore if he is to continue producing his Maxon books, he attempts to regain control over his thoughts and emotions by holding "out his hand, fingers outstretched, back up, as if to prove something."[31] The contemplation of his physical body, specifically the hands that press the keys of the typewriter, reorients him within the safety of the physical domain and helps exclude the realm of the imaginative.

It is implied, therefore, that Murray's mechanistic approach to writing, his deliberate rejection of the aesthetic for the commercial, is a conscious decision, one that he must maintain, perhaps against his own natural inclinations, to perpetuate his successful writing career. Murray seems to have successfully accomplished domination over his aesthetic sensitivities, subduing any potential intrusion into his writing from the muse. However, in addition to the reference to Dylan Thomas above, Murray also betrays his own aesthetic sensitivities in several other ways, suggesting that there are the remnants of an artist at his core. When his carefully orchestrated writing process is violently interrupted by the arrival of Penny, his would-be muse, and Penny seems poised to share her own work, he silences her: "My dear, I'm afraid I don't even like poetry. Even the best."[32] His earlier reference to Dylan Thomas would suggest otherwise, and it seems that he is deliberately excluding aesthetic sensibility from his writing and his public persona. The importance of this idea is evident in Tringham's adapted screenplay, as it acknowledges and develops this suppressed aesthetic, imbuing Murray with far more humanity and potential for change.

The implication that Murray's writing activity has become a siege, a constant battle to keep beauty and inspiration out so that commercial success can persist, is also emphasized in the text by the mechanical and ritualistic way in which Murray approaches his writing. In addition to an intellectual reorientation of his consciousness to the confines of his own physical body, which he accomplishes by contemplating his own hands, he also evinces particular patterns of behavior that also contribute to this grounding of his writing within the empirical and the logical domains, to the exclusion of the cerebral. Specifically, a careful placement of his six "American long-filter cigarettes ... in a neat row" and his practice of always re-setting the alarm clock to reflect a starting time of 9:29, denies the real passage of minutes in the lived world and reflects an artificial time during which he must "produce." But again, in spite of these attempts to keep the influence of the muses out of his writing process, one item in Murray's writing hut is described as "incongruous," contributing no functional purpose to the clinical writing room, and perhaps hinting at what might be Murray's true aesthetic sense: "a Regency ottoman, six gilt legs ending in ball-and-claw feet, the frame and sides of the end-rest delicately fretted with Attic metopes, also gilded."[33] The item, an exotic piece of art in an otherwise plain and domestic setting, hints at Murray's potential, true identity as an artist.

Reading the story, one witnesses the emergence of his latest novel, *The Venetian Girl*, from Murray's imagination to the page as it is relayed by a third person omniscient narrator, and this allows the reader to witness the effect that Penny's intrusion has on the writer. The use of present tense narrative, anticipating the same device used in *Daniel Martin*, is suggestive of a camera lens capturing the events as they occur: an implied external frame of a detached observing camera relates the two narratives of Murray and Maxon. The complex textuality and metafictionality of this severally framed narrative reflects Fowles's recurrent interest in the process of writing, most prominent in *The French Lieutenant's Woman* as the implied author famously intrudes into his own fictional narration in the much analyzed Chapter Thirteen of the novel.

When Penny interrupts his writing process, Murray is at first infuriated but soon, it seems, he becomes vaguely titillated by the fawning, nubile and Lolita-esque Penny. He decides to play the worldly author and, evidently flattered, accepts her adoration and answers her questions and corrects her grammar until she begins to probe at his own insecurities as a writer, and even as a heterosexual male. When he answers Penny's inquiry regarding the number of women who have been in love with him, and whether they are like the girls in his books, he retorts that girls in books are always "nicer than real ones."[34] This revealing comment indicates the degree to which the encounters he depicts in his books are completely divorced from his lived experience. When faced with a "real" 16-year-old, an apparently willing sexual partner, he is horrified because, in part, as Penny suggests, the unmarried Murray may be repressing homosexual tendencies along with other aspects of his personality, which he must keep under control if he is to maintain his successful writing career.

After Penny reveals herself as the accomplished young woman she really is, Murray ejects her from his study and returns to a violent rape scene in his story, but soon he is interrupted a second time by Penny, this time naked from the waist up and pressing against the window of his writing hut. After she flees, pursued by Murray, he sees her join eight female friends in the distance, her complement of muses, and they take a bow together in Murray's sight, as if concluding a performance.

Returning to his writing, Murray and Maxon's individual consciousnesses merge, as both men simultaneously confront their current state of existence, each acknowledging that he is leading an unrewarding and empty life: "He felt stunned by his blindness, by this relentless rush of a third dimension into his increasingly two-dimensional life. It was as if he had been harboring some wild beast, some evil incubus, without realizing it. For a few moments, it had shown itself just then and in all its hideous viciousness. It had eaten all the decency and humanity out of him, it had left him nothing but a sadistic, meaningless husk." Murray's writing breaks down into a series of incomplete sentences until it gradually stops completely. The author as writing machine is broken and finally, allowing himself to acknowledge the beauty that surrounds him for the first time, Murray "stares out of the window at the splendid view."[35] In Fowles's ending for "The Final Chapter," Murray makes one final, abortive attempt to resume his writing, but even after repeating his ritual pre-writing activities, he is unable to produce a word on the page. In the darkest and most unambiguous ending seen in any of Fowles's fiction, Murray kills himself with a revolver; a literal if highly ironic dramatization of Roland Barthes's "The Death of the Author."[36]

Fowles's ending to his story is shocking for two reasons. First, it denies any possibility for Murray's redemption and this is at complete variance with Fowles's other published works. In no other novel does Fowles completely reject any possibility of redemption on the part of the male. Murray is lost. Also shocking is the degree to which the ending is absolute and unambiguous. Fowles's works both before and after "The Final Chapter" have endings that demand the reader's active engagement in the making of meaning. For example, in *The Collector* the reader infers that Clegg will go on to kidnap another woman, yet the novel ends before one can be sure; the literary freeze-frame conclusion of *The Magus* provides insufficient evidence to determine whether Alison and Nicholas will reunite; and, of course, the last two endings of *The French Lieutenant's Woman* are deliberately unresolved, since part of Fowles's artistic project is dedicated to the realistic depiction of the lived experience, much of which is beyond the abilities of the written word to articulate. Except for "The Final Chapter," Fowles's fiction provides a conduit between the imaginations of the author and the reader, and in this fertile domain, many possibilities exist. Perhaps the determinate ending accounts for Fowles's not having published the story before it was adapted. It is therefore not surprising that David Tringham saw the opportunity to end the story in a less melodramatic way than Fowles had—and in a way that would be consistent with Fowles's wider artistic project.

Although Tringham's adaptation overall is generally a faithful rendition of Fowles's short story text, there are two major ways in which his treatment of Murray deviates from the original: first, Tringham's Murray is a far more sympathetic character than Fowles's original character, who has the potential for redemption and change; second, Murray does not shoot himself at the end of the film, where his suicide is replaced with a more optimistic and ambiguous ending. Tringham's reading of the short story emphasizes Murray's struggle to suppress his artistic talents, which he ultimately releases after Penny reminds him of the insult he has paid to the muses in his rejection of their influence. By contrast, Fowles's original short story is more like a morality play, more intended to punish Murray for his unforgivable crime than to see him recuperated.

In an inspired casting decision, the role of Murray in Tringham's adaptation is played by the accomplished and then well-known actor Denholm Elliot, who plays both Murray and his alter-ego, Maxon, which makes the vicarious existence of the author through his creation even more explicit than in Fowles's original text. Surprisingly, perhaps, Elliot was not Tringham's first choice for the part. As Tringham writes:

> I originally wanted Peter Finch for the part, but he wasn't available. He would have been good, maybe a bit too attractive. But maybe not. Second choice was Paul Scofield, but he too was unavailable. So then I turned to Denholm Elliot, who was available and willing to do it. Terrific actor, so many buttons to press, could suggest so much so easily. We all thought he

was terrific, and how lucky to get him on board. (Sort of ravaged but still youthful, bit of a fantasist, bit knowing, world-weary but still a lot of mileage to cover—perfect).[37]

Fowles's text depicts Murray as a loner; someone whom the reader sees only within the context of his writing and his brief but stunning exchange with Penny. He has been interacting with no one else in the work but the characters in his imagination. As a result, the reader tends to judge Murray in the same way that Penny does: as a rather sad, lonely, cynical man who has chosen to sublimate his own artistic abilities in favor of a comfortable income.

From the unpublished typescript of the movie script, it is clear that Tringham saw a different, more sympathetic side of Murray, and that Fowles participated in revising the story for the screen. The Harry Ransom Center for the Humanities holds one complete typescript of Tringham's screenplay (dated 18 January 1971) in addition to two sets of revision pages, dated 1 July 1971 and 15 August 1972, respectively. Each version is followed in the archive by two letters from Tringham to Fowles (dated 4 July 1971 and 22 August 1972) referring to the changes contained in each revision. The second letter accompanied Tringham's final changes in the screenplay for Fowles's review, the changes having emerged from a meeting between the two men on Sunday, August 15th. The significant change was to the ending of the work, which portrays Murray in a more positive light. Tringham has explained that he felt that the original ending was "too melodramatic, a cop-out easy ending, and one that would make the audience feel they had been involved in trying to be seduced by a complete loser—it was far too pessimistic an outcome, we would feel cheated, and also quite unrealistic and unconvincing an outcome. Roy Boulting agreed, the problem was to convince John to alter things, and see it our way. That's when the trouble began! Because flexible and receptive to it he wasn't."[38] Roy Boulting, one of the directors of British Lion, an independent distribution company, which was financing the venture, also placed a time restriction and £25,000 budget on the project—the completed adaptation, *The Last Chapter*, would be a remarkably compact thirty minutes in length. Not surprisingly, Tringham's proposed ending met with hostility from Fowles. In a letter to David Tringham dated 8 July 1971, a clearly enraged Fowles rejected the proposed ending, comparing Murray's lack of integrity with Boulting's, to whom Fowles appears to attribute the origins of this request: "The moral is that if you spit on the muses all your life, there's a price to pay. (Incidentally, it frankly doesn't surprise me very much that the Boult-ings don't like this story line)." Fowles concludes with an insistent para-graph: "Finally, David, let me say that I don't want to screw the project for you but I simply won't have my name connected with this new ending, I don't mind people contradicting the details of what I saw, but I draw the line at the essence. This story is about a man's come-uppance, not his being encouraged to go on as before. Please think about it—and give the Boult-ings my views. And of course let's discuss it all. But I shan't budge on that ending."[39] It must be a tribute to David Tringham's power of persuasion that Fowles eventually did budge. In an earlier letter to Fowles, Tringham had made the argument that he wanted to "make Murray more sympa-thetic without destroying the effect of the encounter with Penny." The sui-cide, to Tringham, made Murray "a rather weak, negative person, and in a way it was a giving in to self-pity," whereas the new ending would be an attempt to "retain some element of self-respect."[40]

Tringham's idea prevailed, but his adaptation underwent a series of revisions before both director and author could settle on an ending that was acceptable to them both. In the first draft of the screenplay, Tringham's Murray does not kill himself as a result of his shame and self-loathing after the visit from his enraged, alienated Muse. Instead, Murray burns his latest typescript along with all of his books, and then he walks "on towards a part of the garden where the large trees are most dominant. As he goes, he puts his hand in his pocket and grips the gun, which would indicate that a suicide might occur off-camera."[41] This version of the screenplay was followed by a second version five months later, in which Tringham removed all suggestions of Murray's suicide from the plot. Instead, as Murray tears up his Chapter 16, a *deus ex machina* appears in the form of Patricia, his secretary, whose report of a telephone call distracts the writer from his contemplation of "one of the shiny barrels." Patricia connects Murray to his American agent who gives him the good news about his reprinting and that "they want to make you a Doctor of Liter-ature, Honorary Degree. Real recognition," after which Murray picks up sheets of paper and seems prepared to start writing again.[42]

This version would be revised again, this time with Fowles and Tring-ham working on the script together on 15 August. Among the new changes in this version would be the interruption of Murray, this time in person, by his secretary, re-named Miss Hornby, who relays news of a large finan-cial advance from his New York publishers and an invitation to speak at the Cambridge University English Club, which she has declined on his behalf because that is his usual preferred response. Surprisingly, he asks her to accept this invitation, because "I might learn something, Miss Hornby."[43] Here is the typical Fowlesian hope for growth by a male protagonist after interaction with the female Muse.

Ultimately, in Tringham's final version and in the released film, Murray has no gun. However, in a kind of implied suicide, in the last scene shown of *The Venetian Girl*, the novel Murray has been writing and viewers have been watching enacted, Murray kills off his secret agent-hero, whom he has been imagining as himself. The enemy spymaster, Kresnick, suddenly appears with a rifle and shoots Maxon, saving the woman Maxon has been tormenting. Another implication of killing off his hero is that Murray is now finished with writing spy novels. But Murray himself lives on and throws his just-written "Chapter 16" onto a pile of burning leaves, even after his secretary has informed him of a large offer just received from New York. Murray replies, "I've had a better offer." In context the viewer is evidently to infer that this better offer may include a resumed relationship with his muse, who will redeem rather than punish the formerly commercial writer. The change provoked Fowles, but Tringham is philosophical. He observes that Fowles "always had trouble with his endings, didn't know how to tie things up, didn't want to tie things up, liked the idea of indetermination, of leaving loose ends—and in *The Last Chapter* it became a real bone of contention. But I think even then, at the end, when we finally worked it out, agreed on a compromise, I think he still enjoyed the process—which is why he continued to be so supportive. This was fun, sort of!"[44] Fowles may also have liked—or even suggested—the concluding image at the end of a pile of burning leaves, which is also the final image of *The Magus*, whose last two words, "burning leaves," convey a double meaning of tree leaves and manuscript leaves.[45]

Perhaps one reason that Fowles agreed to an ending where Murray survives is that the last line of dialogue undercuts the idea that Murray will reform: he tells Patricia, "Say yes to New York." This line seems inconsistent with his previous burning of the last chapter, which he will now have to re-write for his publishers. Indeed, Murray seems to want his future both ways, as a writer of serious, less formulaic fiction who will continue to rely on commercial fiction for his income. Murray's last statement subverts the moral Fowles wanted, but Fowles may have felt compensated by the new ambivalence of the ending. In any case, the fact that

Tringham was able to make such a dramatic change to Fowles's work and still earn the author's endorsement of the adaptation is a testament to the collaborative spirit that seems to have existed during this project.

The character Penny is another variant on the Fowlesian female magus-muse. In this case, however, Murray seems to have squandered his opportunity to benefit from her influence, having consciously barred her inspiration from his work. In the three decades of Fowles's publishing career, the increasing centrality of his female characters was accompanied by a growing focus on the mysterious and the uncanny. Fowles's work increasingly associated mystery with creativity, femininity, and the mythic; it suggests that mystery is essential for growth and change, both in society and in the novel form itself, and implies that women, rather than men, are naturally predisposed to embrace it.[46] Fowles's novels reflect a worldview that challenges an over-reliance on the empirical and rational to the exclusion of the mysterious and the intuitive. Despite the realism of Fowles's novels, his work increasingly moves towards the mythopoeic, constantly testing the limits of what can be apprehended and articulated in language, striving toward a realism that appears to be universal and transcendent.

The interpenetration of the everyday with the otherworldly and uncanny is a recurrent theme in Fowles's work, where protagonists often experience epiphanic episodes, sudden glimpses of a world that lies at the periphery of consciousness. Penny's intrusion into Murray's clinical writing process forces an awareness of what Freud describes as "the uncanny" in his celebrated 1919 essay. The uncanny might be summarized as our recognition of the point at which our confidence in scientific or empirical knowledge of the world is momentarily fractured or pierced, and we become aware of the (sometimes repressed) pre-scientific explanations for such feelings or events. Thus we confront a common, familiar occurrence as if it were unknown to us. In that momentary encounter, we acknowledge, just as Murray does in *The Last Chapter* our fragility and our doubts. We experience a slippage—embracing, perhaps only fleetingly, that which cannot be explained by post–Enlightenment rationality. Freud recognizes what Fowles would later exploit in his work: that "fiction affords possibilities for a sense of the uncanny that would not be available in real life."[47] Penny's confronting an author who has deliberately shut out the muse is therefore a further indication of Fowles's interest in the interpenetration of lived and imagined lives as well as another incidence of a female magus-muse confronting a collector male with the inauthenticity of his life.

Unlike the muse in *Mantissa* whose name, Erato, identifies her directly as the Greek goddess responsible for love poetry, Penny is to be identified with Penelope, a more complex archetype historically identified with the most revered and chaste of women, but one who has relied on deceit in weaving a deceptive shroud—a metaphor widely associated with storytelling. Like her magus-muse precursors, especially Sarah Woodruff in *The French Lieutenant's Woman* and Julie in *The Magus*, Penny is a master storyteller. She assumes the role of adoring fan, gushing that "I just wanted to tell you how absolutely thrilling I think your books are."[48] Like Homer's Penelope, Penny is adept at keeping a male interested in her story via the familiar veiling and revealing of her story, suggesting a narrative that must be coaxed from the magus female, which, of course, makes her story even more beguiling to the collector male. When Murray asks her why she did not ask him her questions at a recent sherry party, she maintains that she did not want to talk to him in front of "all those people," again assuring the collector male that her narrative is for his ears only.

Fowles's Penny also amplifies the effect of her presence on Murray by aligning herself with clichés associated with the coquette, exposing "white legs and thighs, then pink cheeks, "dropping her pen, having to get on her knees to retrieve it."[49] She also feigns ignorance, placing Murray in the dominant position both intellectually and physically, by pretending not to be able to read her own handwriting, revealed ironically in her implied misreading of her notes: "Do you drink a lot—oh gosh, no. It's my writing. Do you *think* a lot before you write a book?"[50]

Her seemingly innocent questions gradually begin to probe Murray, making him uncomfortable and defensive as he is forced to acknowledge doubts about his writing and his repute. For example, when Penny effusively compliments the film adaptations made of his books, he responds that "movies of their books very rarely seem super to writers," and when Penny presses him, asking whether it's "because they alter things?" he hesitates: "He means to say something, but changes his mind, smiles and nods. 'Because they alter things.'"[51] The hesitation might suggest that it may not be the changes made to his books that are the heart of his dislike of the movie adaptations but, rather, that the change of medium makes other changes inevitable. Most likely "they alter things" hints at Murray's own thoughts about how he is perceived as a writer, and suggests that he has his own insecurities because he has consciously suppressed all of his aesthetic instincts.

Their final confrontation, however, is provoked when Penny returns to the writing hut after having been physically ejected, and proceeds to question Murray's sexuality. She maintains that she came to disprove a school friend's theory: 'She says you're a ... you don't really like women."[52] The implied accusation of homosexuality seems to provoke Murray into calling her bluff, reverting to the overtly masculine behavior of his alter-ego, Maxon, but, after Penny appears shaken by his changed attitude, he launches into a tirade against women. His comments are suggestive of a deep-seated misogyny, reminiscent of the warped attitudes seen in Frederick Clegg. Murray rails against "empty-headed" women like Penny, for whom there exists a thin wall between them and "a lifetime of moronic mess" as "thin as that piece of skin between your legs."[53] Murray's crude bifurcation of women into the innocent and the defiled is a manifestation of what Freud has described as the "Madonna-Whore complex."

Interestingly, this extreme bifurcation of women into these two categories is often amplified and extended by Fowles in his fiction. He frequently represents twins or sisters, one of whom is sexually adventurous and the other chaste, who are both cast variously in relationships with the male protagonist. For example: the seemingly repressed Julie/Lily and the sexually experienced June/Rose in *The Magus*; the sisters Nell (sexually accessible) and Jane (seemingly cold) in *Daniel Martin*; or "the Mouse" (chaste) and "the Freak" (available) in "The Ebony Tower." Miranda Grey epitomizes both ends of this continuum in *The Collector*, as she is viewed by Frederick Clegg at first as his perfect woman when she adheres to his vision of her as virginal "Madonna" but is later left to die from pneumonia when, in his eyes, she becomes the "whore" who has tried to seduce him to secure her freedom. The enigmatic Sarah Woodruff similarly appears to encapsulate both extremes simultaneously, since she is a virgin before her single sexual encounter with Smithson and is directly compared with Mary the mother of Jesus in Chapter 18, yet has the reputation in Lyme as "the French Loot'n't's Hoer."[54] In Fowles's final published novel, *A Maggot*, Rebecca Lee—a whore recruited from a bordello—participates in a mysterious rite central to the plot, during which she is adorned as the May Queen in what appears to be an abortive attempt at virgin sacrifice.

Rather than being symptomatic of male chauvinism in Fowles, instead this seemingly reductive, artificial bifurcation of women could be read as a symptom of two elements of the male psyche which Fowles seeks to interrogate in his work. First, Fowles foregrounds a male protagonist's compulsion to label and to know—part of his "collector compulsion"—the urge to solve complexities in human emotions and behavior by imposing artificial and ultimately reductive labels on women in a desperate attempt to understand them. Second, the artificial polarization of women into "madonna" or "whore" is indicative of what Bruce Woodcock characterizes as a "Victorian middle-class man's misreading of women." Such a misreading, Woodcock explains, occurred when Victorian men, in response to a worrisome emergent feminine emancipation, felt compelled to keep women in their place. He writes that "Victorian patriarchy produced its own versions of those archetypes common to male-dominated societies, the Madonna-Magdalene syndrome, as part of its social control.... For Victorian women this involved living up to male imagery that both condoned and condemned their sex, the redemptive domestic angel and the outcast harlot." As a Victorian phenomenon, it is not surprising that the Madonna-Magdalene syndrome appears writ large in *The French Lieutenant's Woman*, but this syndrome is not confined to this one, historically contingent, novel. Woodcock suggests, convincingly, that *The French Lieutenant's Woman* charts the male anxiety of the late 1960s over a "newly-emergent female autonomy" rather than one born a century earlier.[55] This might explain why a writer of Fowles's generation, close to and informed by the Victorian age, would be so influenced by its extreme gender stereotyping. Fowles's numerous depictions of Madonna-Magdalenes in his novels are, as Woodcock suggests, indicative of the writer's own attempts to deal with his own male anxiety. Therefore, as Woodcock posits, much of the criticism leveled at Fowles's allegedly dubious feminism could be countered by an acknowledgment that Fowles's novels are, in part, a feminist deconstruction and interrogation of "masculinity ... the myths that contemporary men impose on themselves in their perpetuation of power [which] have a historical root in the legacy of Victorian England."[56] In short, Fowles is not Clegg, Smithson, or Murray. These are ironic personas used by Fowles to examine the status of men and women in society.

For *The Last Chapter* Tringham cast the unknown Susan Penhaligon as his Penny. She was Tringham's first choice, after he had rejected other candidates. David Tringham reports that Roy Boulting had suggested Jane Seymour. Fowles had suggested "Cherie Lunghi, ... a friend of his stepdaughter. Tringham interviewed her, but did not think she would be right for the part, a bit too conventional and ... not for me." Penhaligon was the right one. Tringham had first seen her in Picasso's play *Five Little Girls* at a fringe theatre called The Open Space. Penhaligon was playing the lead, and Tringham remembers that since during "most of the play the cast were completely naked, I knew I would have no problem in the semi-erotic scenes in the film. Plus she was a really good actress, perfect for the part, seductive, alluring, innocent but maybe not—all the qualities the film required. We met and got on and she decided to do it."[57] This turned out to be Penhaligon's big break since, as Tringham relates, after 1972 "she used the film as her calling card, because until then nobody had heard of her—she went on to do fantasy films like 'The Land That Time Forgot,' and 'Bouquet of Barbed Wire'—a giant TV success."[58]

In *The Last Chapter* Penny (Susan Penhaligon) plays an admiring reader who turns out to be a feisty incarnation of a Greek muse (Charter Film Productions).

The Last Chapter was filmed at Shepperton Studios, London, in 1972, and Fowles evaluated the finished film on November 13th. His comments reveal the surprising fact, given the obvious clash of opinions regarding the ending, that he approved of the adaptation: "Not too bad for a first attempt, and I didn't have to put on a mask to say so to David afterwards."[59] The film was not released to the public until 1974. It was delayed so that it could be presented as a supporting feature for the Boulting Brothers' *Hard Beds Soft Battles*, which was not finished until that year. Tringham recalls the positive reception that met *The Last Chapter* at the Richmond Odeon: "the audience were laughing and showing their appreciation throughout, even in places I never imagined would get such a reaction. Very invigorating!"[60]

After the screening, Tringham was invited to work on another Fowles adaptation. After seeing *The Last Chapter*, Tringham recalls, "John sent me his screenplay 'Zip', asking if I would be interested in directing it as a film, but I had to confess it wasn't for me, which seems profligate now. But it seemed too muddled and uninvolving to be made into a movie, there was something lacking at the core—so I declined!"[61]

There were also discussions of another possible Tringham-Fowles collaboration, since Twentieth Century–Fox was interested in acting as distributor. This time, Fowles responded with *The Girl from Nowhere*, which eventually became *The Black Thumb*. Tringham recalls it having

> lots of elements and incidents which appealed to me, and to John also. It was a sort of homage to film-makers like Jean Cocteau and Rene Clair, with an undercurrent of black humor and a thread of existentialism thrown in. It was also very cinematic, most of it taken up with driving down to the West Country, and various accidents which occurred en route. And it was very funny in a warped kind of way, demonstrating John's command of the vernacular and idiom, and very inventive.[62]

Unfortunately for Fowles and Tringham, Fox decided they didn't have the funds. Tringham still laments the loss of a work that, either published or scripted and produced, would have shown "a side of John Fowles that nobody knew about, and would have opened up a whole area of discussion that has remained hidden."[63] That hidden "side" would be the cinephile that Fowles privately was, and the missing "discussion" might indeed have provided a more nuanced view of Fowles's relationship to the cinema.

With regard to *The Last Chapter*, it is perhaps ironic that Fowles ultimately liked the video adaptation despite the fact that Tringham had changed the story so much, and despite the often acrimonious exchanges that occurred between the two men. Probably Fowles came to recognize that his story had not lost its moral force just because his selfish protagonist is rehabilitated rather than killed off. The absence of any damning comments about the project in Fowles's journals and his subsequent willingness to work again with Tringham suggest that Fowles held *The Last Chapter* in uniquely high regard as an adaptation of his fiction.

Another irony is that *The Last Chapter* has obtained a second life from its 2010 re-issue on DVD, which has prompted a number of positive reviews. One reviewer's online praise is typical: "It's doubtful that this bewitching short film would have ever again seen the light of day if it were not for the BFI release; and, as it turns out, it's a thoroughly engrossing little oddity shot at Shepperton Studios, with both Elliott and Penhaligon in top form, and showcasing some attractive photography by Jack Hildyard."[64] Fowles would have been gratified to know that the video project he admired ultimately gained public and critical approval.

Notes

1. Fowles wrote of Tringham's request for permission to adapt "The Final Chapter" on 17 October 1970, according to *The Journals: Volume 2*, p. 95.

2. Although Guy Green's 1968 direction of Fowles's screenplay for *The Magus* has recently become something of a cult classic, at the time it was deemed both a commercial and critical failure. Woody Allen, when asked whether he would change anything if he could live his life over again, is reported to have said, "I would do it all exactly the same— only next time I'd skip seeing 'The Magus'" (reported in "John Fowles, Author of *The French Lieutenant's Woman*, Dies Aged 79," *The Scotsman* 8 Nov. 2005).

3. Letter from David Tringham to John Fowles, 11 May 1970, generously shared by Vic Pratt of the British Film Institute.

4. Email from David Tringham to Michelle Buchberger, 21 Mar. 2013. Letter from a collection held by Vic Pratt of British Film Institute.

5. According to David Tringham, Fowles "was appalled when *The Collector* was advertised as William Wyler's *The Collector*—because Wyler was only the director, the story, the characters and concept were of course all John's work, and for Wyler to be given such a credit really got up his nose … [so] when *The Magus* deal was done, it was only done on condition that John wrote the script, and had approval on any alterations or amendments—which left John, never having written a screenplay before, talking it over with Robert Rossen, who explained the basic principles (apparently), and gave him a copy of the script of 'The Hustler' for the format" (email from David Tringham to Michelle Buchberger, 21 Mar. 2013).

6. Letter from John Fowles to David Tringham, 14 May 1970.

7. *Ibid.*, 5 Oct. 1970.

8. Fowles, "Notes on an Unfinished Novel," in *Wormholes*, p. 13.

9. *Ibid.*, p. 25.

10. *Ibid.*, p. 13.

11. For more information on Fowles and metafiction, see Linda Hutcheon, *A Poetics of Postmodernism* (New York: Routledge, 1988), Robert Scholes, *Fabulation and Metafiction* (Urbana: University of Illinois Press, 1979), and Mahmoud Salami, *John Fowles's Fiction and the Poetics of Postmodernism* (Cranbury, NJ: Associated University Presses, 1992).

12. See Eileen Warburton, *John Fowles*, p. 326.

13. Fowles, *The Journals: Volume 1*, pp. 543–54.

14. *Ibid.*, p. 550. Jonathan Cape had bought the publishing rights for *The Collector* in 1962, but even before the book was on shelves, Columbia Pictures had purchased the film rights.

15. *Ibid.*, p. 379. Fowles's first mentions the novel in the entry for 25 August 1956: "Halfway revising *The Joker*—now *The Magus*." Since the novel was not published until 1965, *The Magus* evidently took Fowles at least nine years to write.

16. Fowles, *The Journals: Volume 1*, pp. 452, 458. The first reference to *The Collector* appears on 2 December 1960, when Fowles noted that he had started writing the novel. On 31 March 1961, he noted that his wife had read the novel.

17. Fowles, *The Journals, Volume 2*, p. 49.

18. *Ibid.*, p. 103.

19. *Ibid.*, p. 105.

20. Warburton, *Fowles*, p. 326.

21. Bruce Woodcock, *Male Mythologies* (Totowa, NJ: Barnes and Noble), p. 11.

22. The complete manuscript of the unpublished "The Last Chapter" is part of the John Fowles Collection at the Harry Ransom Center for the Humanities, in Austin, Texas.

23. It is interesting to note that the Penny character refers to "seven" muses in the screen adaptation. This inaccurate reference to the number of muses is present in the screenplay on p. 29 and can be traced to an exchange between David Tringham and John Fowles as they were working on the script. As Tringham recalls, he made this same slip referencing the number of muses, and was corrected by Fowles, but Fowles suggested that they "use that in the dialogue, (which we did), and it was when he said whenever

you think of anything like that, a good point or phrase or observation, always write it down immediately, because you will never remember it later, not the actual words" (email from David Tringham to Michelle Buchberger on 21 March 2013). Why Fowles thought that his muse-character's slip would be a "good" idea is obscure.

24. "The Final Chapter," draft manuscript, Folder 14, Box 19, Harry Ransom Center for the Humanities, Austin, TX.

25. A more extended exploration of Fowles's bifurcated view of male and female traits appears in "Adam and Eve," in Section 9: A New Education, in the second edition of *The Aristos* (Boston: Little, Brown, 1970), pp. 165–67.

26. Fowles, *The Aristos*, p. 157.

27. Fowles, *The Magus: A Revised Edition*, p. 58.

28. Fowles, *Mantissa*, p. 120.

29. "The Final Chapter," pp. 24, 26.

30. *Ibid.*, p. 2.

31. *Ibid.*, p. 25.

32. *Ibid.*, p. 12.

33. *Ibid.*, p. 3–4.

34. *Ibid.*, p. 15.

35. *Ibid.*, p. 30.

36. Roland Barthes, *Image-Music-Text*, trans. Stephen Heath (1977; rpt., New York: Hill and Wang, 1978), pp. 142–48.

37. Email from David Tringham to Michelle Buchberger, 21 Mar. 2013.

38. *Ibid.*, 12 Mar. 2013.

39. Letter from John Fowles to David Tringham, 8 July 1971.

40. Letter from David Tringham to John Fowles, 4 July 1976.

41. Tringham, "The Last Chapter," version 1, 18 Jan. 1971, p. 50.

42. *Ibid.*, version 2, 1 July 1971, p. 48.

43. *Ibid.*, version 3, 15 Aug. 1971, p. 49.

44. Communication between David Tringham and Michelle Buchberger, 13 Mar. 2013.

45. Fowles, *The Magus*, p. 656.

46. See Fowles, *The Aristos*, p. 90.

47. Sigmund Freud, *The Uncanny* (London: Penguin, 2003), p. 157.

48. Fowles, "The Final Chapter," p. 10.

49. "The Final Chapter," p. 13.

50. *Ibid.* The emphasis is in the original.

51. *Ibid.*, p. 16.

52. *Ibid.*, p. 20.

53. *Ibid.*, p. 23.

54. Fowles, *The French Lieutenant's Woman*, p. 77.

55. Woodcock, p. 82.

56. *Ibid.*, p. 11.

57. Email from David Tringham to Michelle Buchberger, 13 Mar. 2013.

58. *Ibid.*, 21 Mar. 2013.

59. *The Journals: Volume 2*, p. 126.

60. Email communication, 13 Mar. 2013.

61. Email from David Tringham to Michelle Buchberger, 21 Mar. 2013.

62. *Ibid.*, 13 Mar. 2013.

63. *Ibid.*, 21 Mar. 2013.

64. Movie reviews at http://www.horowview.com/movie-reviews/private-road.

Safe Dreams:
The Enigma on Video

Michelle Buchberger

Enigma and mystery are familiar fare for readers of John Fowles. Often as confused by the bewildering happenings as the protagonist, readers must attempt to make meaning in these complex works, which are often misleadingly straightforward in terms of narrative structure, seeming to adhere to the conventions of realism and familiar genre codes only to subvert them. Such literature seldom transitions effectively to the screen, and so it is perhaps surprising that Fowles's fiction has been the credited source of three major Hollywood film productions and also of several smaller-scale works for television—despite the author's own ambivalence towards the visual media as well as the inherent difficulties that his complex and ambiguous works invariably present for an adaptor.

Fowles's thoughts concerning a visual versus a literary articulation of the human experience are widely documented. For example, remarks made during an interview with Devon McNamara in 1979 typify his attitude towards the visual, as Fowles criticized the "distressingly amoral" nature of film and television, "possibly because the photographed image denies the spectator virtually all use of his own imaginative powers."[1] Further evidence of his suspicions regarding the cinema can be found in his 1979 novel, *Daniel Martin,* in which the shortcomings of a cinematic representation of lived experience, compared to a rendition in prose narrative, constitute a central theme of the work. The protagonist, eponymous hero, and ersatz author ultimately chooses to reject screenwriting to resume work on a novel because the former medium lacks the ability to transcend the present and articulate the real. Daniel Martin himself articulates many of Fowles's own previously documented concerns about the medium, particularly his mistrust of the screen's seductive appeal, its reductive ten-

In *The Enigma* John Marcus Fielding, a Member of Parliament, has mysteriously disappeared. His corpse may lie beneath the lake near his house, shown here, but the case remains unsolved at the end of Fowles's anti-detective story (BBC Broadcast Archive/Getty).

dency: "Film excludes all but now; [it] permits no glances away to past and future; is therefore the safest dream. That was why I had given so much of my time and ingenuity to it."[2]

If these limitations hold true, then I suggest that a successful visual adaptation of Fowles's work would incorporate this complex, multiplicity of insights to avoid rendering merely a safe dream. Additionally, to mitigate what Fowles characterizes in *Daniel Martin* as the inherently fascistic nature of the moving image, its tendency to "overstamp the truth, however dim and blurred, of the real past experience," a successful adaptation should also retain some of the ambiguity inherent in the original prose narrative, allowing room for the viewer's imagination to play a part in making meaning.[3] Finally, a successful adaptation should include the original's core themes and artistic kernel. If this could be accomplished, the work might approach *Daniel Martin*'s "whole sight," the opening words

In *The Enigma* Isobel Dodgson (Barbara Kellerman), a graduate in English studies, employs creative thinking to help detective Michael Jennings (Michael
Thomas) with the case of a missing Member of Parliament. This romantic get-
together provides some closure to Fowles's otherwise open-ended story (BBC
Broadcast Archive/Getty).

of the novel and the holy grail of realist depiction toward which Martin,
like Fowles, constantly strives.

In 1979 Malcolm Bradbury, himself a successful novelist, wrote a
screenplay based on Fowles's short story "The Enigma," the very title of
which warns of its nebulous content, indeterminate even for Fowles. The
story was from the author's 1974 collection, *The Ebony Tower.* Bradbury's
adaptation was directed for British television by Robert Knights, who
would later go on to direct *The Ebony Tower,* based on the title story from
the same collection. *The Enigma* was first broadcast in February 1980 as
part of the BBC2 television *Playhouse* series.

Bradbury's adaptation can reveal the degree to which any adaptation
is able to articulate the complexity of a short story, in this case one that
is reliant on an omniscient narrator and extended dialogue to articulate
the nuances of the story's central relationship between Isobel Dodgson
and Michael Jennings and, by association, her relationship with a missing

Member of Parliament. Bradbury's screenplay also proposes cinematic techniques to create extended visual metaphors associated with one of the key themes of the story: the disparity between appearance or mask, and the existential authenticity that occupied Fowles throughout his writing career. In addition, Bradbury manages to translate the overtly intertextual and metafictional nature of Fowles's story to the screen.

The plot of "The Enigma" is deceptively simple. John Marcus Fielding, "[f]ifty-seven years old, rich, happily married ... owner of one of the finest Elizabethan manor houses in East Anglia ... [and] also a Conservative Member of Parliament," or MP, mysteriously disappears after inexplicably having taken a taxi to the British Museum reading room, where his briefcase is later discovered.[4] This disappearance not only mystifies everyone who knew the unremarkable and predictable Fielding, but also "contravened all social and statistical probability" since, the missing man's profile is outside the demographic commonly associated with missing persons: namely, adolescents, the working class, and/or the financially destitute.[5] The unusual nature of this event, combined with the fact that Fielding disappeared on Friday the 13th, situates the vanishing firmly in a realm outside of one that can be predicted or easily explained using logic—in what is sometimes called the Fowlesian domain. Fielding's disappearance is indeed an enigma, the antithesis of the logical framework with which Special Branch detective Michael Jennings is equipped to solve the mystery.

After local police investigations fail to turn up any clues, Michael is put on the cold case, mainly to assuage the missing man's wife, who has a direct line to the Home Secretary. Michael's subsequent interviews with the missing man's secretary, his wife, her son, his farm manager, and a fellow politician constitute the next part of the short story, followed by Jennings' interactions with the second enigma of the story, Isobel Dodgson, girlfriend of the missing man's son, Peter Fielding. In the text, Jennings' single interview with Isobel has a remarkable effect on him, and the reader is invited to infer that Marcus Fielding may have likewise fallen under her spell. Like her Victorian namesake, the author of *Alice in Wonderland*, Isobel Dodgson plunges Jennings down the rabbit hole of his own self-doubt, eventually providing him with her own "very literary" theory regarding what has ailed Fielding and may have led to his disappearance.[6]

The relationship between Isobel and Michael is crucial to the story and thus also to any adaptation hoping to reflect the central thematic concerns of Fowles's original text. Isobel is a version of the female muse-magus and Michael of the male collector type, the pair of them providing the kind of vehicle through which Fowles likes to investigate different ways of being in and perceiving the world, somewhat divided along gender lines. Often outsiders detached from quotidian social norms of identity and behavior, Fowles's female muse-magus characters elicit a strong sexual attraction from the collector-male and protagonist while simultaneously evincing positive change in them—normally a reorientation towards a more authentic existence. By contrast, the flawed protagonists and collectors (in the metaphorical sense conveyed by Fowles's first published novel), classifiers, list-makers, and logical puzzle-solvers, typically attempting to make solid what "turns into air."[7] The collector-males' logical, scientific, and reductive approach to reality is countered by the intuitive, mythopoeic approach of the female muse-magus, who is more tolerant of ambiguity and flux and more attuned to the existential authenticity to which Fowles's central characters aspire. In Fowles's work, it is this latter attitude that affords a more holistic and therefore more authentic way of apprehending and articulating reality. Ernst Cassirer similarly emphasizes the proximity between mythopoeic thought and its origin and the equivalent relationship between scientific thought and its corresponding stimulus: "...a mere glance at the facts of mythical consciousness shows that it knows nothing of certain distinctions which seem absolutely necessary to empirical-scientific thinking. Above all, it lacks any fixed dividing line between mere 'representation' and 'real' perception, between wish and fulfillment, between image and thing."[8] Thus, like Fowles, Cassirer advocates for mythic thought, rather than scientific thought, as closer to "real" perception, lacking the "fixed dividing line" that is present in empirical-scientific thinking.

Some Fowlesian muse-magus figures are more successful in their attempts to educate their male counterparts than others. In *The Collector*, Miranda attempts but fails to change butterfly collector and photographer Frederick Clegg. In *The Magus* the influences of Alison and Conchis—originally conceived as a female character—reorient the drifting and emotionally desensitized, serial seducer Nicholas Urfe.[9] In *The French Lieutenant's Woman*, Sarah seduces fossil collector Charles Smithson, plunging him into existential despair and a reexamination and rejection of his hitherto vapid existence. In "The Ebony Tower" artist Diana unsuccessfully attempts to lure David Williams away from a safe but sterile existence dissecting the work of others and back to life where he may again create his own art. In *Daniel Martin*, through his reconnection with past love Jane Mallory, eponymous protagonist Daniel Martin realizes that he should be a novelist, rather than a writer of tepid, formulaic Hollywood screenplays. In *Mantissa*, the muse Erato rebukes the male chauvinist author Miles Green for having chosen to write for an audience of literary theorists because "academic readers ... are the only ones who count nowadays."[10] And in *A Maggot* Rebecca Lee, lowly former prostitute, refuses to allow the coldly superior and ratiocinative lawyer, Ayscough, to browbeat her into explaining the disappearance of a missing aristocrat, forcing the lawyer to consider the possibility that the methods of the Enlightenment alone are insufficient to explain all aspects of the human experience.

"The Enigma" proceeds to observe the interactions between the female muse-magus and the collector-male figures and the ways in which the female acts as a catalyst in the male's reorientation towards a more authentic existence. The omniscient third-person narrator affords the author numerous opportunities to identify and interpret this interaction for the reader, and this fact presents a particular challenge for any visual adaptation hoping to capture this dimension of the story—especially since so little of this important information is shared via dialogue. For example, it is important that both Michael Jennings and John Fielding be clearly identified as flawed collector-males because this connection enables an audience to associate Isobel's effect on Michael with respect to Fielding's mysterious disappearance.

In the text, Michael is clearly identified as a collector type. He is a rational puzzle solver, a fact that is equally apparent to both reader or viewer given his occupation: ratiocinative detective. He is also clearly depicted in both media as an analytical list-maker, summarizing what has been gleaned about Fielding into what he calls his "*State of Play*," in which he logically identifies "possibilities and their counter arguments."[11] However, the clearest indication of Fielding's identity as a collector male in the text is downplayed in the adaptation. Specifically, the existence of Fielding's vast collection of scrapbooks, in which he has meticulously pinned and catalogued his existence (a collection that only Isobel has deemed significant to the inquiry) is revealed during Isobel's interview with Jennings as part of the police inquiry. She asks: "'Did you ever see his scrapbooks? ... All bound in blue morocco. Gilt-tooled. His initials. Dates. All his press cuttings. Right back to the legal days. *Times* law reports, things like that. Tiniest things. Even little local rag clippings about opening bazaars and whatnot.... It just seems more typical of an actor. Or some writers are like that. A kind of obsessive need to know ... that they've been known?'"[12] In the adaptation, this important exchange is absent. Instead, Bradbury's adaptation shows Jennings briefly leafing through what could be scrapbooks during his visit to Fielding's home at Tetbury Hall. The implications of this visual substitute for dialogue are almost certainly lost on a viewer. Fielding's need to pin and fix his existence and thus his link to other Fowlesian collector-males such as Michael, is deemphasized in the adaptation, as is Isobel's significant choice of phrase used to describe this behavior that she deduces as evidence of the missing man's feeling of being trapped, his life "[m]apped out ... like a fossil—while he's still alive."[13] The word *fossil* evokes the collecting behavior of Fielding's fellow collector-male in *The French Lieutenant's Woman*, Charles Smithson, whose obsession with fossils is symptomatic of his difficulty understanding the enormity and constantly changing nature of existence, and whose collecting is "a foredoomed attempt to stabilize and fix what is in reality a continuous flux."[14] Thus Fielding's deepest character flaw is largely omitted from the adaptation for television.

Like Charles's muse-magus, Sarah Woodruff, Isobel Dodgson causes the flawed collector-males of "The Enigma" to recognize their own inauthentic existence. Her influence on Michael Jennings is profound, and he progresses quickly through the pattern of behavior with which readers of Fowles will be familiar: increased self-awareness, acknowledgment of self-doubt, even self-loathing, and finally movement towards a new identity as part of a relationship with the female muse-magus. This is doubly significant because as readers sees Michael evolving through these stages, they are also provided with clues that suggest Fielding may also have experienced such an epiphany under Isobel's influence, possibly encouraging him to abscond from his inauthentic life. We read, for example, that Michael is first disturbed by Isobel's way of perceiving the world; that it creates an "abyss between them"; it is, as he muses inwardly, the difference between "people who live by ideas [and] people who have to live by facts."[15] Other inward musings revealed to the reader via the omniscient narrator include Michael's private misgivings about his current identity and occupation, admitting that he "positively disliked the physical side of police work" although it is not until he has met Isobel that he considers that there may be an alternative to his current profession.[16] The text also makes it explicit that it is Isobel who has made Fielding aware that there are other ways of interpreting and being in the world. During Isobel's interview with the detective she recalls how John Fielding told her he was pleased about her relationship with his son, Peter, because of her potential influence on him. Fielding confided that he was glad "Peter had hit it off with me" because "one sometimes forgets there are other ways of seeing life."[17] However, the viewer would have no way of connecting Fielding's newly found awareness of other ways of seeing life with Michael's own increasing self-scrutiny and self-doubt since the latter is not shared in any of the original dialogue. Therefore, the crucial connection between Fielding's rejection of an inauthentic life and Jennings' own increased self-examination, both under the influence of Isobel, is lost. Bradbury's challenge was thus to show the viewer how Isobel affects Michael, and by inference how she affected Fielding, when the original text provides only one interview between Isobel and Michael. To meet the challenge Bradbury adds several scenes to communicate her views and her influence.

A key characteristic of the female muse-magus, and therefore an aspect that a successful adaptation should attempt to reflect, is the powerful sexual attraction she evinces in the collector-male, and it is this initial attraction that is then followed by the male's subsequent self-scrutiny and acknowledgment of his own inauthentic existence and identity. In the text, we read that Michael Jennings "fell for her at once," that he "had not wanted a girl so fast and so intensely for a long time."[18] Again, this development parallels Charles Smithson's rapid awakening of sexual desire for Sarah Woodruff in *The French Lieutenant's Woman*, which is similarly accompanied by Smithson's dramatic, revelatory shift of self-awareness during their first meeting alone on the Undercliff. Here, amid the "luminous evening silence broken only by the waves' quiet wash, the whole Victorian Age was lost."[19] Similarly in "The Ebony Tower," collector-male, David Williams rejects his female muse-magus and the possible future she represents, and consequently he mourns the lost possibility for his own personal growth, reflecting that his relationship with Diana was "far more than sexual experience but a fragment of one that reversed all logic, process, that struck new suns, new evolutions, new universes out of nothingness. It was metaphysical: something far beyond the girl; an anguish, a being bereft of a freedom whose true nature he had only just seen."[20] In Fowles, such increasing sexual attraction is an important component of the muse-magus/collector-male dynamic, and one that is inextricably linked with the collector-male's growing awareness of his own lack of freedom. Thus, a faithful adaptation should likewise communicate sexual chemistry.

Bradbury gives repeated and clear directions in his screenplay to highlight the chemistry that should exist between Isobel and Michael: he indicates that Isobel should have "a strong physical impact.... [W]e should sense not only her strong sexual force but also her containedness," and "[w]e should feel some sexual tension between them"; and in the final scene between Michael and Isobel when their relationship is finally consummated, he adds the direction: "We should sense an element of sexual brutality in her: A power, and enigma, the power of women, the power of the story."[21] From the content of his screenplay, there is no doubt that Bradbury recognized the significance of Isobel's sexual magnetism, her influence on Michael and the importance of conveying this dynamic to the meaning of the work itself. Bradbury and Knights try to take advantage of the visual medium to convey the "sexy young woman" of the text, by putting Isobel in a dress with a plunging neckline, which Mike looks at, repeatedly, as a surrogate for the voyeuristic audience. As film theorists might point out, the intimate dinner together at the end of the story invites the viewer to gaze at her and to identify with him.[22] However, even with the addition of this extra scene between Isobel and Mike, the audience infers only a sexual attraction—not the power of this relationship that is so clearly articulated in the original—because so much of Michael's internal torment does not come across on screen. The story's crucial chemistry, the insights into Michael's gradual transformation under the influence of Isobel, and the inferences that the reader is equipped to make about Fielding's disappearance tend to be lost on the viewer. As a result, the concluding sexual union of Michael and Isobel, which in the Fowles story has symbolic implications of muse-collector blending, in the video adaptation becomes merely a plot device to provide the audience a vicarious release of sexual tension and a sense of narrative closure.

For an informed reader, there are numerous other intertextual cues that identify Isobel as a magus-muse, but they do not make the transition to the screen because in the video adaptation those cues are not provided by an omniscient narrator. Specifically, the reader learns that Michael finds Isobel difficult to label or describe in reductive terms; Isobel seems to evade description, provoking a string of contradictions: "delicate, like sixteen; but experienced somewhere, unlike sixteen, certain of herself despite those first moments of apparent timidity."[23] Readers familiar with *The Magus* will recognize a similarity between this description of Isobel and that of Alison in the novel, who is also described in ways that suggest her qualities are mythical, enigmatic, almost beyond language—a "human oxymoron…," "innocent-corrupt, coarse-fine, an expert novice."[24] Fowles's magus-musethus not only thwarts the collector male's ability to codify her in language, she also challenges his reductive approach to the complexity of lived experience in general and his dependence on scientific logic as a lens through which to examine such complexity.

Similar to Nicholas Urfe at the beginning of *The Magus*, Michael Jennings is too steeped in his logical, analytical approach to resolving complexity to afford much respect for Isobel's different ways of interpreting the world and her apparent ability to understand the enigma of Fielding's disappearance. He half-mockingly describes her insights as "telepathic."[25] Isobel seems unaware of her own intuitive powers, a little embarrassed by her insights and reluctant to give them much credence: "No. Honestly not. I think it was just me. Psychic nonsense. It's not evidence."[26] When pressed to describe why she didn't really like Fielding, she appears to dismiss her insights as "'sympathetic magic'" and begs Michael not to share her words with others: "'You please mustn't say anything about this. It's mostly me. Not facts.'"[27] Finally, before she drops the bombshell that connects her directly with the British Museum reading-room and Fielding's final confirmed sighting, she remarks teasingly: "'It's all so tenuous. I don't even know why I'm bothering to tell you.'"[28] However, by the conclusion of the story the reader recognizes that Isobel's account of events is the only plausible explanation of the disappearance and of Fielding's motivation to abscond. To readers of Fowles, Isobel's seeming reluctance to fully share her insights with Michael is also familiar. The deliberate veiling and gradual revealing of details associated with Fielding's disappearance has the effect of piquing the detective's interest still further. Isobel is exhibiting the familiar power of a master story teller, another characteristic of the magus-muse: she seduces Jennings and the reader into wanting to know more by only providing tantalizing glimpses into the possibilities of her narrative, even possible futures for the collector-male. It is the same kind of spell cast by Sarah Woodruff in her seduction of Charles Smithson and by Diana as she indicates possibilities for David Williams; both involve the males' rejecting their safe, socially sanctioned lives and relationships and plunging into the unknown. And, again like Isobel, Sarah possesses an uncanny ability to assess and understand a person's inner thoughts and motives, as if she had "a computer in her heart."[29] A major part of Sarah's ability to ensnare Smithson is her seeming reluctance to share her story with anyone else but him. Isobel's story likewise culminates in her finally sharing the one clue with Mike that she has been withholding from other police investigators: the fact that she had told Fielding that she would be in the British Museum reading room on the day of his disappearance, thus providing the missing link between the missing man and his final reported sighting. These literary parallels help to confirm the importance and complexity of this central relationship between Isobel and Michael, which is part of a much broader artistic project in Fowles's work.

Malcolm Bradbury responded creatively to the demands of this complexity. Rather than attempting a faithful rendition of Fowles's original text, which as I have suggested above would have been fraught with difficulty, instead he leveraged the strengths of the visual medium by creating numerous added scenes, even additional characters to focus his adaptation on effectively representing three major elements of the work on the screen: first, establishing Fielding's artificial and inauthentic existence; second, suggesting Michael's increasing self-awareness of his own inauthenticity after contact with Isobel; and third, establishing implicit connections between the two central collector male characters and the degree to which their inauthenticity contrasts starkly with the honesty of Isobel Dodgson.

First, to establish the environment of the inauthentic in which Fielding exists, the film makes visual the metaphor of the whitewashed exterior that hides reality to suggest this idea of a mask; one's external appearance as an adopted mask is an important theme in Fowles's work, from his 1962 essay on Robin Hood as the quintessential Englishman, always in disguise, hiding in the woods, to Fowles's digression on the Green Man in *Daniel Martin*.[30] In the opening shots of Bradbury and Knights' adaptation of "The Enigma," the exterior of Fielding's office is presented as one of many identical white-faced townhouses—anonymous, character-less and ubiquitous, their whitewashed fronts suggest obfuscation and artificiality. Similarly, the first visual representation of Tetbury Hall, the Fieldings' country estate, is particularly effective as an extension of the visual metaphor of appearances disguising reality. Only Tetbury's exterior is revealed to the viewer, stressing its superficial and outward appearance, itself a mask. This distancing effect is further intensified by the use of a reflected shot of Tetbury's exterior seen as the building's reflection in the lake. This use of reflected reality, or reality at one remove to suggest artificiality and inauthenticity, will recur in Bradbury's added scenes at the gentleman's club, the site of Michael's revelations about his own inauthentic existence. Tetbury's appearance reflected in water also foreshadows Isobel's increasingly plausible theory that John Fielding has in fact committed suicide after deciding he can no longer continue to live his inauthentic life, his body now lying at the bottom of Tetbury lake, whose presence has been established visually from the onset of the narrative.

Second, Bradbury and Knights make effective use of extreme close-ups, metonymic representations where an individual is reduced to the function performed by one limb or one aspect of his or her body. Fielding is a man who has gradually been diminished to the point of absence, and the filmmakers the use high camera angles with an extreme close-up shot of Fielding's hand to suggest this for the viewer in the opening seconds of the film. The camera gradually pulls back to reveal more of Fielding, but at first only his hand is visible, signing letters on House of Commons stationery, reduced as he is being introduced to the status of a functionary, a cipher, a mere signifier. When Fielding is finally seen in full, it is in a long shot as he quickly disappears into a taxi as he wears the stereotypical uniform of the conservative gentleman, replete with bowler hat—another form to disguise an Englishman's individual identity. After he has left the office, a voyeuristic camera scans Fielding's impersonal room providing more information about the mysterious Fielding. The camera hovers primarily over photographs that reduce Fielding further to the roles he plays: MP, father, and husband—little of the man himself. Fowles frequently associates photography and photographs with the collector impulse to reduce the complexity of human experience to a pinned fragment, as seen in both Clegg's reductive photography of Miranda in *The Collector* and in the extreme close-ups of women's breasts in *The Magus*, which, devoid of context are, as Urfe reflects, "much too obsessive to be erotic."[31] The lingering shots of these photographs in *The Enigma* not only acknowledge this intertextual connection to photography in Fowles's works, but also provide the viewer with fleeting but significant information about Fielding as a character. The inclusion of these numerous photographs of other people who define Fielding, that is, his family and other members of the Conservative party, rather than shots of Fielding enjoying pursuits that define him as an individual, introduces the possibility that Fielding is a man who has been led to adopt an inauthentic role created for him by others— including the unacknowledged author of a metafictional narrative. Finally, in an interesting expansion of the visual metaphor, the whitewashed exterior of Fielding's office in Bradbury's adaptation bears a striking similarity to the exterior of the gentlemen's club where Michael Jennings is depicted interacting with his "master" from the Home Office. The similarity between the two buildings suggests an affinity between the two men, establishing a link between the inauthenticity and obfuscation of Fielding's existence and of the Establishment that is seeking to keep Fielding's disappearance from becoming a scandal. Similarly, the deferred reality of Tetbury, shot as a reflection on the lake in the earlier scene, suggestive of the inauthentic nature of the Fieldings, is recalled by the placement of numerous mirrors in the gentlemen's club, which is especially noticeable in the scene between Fenton and Jennings. Thus in Bradbury's adaptation the visual metaphors of mirrored reality and whitewashed reality intersect in Fielding's places of work, home, and leisure. The mirrors in the gentlemen's club also provide an interesting visual effect of an infinite regression of the reflected image behind Fenton and Jennings, the *mise en abyme* suggesting the mystery of Fielding's disappearance, which no one besides Michael, it seems, wants to solve.

The scenes between Michael Jennings and Fenton are Bradbury's creation. Fenton is an added character, a nameless supervisor in Fowles's original text, so it is interesting that Bradbury cast Nigel Davenport, one of the most well-known faces on British television, to play Fenton. These scenes assume a greater significance to the viewer by virtue of Davenport's stature as an actor. The two added scenes are located before and after Michael's first meeting with Isobel, and this provides Bradbury with an opportunity to depict Michael's evolving attitude towards the Fielding case under the influence of Isobel.

In the text, Michael Jennings is at first nonchalant about his investigation of the Fielding affair. In the first added scene with Fenton, before Michael meets Isobel, he appears complicit with those who wish only to placate Mrs. Fielding, who seems to want to solve the mystery behind her husband's disappearance only if nothing sordid is uncovered. This scene also hints at Michael's artifice, which is extensively described in the text before he first encounters Isobel. The reader learns, for example, that "he took very good care indeed not to show his feelings" toward his superiors in the police force in case doing so might negatively affect his career prospects; the narrator goes as far as to suggest that Jennings' duplicity is "Machiavellian."[32] Additionally, readers are told that Jennings "put on his public-school manner" for his meeting with Mrs. Fielding as part of his attempt to reassure her that the case was not outside his own class.[33] Bradbury depicts Jennings in this first meeting as being very comfortable with Fenton. In the text, Jennings is "fully aware of the situation: he was to make noises like a large squad. He was not really expected to discover anything, only to suggest that avenues were still being busily explored. As he put it to a colleague, he was simply insurance, in case the Home Secretary turned nasty."[34] Consistent with this approach, Bradbury and Knights depict the first scene between the two men as positive. Over lunch in Fenton's club Jennings plays the earnest inspector. The two men are at ease with each other, mirroring each other's behavior and appearance. Thus the scene conveys Jennings' willingness to accept the role he has been assigned.

However, after his meeting with Isobel, the next scene at the gentlemen's club with Fenton is dramatically different. Isobel, as readers learn from the text, has a character that impresses Michael Jennings: she "possessed something that he lacked: a potential that lay like unsown ground, waiting for just this unlikely corn-goddess; a direction he could follow, if she would only show it. An honesty, in one word."[35] After having met Isobel, Michael's attitude toward the Fielding case and his willingness to keep up the charade are much altered; Bradbury and Knights convey this effect visually by contrasting the second meeting with Fenton with the first. In the second meeting, instead of reverse-angle shots showing each man mirroring the other's body language and activity, the camera angles show Jennings' discomfort with his complicity in the choreographed investigation. The men are shown in contrasting poses; there is no mirroring of attitudes or facial expressions, and Fenton is repeatedly shown from behind in a three-quarter turn away from the camera that looks over his shoulder at Jennings in a quarter-turn toward the camera, his face the dominant interest of the shot as he expresses increasing discomfort. Thus in Bradbury's adaptation the meetings between Jennings and Fenton, which occur before and after Michael Jennings' interview with Isobel Dodgson, allow the viewer to witness Jennings' increasing malaise and increasing awareness that he too is reluctantly playing a part in a fiction.

These added scenes with Fenton provide insight into the workings of the male-dominated British establishment, whose old boy network is represented by the addition of another scene with a second new character, a Mr. Wild, one of the members of a board on which Fielding serves. The meeting between Jennings and Wild occurs in another all-male domain: the men's fitness club, and it concludes with Wild meeting a woman, who is obviously not his wife, for a lunchtime assignation. The scene serves to reinforce the idea that the British establishment is a community of inauthentic males, to which Fielding also belonged.

Bradbury's use of visual metaphor is also effectively used to establish Mrs. Fielding's artificiality in comparison with Isobel's honesty. In the text, Mrs. Fielding's responses to Jennings' questions and her accompanying behavior are described in terms that emphasize her artificiality. For example, we read that she displays a "seemingly well-practiced gesture of hopelessness" when Jennings asks her whether she has a theory about her husband's disappearance, and she is further described as "a woman welded to her role in life and her social status, eminently poised and eminently unimaginative."[36] Therefore, Bradbury's choice to depict Mrs. Fielding in terms that define her in contrast with Isobel assist the viewer discerning the difference between the two women and their respective worldviews.

In Bradbury's adaptation Mrs. Fielding is constantly depicted in situations where she is attempting to control rather than exist at one with nature. She is first seen bringing in cut flowers from the garden at Tetbury, and in subsequent interviews with Jennings, she is seen weeding and attending to the gardens of the perfectly manicured grounds. These details are completely absent from the text and thus suggest a deliberate move on the part of Bradbury and Knights to give her character additional weight in its pose of public composure. By contrast, Isobel's rooms are warm and green, brimming with potted, not cut plants, suggesting Isobel is comfortable with nature rather than complicit in controlling it. While Mrs. Fielding's Tetbury is enclosed in fences, Isobel's preferred environment is open, a detail that is emphasized when she requests the open fields of Hampstead Heath as the location for her interview with Jennings. Bradbury and Knights further effectively establish contrast between the Fieldings and Isobel as the viewer is presented immediately with interior shots of Isobel's home, rather than the pompous exteriors of either Fielding's London office or Tetbury Hall. These images reinforce the sense of Isobel's accessibility and honesty.

In the text Peter Fielding is another masked character, a fact that Isobel has detected in him and shares with the reader during her interview with Jennings. In her interview she intuitively characterizes Peter as having two personas; he is "Unmixed. Like oil and water. Two people."[37] Bradbury conveys this image, not by including this dialogue, but instead by adding two original scenes where the viewer can see these two different masks. At the beginning of the adaptation, as in the original text, during his interview with Jennings, Peter is depicted as a self-styled rebel: a pseudo–Marxist who seems to have rejected the privileged class into which he was born. In the text, Mrs. Fielding sees through this mask, and during her interview with Jennings, disputes his inference that Peter does not want to continue his father's legacy running the estate: "'But Peter does want it. He adores this house. Our life here. Whatever he says.' She smiled with a distinct edge of coldness. 'I do think this is the most terrible red herring, sergeant. What worst there was was long over.... Apart from Peter's little flirtation with Karl Marx, we really have been a quite disgustingly happy family.'"[38]

However, in the first of two added scenes, after his father's disappearance, Bradbury takes Mrs. Fielding's observation further by illustrating the shallowness of Peter's political convictions. In the first added scene, Peter is shown stepping seamlessly into his father's shoes, awarding prizes at the local fête, a role historically filled by the most important male in the village, the squire or major land owner; a role that he has previously ridiculed. In the second added scene, Jennings approaches Peter Fielding at Tetbury, to ask whether he has permission to drag the lake for John Fielding's body. Peter has undergone a dramatic physical change in terms of his dress, even his haircut; no longer a political student activist, he now declares that he is the "head of the house" in his father's absence. He denies Jennings' request. He has dropped the mask of the Left-wing political activist and adopted a second mask, that of the country squire, leaving the viewer doubting whether even Peter himself knows what his own authentic existence might be. By showing the effortless assuming and abandoning of masks by both Peter and Mrs. Fielding as they adopt attitudes appropriate for the occasion and company, and by showing her association with controlling and perpetuating artificial order in the face of chaos, Bradbury illustrates the degree to which the Fieldings have incorporated artifice and inauthenticity into their everyday existence. This is contrasted with the effortless honesty and openness of Isobel. In focusing so much attention on these particular aspects of the original text, Bradbury is preserving Fowles's ongoing interest in the concept of authenticity, specifically as an aspect of Satrean existentialism, which Fowles promotes in *The Aristos*: "[T]he true antidote to fascism is ... to re-establish in the individual a sense his own uniqueness, a knowledge of the value of anxiety as an antidote to intellectual complacency (petrifaction), and a realization of the need he has to learn to choose and control his own life."[39] The importance of one's own sense of identity and the autonomy necessary to pursue a path of one's own choosing would seem to be at the heart of the enigma of Fielding's disappearance, the likely result of an existential crisis brought on by his sudden awareness that he has long ago ceded control of his life to some unknown system or authority. Finally, Bradbury was faced by two key elements of "The Enigma" that presented daunting challenges to visual adaptation: first, the work's extensive and explicit intertextual connections, both to the other short stories in *The Ebony Tower* and to Fowles's wider canon; and second, the work's intensively literary, metafictional aspects including experimentation with genre codes and narrative patterns.

As discussed previously, there are evident attempts by Bradbury to foreground some of the overarching thematic concerns in Fowles's fiction. However, the "The Enigma" is part of a self-consciously interrelated set of works titled *The Ebony Tower* which, as Fowles explains in "A Personal Note" to the reader, is a series of variations on themes explored in his other novels. This note appears after the novella "The Ebony Tower" and before Fowles's translation of Marie de France's twelfth century French *lais*, "Eliduc." In this essay-note, Fowles explains his original title for the collection and its significance for the reader. He writes: "The working title of this collection of stories was *Variations*, by which I meant to suggest variations both on certain themes in previous books of mine and in methods of narrative presentation." Fowles replaced this title in part because "the first professional readers, who do know my books, could see no justifications for *Variations* whatever ... beyond a very private mirage in the writer's mind."[40] However, Fowles's decision to highlight this previous, rejected title in a note to the reader serves to stress the author's ambivalence toward this decision. The thematic concerns that are present in "The Enigma" are indeed reiterated in Fowles's other work and are thus imbued with greater significance by the informed Fowles reader, who is aware of these recurring preoccupations. For example, "The Enigma" recalls the extreme circumstance of disappeared persons in *The Collector*, *The French Lieutenant's Woman*, and *A Maggot*. It also revisits the recurring motif of the creative female artist, who is able to connect the male protagonist with a more authentic life. It anticipates *Daniel Martin* and its preoccupation with English class and role playing, as well as with the nature of fiction, its creation, its relationship with reality, and the codes that it follows or rejects. The possible associations and connections that may be evident to a reader of Fowles's other works are, of course, impossible to anticipate, but it is certain that readers of *The Ebony Tower* alone cannot avoid becoming aware of the author's wider philosophical interests. It would be unrealistic to expect the same level of intellectual engagement in an adaptation of a single work from this collection, let alone an adaptation for a television audience.

Fowles's "A Personal Note" also draws the reader's attention to the book's Celtic romance, "Eliduc," which, Fowles reminds us, is the ancestor of the English novel: "I believe that we also owe—emotionally and imaginatively, at least—the very essence of what we have meant ever since by the fictional, the novel and all its children, to this strange northern invasion of the early medieval mind. One may smile condescendingly at the naïveties and primitive technique of stories such as Eliduc; but I do not think any writer of fiction can do so with decency—and for a very simple reason. He is watching his own birth."[41] Such a statement stresses the interconnectedness of the stories in the collection, their collective relationship to this seminal work, as well as drawing attention to the metafictional nature of the collection. By drawing attention to the modern novel's position on a historical continuum, as well as focusing on the writing process itself (an explicit feature of Fowles's story "Poor Koko," also in *The Ebony Tower*), Fowles reminds the reader of the work's identity as a constructed artifact.[42] Relationships between reality and existence, between the past and the present, and between people are, "The Enigma" suggests, more complex and demanding than a reductive or simplistic solution would imply. Separating one short story for adaptation, particularly one that is so intrinsically associated with a wider conversation about the nature of reality, is fraught. "The Enigma" continues Fowles's exploration of the complex nature of the lived experience; it presents a mystery that draws us in, that panders initially to our post–Enlightenment zeal for puzzle-solving only to remind us that life's mysteries are seldom resolved so neatly. Fowles was well aware of the enduring need for thrillers and detective stories, positing in a 1977 interview that they were "obviously fulfilling a deep need" because "situations of mystery have become very rare in the personal lives of the twentieth century."[43] With "The Enigma," however, in *seeming* to adopt the form of the detective story, Fowles is not pandering to the vicissitudes of the reading public. Instead, he adopts the familiar genre codes and narrative patterns of detective fiction, but, importantly, he refuses to provide the neat solution to a mystery that would render the story a simple detective story.

In this sense, "The Enigma" is the perfect metaphor for the trait of

Englishness with which Fowles is increasingly fascinated: the propensity to present as one recognizable thing while retaining a mysterious core self behind the mask. Fowles's experimentation with genre codes and the expectations engendered in a reader of "The Enigma" is suggestive of the author's broader interrogation of simplistic notions of realism in his attempt to more accurately apprehend reality in his work. As in *The Collector*, the reader is drawn into what *seems* to be a typical thriller, as the protagonist stalks and then imprisons Miranda Grey. But expectations of Miranda's escape, or at the very least, of Clegg's apprehension and prosecution for her murder, thus restoring order in the manner of a typical thriller or detective story, are thwarted. Clegg not only seems to have successfully evaded capture at the end, he is sufficiently emboldened by the experience to look for a second victim after Miranda's death. Likewise, the protagonist in *The Magus* draws the reader into a vicarious attempt to solve the mysteries Nicholas Urfe encounters on Phraxos, only to find that Urfe himself eventually reflects that all attempts to solve these mysteries are pointless because life is simply not a mystery to be solved: "That was the meaning of the fable. By searching so fanatically I was making a detective story out of the summer's events, and to view life as a detective story, as something that could be deduced, hunted, and arrested, was no more realistic (let alone poetic) than to view the detective story as the most important literary genre, instead of what it really was, one of the least."[44]

A major departure from the original, then, is Bradbury's decision to present *The Enigma* as that which Fowles's story assures us that it is not: a detective story. In the text, the traditional detective novel pattern is suspended because there are no clues to follow; instead, it is the creative writer, Isobel, rather than the detective who must solve the mystery. Isobel suggests two endings, one that would satisfy the expectations of the reader of a detective novel, and one that refuses to adhere to these expectations. Isobel first invites Jennings to "pretend everything to do with the Fieldings, even you and me sitting here now, is in a novel. A detective story. Yes? Somewhere there's someone writing us, we're not real." In this first hypothesis, Isobel provides an explanation for Fielding's visit to the British Museum, one that would provide an acceptable ending to a detective novel, because "[y]ou can't have a mystery without a solution."[45] She suggests that Fielding might have gone to the British Museum reading room and, not finding her there, proceeded to call her at the publishing house where she worked, broke down, and asked her to help him stage his disappearance.

Ultimately, Isobel rejects this ending, because it adheres to readerly expectations of detective fiction and is thus contrived, artificial, and therefore suspect. Instead, she proposes an ending that diverges from expectations of detective fiction readers, but one that is eminently plausible both because it does not adhere to any formulaic pattern and because it is grounded on her explanation of Fielding's motives which she explains using the extended literary metaphor of the author and his characters. Isobel proposes that Fielding recognize that "there was an author in his life. In a way. Not a man. A system, a view of things? Something that had written him. Had really made him just a character in a book," "a zombie, just a high-class cog in a phony machine." The nature of his disappearance was therefore crafted not only to escape "both the rot and the pain" but also to imbue him with the immortality that accompanies a mystery, because "the one thing people never forget is the unsolved. Nothing lasts like a mystery."[46] Isobel suggests that this second posited theory is the more plausible because it flouts readerly expectations: "[I]f our story disobeys the unreal literary rules, that might mean it's actually truer to life."[47] In other words, surface reality—a perceived adherence to quotidian norms—should be considered suspect. What lies beneath that layer, might be a more authentic version of the real.

In the adaptation, however, Bradbury presents Isobel's first ending, the one where she has colluded with Fielding to bring about his own disappearance, a fact that is dismissed by Isobel as being too tidy, too much in the vein of a detective story. Bradbury concedes that, in general, television dramas must provide an ending that would satisfy a television audience rather than one that conveyed the subtle nuances of the original story. He reflects that Fowles's original ending "undermines much of the story, and leaves us in several different kinds of doubt, a lesson in our very sense of fiction"; a faithful rendition of this ambiguous ending would result in "upsetting an audience who has devoted 75 minutes to watching what is apparently a detective story, and who are likely to feel disappointed if that story offers no solution, only a continued enigma."[48] In making the story less enigmatic, Bradbury has changed an intellectually-stimulating work of fiction into a cinematic work of middle-brow entertainment.

Despite these changes, Bradbury and Knights' adaptation of Fowles's "The Enigma" was, according to Craig Brown's review in the *Times Literary Supplement*, a critical success; an adaptation, which "improves upon and enriches the original story." Tellingly, he characterizes *The Enigma* as a "cracking good yarn in the Agatha Christie tradition," which confirms that Bradbury was probably wise not to preserve the original story's overt experimentation with the detective novel formula.[49]

There is little evidence regarding Fowles's own view of Bradbury and Knight's finished work, other than the fact that according to Eileen Warburton's biography of the writer, Fowles "retained script oversight and consulted with Bradbury before production."[50] He must have recognized that Bradbury's adaptation is simply one of those "safe dreams" that deny "the spectator virtually all use of his own imaginative powers" and exclude "all but now; permit[ting] no glances away to past and future."[51]

In his preface to Pinter's screenplay for *The French Lieutenant's Woman*, Fowles acknowledged the overlap between the two narrative domains of the cinema and the novel, but also suggested there were "no-go" areas for both. The cinema's domain, and one where the novel should not go, he characterizes as the "visual things the word can never capture ... [like the] endless nuances of facial expression."[52] I suggest that for the televised version of "The Enigma" Bradbury and Knights effectively use the visual in their depiction of setting, in their use of interior and exterior shots, and in the extreme close ups to convey information about the Fieldings and about Isobel that is provided to a reader by the narrator and implied author of the story.

But cinema, and by extension television, should not trespass in the domain of "the things the camera will never photograph nor actors never speak," which Fowles characterizes as the "long paragraphs of description, historical digression, character analysis and the rest that the vast portmanteau of novel form was specifically evolved to contain." I suggest that this is the aspect of Fowles's story that is lost as Bradbury adapts it to the medium of visual performance. Bradbury was dealing with a difficulty that must be faced when adapting any work of fiction written in the latter part of the twentieth century and beyond, since the novel form in general and Fowles's work in particular have become increasingly concerned with "aspects of life and modes of feeling that can never be represented visually."[53]

Fowles's work increasing embodies a mythopoeic realism not based in the realm of mimetic verisimilitude or scientific observation and labeling, but on a richer and more elusive apprehension of reality. This deeper reality is the means by which Fowles attempts to capture an increasingly complex reality that demands a different approach from traditional realistic narrative to facilitate its apprehension. The mythopoeic is inextricably linked with storytelling, the origins of language, and creativity. Fowles's female characters are more able to apprehend a reality that lies beyond surface quotidian norms because they are more aligned with the mythopoeic: privileging the intuitive over the scientific, they are more receptive to possibilities beyond the status quo.

The broader range afforded by prose narrative, its ability to acquaint the reader with a character's past, his inner thoughts about other characters and his own existence are typically lost in a cinematic adaptation of a work of fiction, and *The Enigma* in particular is impoverished by the absence of this missing component. There are missing glances "away to past and future," the restriction to the "now" which renders the adaptation a "safe dream." It is the same challenge faced by Daniel Martin, who ultimately rejects screenwriting for these very reasons. The camera is unable to capture the complexity, particularly of the English psyche, that might still only yet be hinted at by prose narrative, leaving the ersatz author, Daniel Martin yearning for a totality of consciousness:

> [Longing for] a medium ... would tally better with this real structure of my racial being and mind..., something dense, interweaving, treating time as horizontal, like a skyline; not cramped, linear and progressive. It was a longing accented by something I knew of the men who had once lived at Tsankawi; of their inability to think of time except in the present, of the past and future except in terms of the present-not-here, thereby creating a kind of equivalency of memories and feelings, a totality of consciousness that fragmented modern man has completely lost ... so infinitely beyond camera and dialogue and dramatic art, as unreachable as all the landscapes beyond the limits of my eye.[54]

Oral and written storytelling maintains an attractive imprecision that is absent in film. It forces the readers' imaginations to strain to make meaning, often approaching the boundaries of what can be understood about the lives depicted in stories heard and read. Bradbury's adaptation is, unavoidably, a safe dream because the nature of the medium is what Fowles discounts as safe. "The Enigma" takes as its subject the internal life—the ability of the individual to imagine possible futures and the conflict that exists between the roles that we are expected to play versus authentic existence. It considers the mythopoeic imagination to be connotative, evanescent and transcendent and contrasts it with the rational and scientific as they encounter this enigma. Put succinctly, Fowles points out the challenges inherent in conveying the complexity of human perception and experience using still or moving images rather than using the less precise medium of language. In Fay Godwin's collection of photographs, *Land*, Fowles's accompanying essay contrasts two versions of the same subject: one a photograph and one a description in prose, a passage called *"la bonne vaux"* from Restif de la Bretonne's *Monsieur Nicolas*. In this essay Fowles encapsulates the challenge inherent in trying to capture what one can only hope to suggest or to hint at, what is somehow diminished with the clarity and precision of the mimetic verisimilitude of film:

> The passage is imprecise in almost all the ways where a photograph must be precise; yet for me it has an emotional vividness, an accuracy over an experience that every child has known, the first discovery of a secret place or landscape, which photography—even cinematography—is eternally barred from. The effect here is gained not just because the writing is sequential, describing a series of events, thoughts, reactions, but above all because it is so vague in its general detail that no reader will envision the place in the same way. It is both "so far" and intensely close at the same time, like the memory ... of an older person; and this, I believe, is a faculty beyond exact representation; that is, even if exact representation of the bonne vaux had been possible—had Restif also been a ten-year-old genius with a pencil—it could only have diminished, not enhanced the experience. One can go blind with seeing, in more ways than one.[55]

So Bradbury and Knights' *The Enigma* is not equivalent to Fowles's "The Enigma," but that is so because certain kinds of equivalence across different media are not possible. In its own right, as a television production, *The Enigma* is serviceable entertainment, without the original work's complexity and nuance—a safe dream.

Notes

1. Devon McNamara, "Staying Green: An Interview with John Fowles the Novelist," *The Christian Science Monitor* 1 February 1979, p. 20. Rpt., in Vipond, *Conversations*, p. 66.
2. John Fowles, *Daniel Martin* (Boston: Little, Brown, 1977), p. 155.
3. *Ibid.*, p. 87.
4. Fowles, *The Ebony Tower* (Boston: Little, Brown, 1974), pp. 191–92.
5. Fowles, "The Enigma," *The Ebony Tower*, p. 191.
6. *Ibid.*, p. 235.
7. Karl Marx, qtd. in Marshall Berman, *All That Is Solid Melts into Air* (London: Penguin, 1988), p. 89.
8. Ernst Cassirer, *Mythical Thought* (New Haven: Yale University Press, 1971), p. 36.
9. John Fowles, "Notes on an Unfinished Novel," *Harper's* July 1968, p. 94; rpt., *Wormholes*, p. 23.
10. John Fowles, *Mantissa* (Boston: Little, Brown, 1982), p. 120.

11. Fowles, "The Enigma," p. 203.

12. *Ibid.*, pp. 240–41.

13. *Ibid.*, p. 240.

14. John Fowles, *The French Lieutenant's Woman* (Boston: Little, Brown, 1969), p. 49.

15. Fowles, "The Enigma," p. 239–40.

16. *Ibid.*, p. 213.

17. *Ibid.*, p. 233.

18. *Ibid.*, pp. 223, 226.

19. Fowles, *The French Lieutenant's Woman*, p. 72.

20. Fowles, "The Ebony Tower," *The Ebony Tower* (Boston: Little, Brown, 1974), p. 102.

21. Malcolm Bradbury, screenplay for *The Enigma*, in *The After Dinner* Game, 2d ed. (London: Arena, 1989), pp. 88, 96, 126.

22. Laura Mulvey, "Visual Pleasure and Narrative Cinema," *Screen* 16.3 (1975): 6–18.

23. Fowles, "The Enigma," p. 225.

24. John Fowles, *The Magus: A Revised Version* (Boston: Little, Brown, 1977), pp. 24, 28.

25. Fowles, "The Enigma," p. 229.

26. *Ibid.*, p. 228.

27. *Ibid.*, pp. 229.

28. *Ibid.*, p. 234.

29. Fowles, *The French Lieutenant's Woman*, p. 52.

30. Fowles, "On Being English, but Not British," *Texas Quarterly* 7.3 (Autumn 1964): 157–58; rpt., *Wormholes*, pp. 83–85; *Daniel Martin*, pp. 275.

31. Fowles, *The Magus*, p. 101.

32. Fowles, "The Enigma," pp. 198, 203.

33. *Ibid.*, p. 219.

34. *Ibid.*, p. 202.

35. *Ibid.*, p. 236.

36. *Ibid.*, pp. 220, 222.

37. *Ibid.*, p. 233.

38. *Ibid.*, p. 221.

39. Fowles, *The Aristos*, rev. ed. (Boston: Little, Brown, 1970), pp. 121–22.

40. Fowles, "A Personal Note," p. 117.

41. *Ibid.*, pp. 118–19.

42. Fowles, "Poor Koko," page 145.

43. Richard Yallop, "The Reluctant Guru," *The* Guardian 9 June 1977. p. 8.

44. Fowles, *The Magus: A Revised Version*, p. 552.

45. Fowles, "The Enigma," p. 236.

46. *Ibid.*, pp. 240, 242.

47. *Ibid.*, p. 239.

48. Bradbury, *Enigma*, p. 22.

49. Craig Brown, "Evading Authority," review of *The Enigma* (BBC2), *Times Literary Supplement* 15 February 1980, n.p.

50. Eileen Warburton, *John Fowles* (New York: Viking Penguin, 2004), p. 402.

51. Devon McNamara, "Staying Green: An Interview with John Fowles the Novelist," *The Christian Science Monitor* 1 February 1979, p. 20; Fowles, *Daniel Martin*, p. 168.

52. Harold Pinter, screenplay for *The French Lieutenant's Woman* (Boston: Little, Brown, 1981), p. ix.

53. Pinter, screenplay for *The French Lieutenant's* Woman, pp. ix–x.

54. Fowles, *Daniel Martin*, pp. 351.

55. Fowles, "Essay by John Fowles," *Land*, by Fay Godwin (Boston: Little, Brown, 1974), p. xi.

Situating Sarah:
The French Lieutenant's Woman on Film

CAROL SAMSON

*I wish it were possible to explain the impression made upon
a young girl whose experience so far had been quite remote
from art, by sudden and close intercourse with those to whom
it was the breath of life.*—Georgiana Burne-Jones

In the summer of 2002, I had tea with John Fowles at a hotel outside
of Lyme Regis, the tearoom window opening to the vast seaside. Fowles
was frail at the time, but congenial, courtly, robust of memory. I asked
him about Sarah Woodruff in his novel *The French Lieutenant's Woman*.
I wanted to know where he found her. He smiled, and he told me a story
about walking through the bookshops off Leicester Square in London. He
said that many years earlier he had seen a painting of a Victorian woman
in the window of one shop, and he never forgot the image. He said he
went back several times and, one day, asked the shop owner if he could
buy the painting. The shopkeeper said it was not for sale, but Fowles said
that he kept that image in his mind, that he found Sarah there. In an earlier
interview, in *Harper's*, Fowles had suggested another genesis, explaining
that he found Sarah in a picture that came to his mind in late 1966: "A
woman stands at the end of a deserted quay and stares out to sea. That
was all.... These mythopoeic 'stills' (they seem almost always static) float
into my mind very often. I ignore them, since that is the best way of finding
whether they really are the door into a new world."[1] Either way, the image
was indelible. Fowles conceived this woman as an iconic figure, not necessarily of an historical period, but as a figure from myth or dream or chance
encounter, as if she were drawn from his knowledge of women who stand

in the spaces where love makes its assault on nothingness, of women who attempt to take something back from their own lonely silence.

In adapting *The French Lieutenant's Woman* to film, screenwriter Harold Pinter and director Karl Reisz also attended to this image, a solitary woman on a deserted quay looking out to sea, carefully orchestrating it in their 1981 film. Early on, they focus on the woman and on an exchange of male and female gazes, the watcher and the watched. When Sarah and Charles meet on the Cobb in the novel, Sarah returns Charles's look with a powerful stare: "Again and again, afterwards, Charles thought of that look as a lance; and to think so is of course not merely to describe an object but the effect it has. He felt himself ... both pierced and deservedly diminished."[2] In the film, Sarah appropriates Charles's traditional male gaze, constituting a gaze of her own, becoming the one who judges, the voyeur. Put simply, Sarah looks back, and her silence is not mere mute gesture. She is constructing meaning and allowing time for a presencing. Her gaze creates, in Roland Barthes's terms, a *punctum*, a moment wherein Charles is "pierced" by an image.[3] Harold Pinter's 1981 screenplay reads: "She turns sharply, stares at him. He stops speaking."[4] In a series of reverse-angle shots, we see Sarah's gaze interspersed with Charles's reaction. We see her cloak, her back. He calls "Madam." She turns. The camera closes in on her face. She looks up and beyond the camera past Charles, focusing on him, measuring him. Then she turns away, having made note of him, having assessed him as potential lover or mentor or protector. Sarah returns to her view of the sea. She is, once again, solitary, singular.

In situating Sarah throughout their film, however, Pinter and Reisz most often choose to draw heavily on images that support the male gaze. They offer up a montage of painterly visions, borrowing poses which establish the male gaze of the Pre-Raphaelite Brotherhood, who led what Fowles describes in the novel as "the revolutionary art movement of Charles's day."[5] Later, in his early post-modernist way, Fowles brings these historical figures into his fictional narrative as Sarah's co-habitants in the historical Tudor House at 16 Cheyne Walk, in Chelsea.[6] The film suggests works by various Pre-Raphaelite Brotherhood artists, particularly John Everett Millais, James McNeill Whistler, and Dante Gabriel Rossetti.

Of particular relevance to the Pinter-Reiz film is the etching on paper, *The Bridge of Sighs* (1858), by John Everett Millais, for the image seems to be a prototype of the pose of Meryl Streep in her first appearance as the character of Sarah in the film. Millais' study, filled with dark and web-

The Bridge of Sighs, by John Everett Millais (1858). This etching seems to be not only a prototype image for first appearance of Sarah in the film, but also a suggestion of its romantic theme. In the background, Millais offers a looming dome, perhaps St. Paul's Cathedral, image of the dominant moral order, and then he counters the solidity of the monumental dome with a play of gaslights on the bridge, lights that create spaces of possible romantic sentiment by opening up a haunted and ephemeral otherness, a shimmering world reflected in the water (© Victoria and Albert Museum, London).

like markings, presents a solitary woman shrouded in a long black cloak, her hand clutching her wrap or, perhaps, securing the drapery of her cloak in order to disguise her pregnant condition or even to hide an infant she has hidden under the folds. The etching presents a London night, quiet and misty. The figure stands alone at the river's edge, near Victoria Bridge, called the Bridge of Sighs, a place known in the Victorian period as the site of tragedy and despair, as the location where unmarried mothers and destitute prostitutes took their own lives, seeking to escape their shame and poverty. At the background of the etching, Millais offers a looming dome, perhaps St. Paul's Cathedral, a certain image of the dominant moral order, and then he counters the dark solidity of the dome with a the play of gaslights on the bridge, lights which create spaces of Romantic possibility, if not sentimentality, by opening up a haunted and ephemeral otherness, a shimmering world reflected in the water. Framed by the bridge and water, the young woman, Poor Tragedy herself as Fowles might call her, metes out her lonely existence, her eye arresting on something or someone forever in the distance.

Similarly, in several moments from the film and especially in still photographs of Meryl Streep as Sarah, the designers replicate elements borrowed from James McNeill Whistler, another member of the Brotherhood, and make particular use of his *Symphony in White*, also known as *The White Girl* (1862). This painting is a portrait of the artist's mistress dressed all in white and standing against an all-white brocade drapery. In one on-location, still shot, the film designers transform Whistler's all-white palette to an all-green setting, reiterating Whistler's pose and theme. In this photograph, Streep, as Sarah, becomes a woodland creature dressed in forest green, standing alone at the center of a dense wood. All is nature and greenery and Eden come again. Then, later in the film, in the final scenes at New House, the designers return to Whistler's painting even more directly

Opposite: James McNeill Whistler: *Symphony in White, No. 1,* or *The White Girl* (1862). In one of the still photographs made to promote the film, Meryl Streep as Sarah, wearing a hunter's green dress, stands amid woodland greenery. The natural textures of trees and leaves are monotone green, her face and hair the only contrast; as in the Whistler painting, all is rich texture, silk fabric and tapestry and bear-hide, carpet weaving and brocade, all pleat and fold. In either image, the girl becomes a mere design element. She stares back at the viewer as if to ask if we can see the paradox that she is both female figure and aesthetic pattern, as if to judge whether we understand the grammar of ornament (courtesy National Gallery of Art, Washington).

as Streep's Sarah reunites Charles in an all-white studio in the New House. Here she is dressed in all-white, the shoulders of her gown rounded and finished with the suggestion of a puffed sleeve, her bodice defined in pleats—all of the details repeating Whistler's choice, emphasizing aesthetic texture, minimizing tonal contrast. In the Whistler painting, all is fabric, silk and bear-hide, flower design and carpet and brocade, pleat and fold. Looked at in a certain way, the Whistler girl herself becomes a stately element of design, an art object for art's sake. She gazes directly at the viewer, her hair flat at the brow and opening to a sensuous halo of red, and she is frozen against the background, unmovable. She stares back at us as if to ask if we can see the paradox that she is both female figure and aesthetic pattern, as if to judge whether we understand the grammar of ornament.

In addition to references to the works of Millais and Whistler, the filmmakers also appropriate images of costume and pose from the works of Dante Gabriel Rossetti. One of Rossetti's watercolors, *Writing on the Sand* (1859), suggests not only ideas for the hairstyling and bushy Dundreary whiskers of Jeremy Irons, as Charles, and the Garibaldi-hoopskirt possibilities in the costumes of Meryl Streep and the other ladies, but also concepts relating to Fowles's theme of woman as Muse. In this work, a Victorian couple, hand in hand walk along a windy beach, the gentleman glancing at his companion and reaching with his cane to draw her picture in the sand. The sea and wind are turbulent, the bodies of the couple twist against the elements, yet the gentleman-artist is intent on translating her beauty, if only in the most transient of ways, by creating a portrait on a canvas of shifting sand. In another instance, the filmmakers allude to one of Rossetti's last portraits, *The Day Dream* (1880), as Streep, once again in the woodlands, sits in the cradle of a tree, framed by the branches. In *The Day Dream*, Rossetti, much like the gentleman-artist in the watercolor who records his lady friend, paints his own personal Muse, the model Jane Morris, wife of William Morris. She is a monumental figure, seated in a sycamore tree, its leaves reminiscent of the designs in William Morris wallpapers. In her lap, the woman holds both a sweet branch of honeysuckle, a Victorian love symbol, and a book of poetry. Alone in her reverie, she cradles a flower in one hand and holds a branch in the other. Like Whistler's girl dressed in white, she is both woman and design element, but Rossetti creates her as iconic figure, as myth. She is Daphne and tree nymph. She is Eve caught up in the Tree of Knowledge. She is, or so Ros-

Dante Gabriel Rossetti: *Writing on the Sand* (1858–59). This watercolor offers an unmoored sea and a sandy beach where lovers walk hand in hand. The sea and wind are turbulent, the bodies of the couple twist against the elements, yet the gentleman-artist is intent on translating her beauty, if only in the most transient of ways, by creating her portrait on a canvas of shifting sand (British Museum, London).

setti might wish his mistress-model Jane Morris to be, Baucis to his Philemon.

While relying on Rossetti's paintings for visual designs, the filmmakers also chose to blend in references to photographs and to *carte de visite* images of the period. As Streep plays the Hollywood actress called Anna in the film, her hair is styled in a contemporary bob, but, then, as the Anna character becomes Sarah Woodruff, Streep is bedecked in a red wig, sometimes tightly curled and caught up at the nape of her neck, often, though, loose and flowing, and in these more Romantic moments, the character of Sarah slowly comes to adopt the persona of a Pre-Raphaelite model, a woman of beauty referred to as a "stunner" by the Brotherhood. The beauties were offered up to the male gaze in paintings, the male percipient thus allowed to study the women as vessels of perfection, as sensual objects. Not surprisingly, the film references the luxurious red hair of some of Rossetti's models. In one of the still shots, Streep lies on a barn floor in the hay, her hair a halo of red much like the model in Rossetti's *Head of Andromache* (1868). At other times, in the forest scenes outside of Lyme Regis, she is coy, flirtatious, her face reminiscent of Rossetti's painting of *Helen of Troy* (1863). Actual photographs of Rossetti's models do, however, create a counter version of the Victorian "stunner" persona. In a *carte de visite* made of Jane Morris, we see a sturdy woman gazing at us directly, an official self, her hair parted in the middle and curled in sea waves at her temples. She is serious, one could even say, ordinary, plain. The filmmakers replicate this *carte de visite* self in some of the still photographs, especially in the images of Streep as Sarah when Sarah must play her role as conventional Victorian woman, as lady's companion, as servant. In these scenes, her hair is tightly controlled, a solid cap of respectability. In these photographs, Streep is no longer the mysterious stunner. She views us with an intelligent regard, with an awareness of her place in the scheme of things. There is no daydream here.

Interestingly, though, this idea of the "stunner," this concept of the female surrendering to a male viewer as part of the Pre-Raphaelite Brotherhood's vision of the feminine ideal, is an argument that the Fowles novel does not critique, except perhaps in the moment when Charles considers the criticism he has heard of Dante Gabriel Rossetti's friend, the poet Algernon Charles Swinburne, a Brotherhood member, in Charles's remembered reference to Swinburne as the "libidinous laureate of a pack of satyrs" or, once more, in the scene inside the Rossetti house when Charles anticipates meeting Christina Rossetti and recalls that the magazine *Punch* called her a "sobbing abbess" and "hysterical spinster."[7] Rather, as Sarah reunites with Charles in the novel, she defends her life with the Rossetti clan and explains her new philosophy in terms of their Art and Aesthetics. She tells Charles that she has considered the faults and vices of the artists who

Dante Gabriel Rossetti: *The Day Dream* (1880). Like Whistler's girl dressed in white, Rossetti's daydreaming woman is both woman and design element, but Rossetti creates her as an iconic figure of myth. Seated in a woodland setting, this monumental woman is Daphne. She is Eve caught up in the Tree of Knowledge or, as the painter Rossetti might have wished his mistress Jane Morris to be, is Baucis to his Philemon (© Victoria and Albert Museum, London).

abide at Tudor House, but she deems them to be people "of noble purpose."[8] She accepts their allegiance to Beauty, and she seemingly adapts to the Pre-Raphaelite Brotherhood vision, aligning their genius with her own personal sense of self and womanhood and of New World possibility. Sarah's explanations to Charles at the end of the novel reveal that she has been gazing back at the Brotherhood. She has reckoned them, perhaps, much in the same way the model, Jane Morris, regards the painter Dante Gabriel Rossetti in several of her painted portraits—with a deliberate and calculating and, of course, alluring eye.

Sarah's commitment to this clan has, as Fowles constructs it, evolved as a result of her own calculated agenda. In order to come to her moment of choice, her decision to reside at the Rossetti house, she herself has had to become what the Brotherhood called "a stunner," that is, an alluring female model. Fowles allows her the skill of assessing a situation and playing a deliberate role. Aware of the hierarchy and the fallibility in the construct of her Victorian world, Sarah anticipates the independent mindedness of the New Woman of the 1890s by finding a way to manipulate that world, to read the *kairos* of the moment, and to adapt it to her advantage. In a recent study of the Pinter film adaptation, Brenda Allen notes that Sarah can be a "temptress or tragic victim to gain Charles's affections" or, late in the novel, reunited with both Charles and daughter Lalage, "an agent of Providence" who willingly accepts the Angel role, or, in the alternate ending, an "Iago to Charles's Othello, concealing the truth from him in the interests of propelling him in the direction of his own destruction."[9] Admitting, like Fowles, that Sarah Woodruff is not to be explained, Allen reads the Pinter screenplay ending, the scenes with Sarah situated as a tutor at a Lake Windermere mansion, as fitting, for she understands that Sarah must claim Charles as protector. In the film we see them, at last, together in a small boat issuing out of a dark tunnel and emerging as a bright couple, Charles taking command of the oars, rowing them to domestic bliss. Allen argues economic need and gender issues as the motive for Sarah's choice:

> Sarah must find herself a protector, and although her protector is for a brief time the formidable Mrs. Poulteney, in the novel she ultimately allies herself with the artist Dante Gabriel Rossetti ... [and] like the [pre–Raphaelite] Brotherhood's members, Sarah resists convention, considers herself intellectually superior to others of her station, and takes what she needs while giving little back in order to achieve her own ends. Unlike the Rossettis, but like other pre–Raphaelite artists, Sarah is poor; she can

place herself outside of society but she cannot easily support herself. Outside the storyworld Fowles's solution for Sarah is less than convincing because the chances of gaining such patronage are remote.[10]

Allen goes on to note that Pinter's screenplay, his choice to place Sarah with an architect's family in the Lake District, is more credible than the alternative with the Rossettis at Tudor House in London. Herein Allen privileges male patronage and stability in Pinter's script, his placement of Sarah "in the house of a well-known, untitled, less wealthy and less famous artist than Rossetti—one who has lived a more conventional married life … [one] who accepts the need to care for others as part of his world-view … [one who] may well encourage the development of another artist or take care of a pregnant model."[11] In Allen's view, the Rossettis were problematic people of extreme privilege who would demand subservience from Sarah, so that Sarah's adoption of a conventional role, that is, her placement as a governess for a kindly architect's family and, later, her life as wife-mother under Charles's protection, is more realistic and, thus, preferable in a film adaptation.

Interestingly, though, in the text of the screenplay, Pinter offers a gentle, if not coy, reference that implies other possible meanings in the Lake District setting, subtle references to an emerging modernism within Victorian order. As Pinter situates these final scenes, Charles ascends a wooded bank and looks through the scenery for a sign of life. In the screenplay, this Lake District house is called "The New House," and it belongs to a man named Elliott whose son is Tom Elliott, a not-so-hidden nod to Thomas Stearns Eliot and a modernist tradition nascent in the historic moment. The House is white and surrounded by shrubbery and stones walls. From somewhere beyond the wall comes the sound of children at play:

[Scene] 228. LAKE SHORE. DAY.
CHARLES ascending a wooded bank. Behind him, the lake.
Piano music.
CHARLES looks through shrubbery at the white house.
He begins to skirt it. He waits for signs of life.
[Scene] 229. THE NEW HOUSE DAY.
CHARLES' view—a glimpse of white walls through dense shrubbery.
The sound of playing children.[12]

In this moment, a child of twelve years appears, announcing himself to be called Tom Elliott, his name a homonym for that other Tom Eliot, the poet T.S. Eliot, and his arrival, caught up as it is in images of a garden and a wall, suggest Eliot's *Four Quartets*, specifically the "Burnt Norton" sec-tion—"Go, said the bird, / for the leaves were full of children, / Hidden excitedly, containing laughter"—with its theme of a human kind who "can-not bear very much reality" and who, like the reunited Charles and Sarah perhaps, know that in this reunion moment "Time past and time future / What might have been and what has been / Point to one end, which is always present."[13] This brief allusion to modernism, to the New House and the New Woman, is, however, countered in the script and film as the adaptation returns to images of the domestic, to talk of children and family contained, and even to Romantic constructs in architecture, the room for the reunion an alabaster space, a tower, and the maiden, Sarah, dressed like Whistler's *The White Girl*, awaiting her knight. The New House, while tentatively suggestive of new "Eliot" beginnings, remains a Victorian "Elliott" domicile with a kindly tutor governess, reminiscent of Victorian concept of the "Angel in the House."

Pinter's use of art images at this point further serve the domestic and the art themes in the film as Charles meets Sarah inside the house in a room that is "*white, full of light... Pictures on walls. A trestle table. Piles of drawing. A drawing in progress on a small table.*"[14] Encouraged by the architect-owner of New House to explore, if not teach, her art, Sarah has a space for artworks which, as Charles notes immediately, are all drawings of children. He tells her she has found her gift—rendering children. Their dialogue here seems the stuff of Victorian melodrama and, more impor-tantly, a rejection of the existential modern, of that "damned freedom" in Sarah that, as Charles proclaims, twists the heart. The action is nineteenth century theatre: Charles flings Sarah to the floor. She smiles. They forgive each other. They kiss. Enter sunlight.

CHARLES: To make a mockery of love, of all human feeling. Is that all Exeter meant to you?
   One brief transaction of the flesh? Only that? You have planted a dagger in me and your "damned freedom" gives you license to twist it in my heart. Well, no more!
   He strides to the door She seizes his arm.
SARAH: No!
   He flings her away, violently.
CHARLES: Yes!
   She falls to the floor, hitting her head. He stops
   She sits up, holding her head. He stares down at her.
   She looks at him. She smiles.

SARAH: Mr. Smithson ... I called you here ... to ask your forgiveness.
>   *Pause.*
> You loved me once.
>   *Pause.*
> If you still love me, you can forgive me.
>   *She stands.*
> I know it is your perfect right to damn me.
>   *Pause.*
> But if you do ... still ... love me ...
>   *They look into each other's eyes.*
CHARLES: Then I must ... forgive you.
>   *Pause.*
SARAH: Yes. You must.
>   *A piano is heard.*
>   *Sunlight falls across the room.*
>   *CHARLES and SARAH move towards each other.*
>   *The camera tracks closer and stops.*
>   *They are embracing.*
>   *They kiss.*[15]

As Pinter frames his script in meta-cinematic terms, the next moment extends his binary structure. Everything changes as this scene of melodramatic reunion at the New House is juxtaposed with a contemporary postmodern scene of Hollywood-style partying and decadence. Suddenly, the New House, still the scene's setting, takes on new meaning as the script defines the space as twentieth-century frivolousness with actors at play, scenes of Anna and Mike, still dressed as Sarah and Charles, posing in front of the New House garden, other actors celebrating the completion of the filming. Even in the next film scene as the Pinter-Reisz team change the New House space into Mike's own London mansion, it is still all Hollywood cavorting and post-modern surface, jumble and chaos. The actors, mostly in modern clothes, some drunk, frolic—the actor who played the doctor, Grogan, dancing with the actress who played Mary, the actor who played Sam dancing with Mrs. Poulteney, the prostitute figure cavorting with Mr. Freeman. When the actress who played Ernestina appears, she wears a fur coat and boots. She enters, to applause and whistling, steps onto a platform and begins a burlesque parody of a fan dance, "opening and closing her coat," "reveal[ing] that she is dressed in a Victorian corset."[16] We, as watchers, are no longer mere spectators at a melodrama, for the film, with its imposed binary frame, turns us into voyeurs. We experience a blurring of Victorian and modern frames, and as a result, we see all things turned inconsequential, illusory, decadent. As two critics have viewed it, the filmmakers

> successfully remind the audience of how artificial their lives are, with the pressures of history, ideology, psychology and social convention forming the scripts of their lives.... [Then Victorian story, modern frame, and audience lives] "merge, to remind us again of the fragile and ambiguous boundaries distinguishing our own realities, which, if we heed the screenplay, seem increasingly illusory."[17]

The script concludes with Mike searching for the actress Anna, finding her white dressing room empty, her long red wig hanging from a block of wood. She is gone. At the window he calls, "Sarah," conflating her two identities, the Victorian heroine and the existential New Woman, denying boundaries.

This meta-concept of film and literature, of reflexive cinema, is, of course, not new to us. But, caught as we are now in a post post-modern world, we sniff out a falsity in binaries. Allen might realistically perceive that Sarah, in the patriarchal world of 1868 London, needed to find a protector, but thirty years after the Pinter-Reisz film, we might also deconstruct the alternate ending, calling for a screenplay to explore the cultural bindings in Sarah's choice to live at the Rossettis' Tudor House in Chelsea, at the address given in the novel, the legendary site of poets and philosophers, of Lady Tragedy and Lady Beauty, of the sublime and despondent. This Tudor House is, for Sarah, it would seem, a place of existential freedom without promise of conventional security. It is a brush with genius, a space that teases her intellect, tempts her senses. It is, as Fowles suggests strong concepts should be, a door to a new world. To situate Sarah in the light of the Tudor House is to place her in an eccentric and bohemian community, to offer her a third space, a "wonderland" with the Rossetti clan, something beyond platitudes and Angels in the House, or perhaps one should say, a space with a different variety of Angel, for the House held not only the Pre-Raphaelite Brotherhood, but also a Pre-Raphaelite Sisterhood, female models and artists and biographers, weavers and wives— women passionate, if unknown, working to constitute their own gaze.

Living in the Tudor House at the end of the novel, Sarah explains she has been "admitted to the daily conversation of genius ... [a place where she finds] a community of honourable endeavor."[18] In terms of a new adaptation of the novel into film, the question becomes: What exactly did Sarah find at Tudor House? In addition, given the Pinter-Reisz script's use of allusions to the images of the Pre-Raphaelite Brotherhood, are such images, with their male gazes, sufficient to define the place? The fact is, they are not. The House was, of course, a feminized context, a space saturated with paintings of and by women, filled often with poetess types and models of varied temperament, with mistress-strumpets, with wives and sisters of male artists, and, of course, a place noteworthy for its eccentricities. Fowles, in fact, took his cue to use such a space from another strong woman by listening to his wife Elizabeth who was disappointed in the conventional marriage ending of an early draft and who told Fowles he could do better. And it was Elizabeth who directed him to "bang her somewhere in the centre" of the household and its eccentric and philosophical art movement—artists, poets, academics, and rascals—all living or passing through Tudor House.[19] In this House, Sarah Woodruff becomes both the artist's amanuensis and model, another Muse, not a Penelope this time, rather a Beatrice. Fowles directs Charles Smithson, much like Virgil guiding the Italian poet Dante, up to the "fatal gate" of 16 Cheyne Walk, where he will find not only Sarah, but also another Dante—this one a Rossetti.

Dante Gabriel Rossetti and the house were legendary, even notorious, by 1869 when Charles arrives to claim Sarah. Interestingly, on October 7, 1863, Lewis Carroll had carried his heavy camera equipment up to Tudor House, to photograph the Rossetti clan. Carroll was, as biographer Diane Roe states it, "about to experience the Rossetti effect."[20] It is a fact that Lewis Carroll admired Christina Rossetti, and he would come to borrow one of her lines from *Goblin Market*, "Eat me, drink me, love me," adapting it for his own *Alice's Adventures in Wonderland*, and Carroll would have known that the fashionable Cheyne Walk collected celebrity, male and female alike. The neighborhood was full of genius. Elizabeth Barrett Browning had been born at number 93, JMW Turner died at number 119. Other residents of fame included George Eliot, Whistler, and Bram Stoker. Henry James would die at number 21.[21] According to Roe, as Lewis Carroll entered the drawing-room which ran the length of the first floor, he would have found sea-green walls lined with mirrors and looking-glasses of all shapes and sizes. He would have found the few remaining spaces filled with framed paintings whose female subjects surveyed the elegant clutter of the room with dark eyes.[22]

Through accounts in letters, we know that three large bay-windows framed the Thames, that daylight played on the blue-veined Delft tiles of the fireplace, that mandolins, lutes and dulcimers were scattered on the

Henry Treffry Dunn: *Rossetti Reading Proofs of* Ballads and Sonnets *at 16 Cheyne Walk* (1882). According to Rossetti's biographer Diane Roe, as visitors entered this drawing-room which ran the length of the first floor, they would have found sea-green walls lined with mirrors and looking-glasses of all shapes and sizes. In *The French Lieutenant's Woman*, Charles would have found the few remaining spaces filled with framed paintings whose female subjects surveyed the elegant clutter of the room with dark eyes (© National Portrait Gallery, London).

oriental rugs. There was an English china cupboard filled with Spode ware as well as Belgian brass sconces. There were gold ornaments, earthenware pots decorated with birds, carved oak furniture from an antique dealer, Japanese prints, woodcuts and cabinets reflecting the new "Japanese Mania"—all of it meant to startle and delight visitors. As Roe defines it, it was "like a dream, a great core sample mined from the Victorian subconscious and manifested as interior design"—a Pre-Raphaelite painter's vision of bohemian paradise. Rossetti's fantasy women, of course, transformed the space, the walls hung with drawings of his deceased wife, Lizzie Siddal, and rooms set aside for séances he held to contact her spirit. Apparently, guests there were often rowdy, and Lewis Carroll would claim later that the afternoon he spent at Tudor House had inspired the Mad Tea Party chapter of his fantasy *Alice in Wonderland* (1865) where he saw the expatriate American painter James Whistler as the March Hare, Algernon

Swinburne as the Dormouse, and Dante Gabriel Rossetti as the Mad Hatter. And, if the human clamor was not enough to suggest wonderland, Rossetti kept an exotic menagerie of parrots, peacocks, wombats, a kangaroo, and a Brahma bull, whose eyes, he insisted, reminded him of Jane Morris.[23]

By 1869, when Charles arrived at the Chelsea House, he would have had justifiable trepidation. In making his visit and attempting to sort out Sarah's destiny, before he ascends the stairs, he recognizes Rossetti's monogram on some of the "crowded paintings and drawings."[24] He would have seen collections of images of women on the walls, there, many of them portraits of Lizzie Siddal, Rossetti's model and wife, an artist herself who had died as result of a laudanum overdose in 1862. Here, Charles might have concluded, is an argument for the possible tragic end for any woman choosing an existential course. Among Lizzie's own paintings and Rossetti's drawings of her that filled the walls would have been Rossetti's *Beata Beatrix*, the memorial painting of Lizzie wherein Rossetti attempted to assuage his guilt for his infidelity. Indeed, these images of Lizzie were a blueprint of Poor Tragedy herself: a young girl found working as a hatmaker; a Beauty chosen to be an artist's model, posing in water for Millais's famous painting of *Ophelia* (1851–52) and contracting pneumonia, subsequently becoming a woman never healthy, an artist working at her own art, living with Rossetti, marrying him, birthing a stillborn baby, dying of an overdose. During their time together, Rossetti drew Lizzie's portrait again and again, and yet some acquaintances said she was not beautiful, her skin pale, her limbs thin. Like Sarah Woodruff, however, she was said to be strangely affecting. She had a poetic sensibility and artistic aspirations, her art technique naïve, self-conscious, romantic, her themes often drawn from the ballad tradition or from Tennyson. In her painting, *Lady Affixing a Pennant to a Knight's Spear* (1858–59), for example, Siddal presents a red-haired woman, a Lady, assisting her Knight with his military banner, as he kneels at her feet in a gesture of chivalric dedication. In Siddal's *Lady of Shallot by Her Loom* (1853), the female figure, drawn from the Tennyson poem, is arrested momentarily in her task of weaving. The victim of a mysterious curse, this Lady is forced to weave images without looking at the world, required to look into a mirror and watch lovers and funerals and parades, to observe world events only as they are reflected in shadows. In time, she confesses, "I am half-sick of shadows."[25] Certainly, fond of poetry and, yet, fragile in her health, Lizzie Siddal would have understood both the Romance of the tale and the depths of the Lady's ennui. When Lizzie died in 1862, Rossetti placed his unpublished poems in her coffin; had Sarah Woodruff stayed at the house, she would have known that Rossetti, ten years after his wife's death, chose to retrieve the poems, sending an associate to open her grave in 1871. Legend says that, when the men opened the coffin, Lizzie's red hair had continued to grow, overspilling the coffin.[26]

That day, when Charles arrived in Chelsea, there were additional issues that would have concerned the female members of the household. At any point, he might have seen a "stunner" like Anna Miller, a blond beauty who would sit for Rossetti as Helen of Troy and who drove Lizzie to jealousy, or he might have encountered the full-figured Fanny Cornforth, the prostitute of good humor whom Rossetti painted in his narrative *Found*, about a man come to retrieve his fallen bride. Ultimately, in this feminized space, the Tudor House, he might have noticed the way Rossetti gave special attention to the model Jane Morris, the woman Rossetti fawned upon and courted as an intimate friend, if not a mistress. Dark-haired and melancholy, she was the woman whose image filled Rossetti's paintings from 1865 to 1880. On meeting her, Henry James wrote: "It's hard to say whether she's a grand synthesis of all Pre-Raphaelite pictures ever made or they a 'keen analysis' of her. In either case, she is a wonder."[27] At first a model for William Morris, Jane married the artist in 1859 and gave birth to two children. By 1868, the date that Sarah Woodruff probably arrives at the Tudor House in the novel, as the Morrises were living in London, Jane Morris was a frequent model for Rossetti, whose admiration became an obsession. She returned his feeling, and, in 1871, Morris and Rossetti took a joint lease on Kelmscott Manor so that Jane and Rossetti might be together. After Rossetti's breakdown, his bouts with the drug chloral, and his experience of delusions of persecution, Jane ended the affair but remained his friend until his death.[28]

The Tudor House in Chelsea was full of the woman's gaze, of women looking back from paintings, of women haunting ghostly séances, of women in conversation in the garden or studio. In Fowles's novel Sarah's choice to live there speaks to her need for a place that would nurture her passion, even obsession, not so much because she needed beauty, but because she needed her mind to be in league with other strong minds and, perhaps, in tune with the spiritual clamor in a Pre-Raphaelite Brotherhood and Sisterhood. Rossetti's house, for Sarah, should be read as an important third space beyond Pinter's nineteenth-century New House with its upper room where Sarah stands, costumed as a conventional and Romantic artist-governess, framed in medieval architecture, waiting for Charles in order to ask for his forgiveness.

Significantly, in the novel Sarah Woodruff has absorbed the language of this third space. She makes a reasoned argument to Charles, adopting the discourse of Art and Aesthetics, mentioning Rossetti's first wife, dead, but not dead in Rossetti's heart, defending Rossetti and the others: "I am *not* his mistress. If you knew him, if you knew the tragedy of his private life ... you could not for a moment be so.... I *have* found new affections. But they are not the kind you suggest."[29] Sarah admits to a kind of madness, but she interprets her decision to stay there in terms of a theory of Art:

> I have since seen artists destroy work that might to the amateur seem perfectly good.... I was told that if an artist is not his own sternest judge, he is not fit to be an artist.... I believe I was right to destroy what had begun between us. There was a falsehood in it.... I remarked a phrase of Mr. Ruskin's recently. He wrote of an inconsistency of conception. He meant that the natural had been adulterated by the artificial, the pure by the impure, I think that is what happened two years ago.[30]

When Charles asks her to speak to him with observations other than Art, she says her art observations are intended to apply to life as well. She tells him she will stay here where she has found herself to be happy: "I am admitted to the daily conversation of genius. Such men have their faults. Their vices. But they are not those the world chooses to imagine. The persons I have met here have let me see a community of honourable endeavor, of noble purpose, I had not till now known existed in this world."[31]

In her own way Sarah has found wonder made legible, a community of philosophical thought and honor and judgment. She has adopted the rhetoric of the group, a level of argument she had not, till now, known possible, and she employs this reasoning to explain her changed relationship to Charles who seems to set aside intellectual women. At one point in the novel, having entered the House and recognized Rossetti or Ruskin in one of the rooms, Charles waits in a drawing room, anticipating that the poet Christina Rossetti will appear. Wary of her sensibility, Charles credits Christina Rossetti with Sarah's new vision of self:

> [Charles] divined at once whom he was about to meet. It was her employer's sister, the poetess (I will hide names no more) Miss Christina Rossetti. Of course! Had he not always found in her verse, on the rare occasions he had looked at it, a certain incomprehensible mysticism? A

passionate obscurity, the sense of a mind too inward and femininely invo-
lute...? He saw now who was to blame for Sarah's philosophy of life—she
whom *Punch* had once called ... the hysterical spinster of the Pre-
Raphaelite Brotherhood.[32]

Fowles's narrator deliberately identifies Christina Rossetti as a source of
the intellectual energy in the house. If Jane Morris and the others were
"stunners" or "strumpets," Christina was the poet-interpreter of the place
who would become a major figure in Victorian poetry. Clearly, she
observed and came to understand the male gaze, working to render her
brother Dante Gabriel's intense affection for and obsession with his model,
Lizzie Siddal, in her poem "In the Artist's Studio." She writes:

> One face looks out from all his canvases,
>   One selfsame figure sits or walks or leans;
>   We found her hidden just behind those screens,
> That mirror gave back all her loveliness.
> A queen in opal or in ruby dress,
>   A nameless girl in freshest summer green,
>   A saint, an angel;—every canvas means
> The same one meaning, neither more nor less.
> He feeds upon her face by day and night,
>   And she with true kind eyes looks back on him,
> Fair as the moon and joyful as the light:
>   Not wan with waiting, not with sorrow dim;
> Not as she is, but was when hope shone bright;
>   Not as she is, but as she fills his dream.[33]

Here the poetess presents the male gaze as a gesture of "feeding" or con-
suming of feminine beauty while the woman, the stunner, a saint or an
angel, looks back at her worshipper with a kind face. This model, the perfect beauty, is "fair" and "joyful," and the male artist sees her as the source
of his personal dream fulfillment, never considering, it would seem, her
sad "waiting" or her "sorrow dim." In addition to this poem, and perhaps
with direct relevance to *The French Lieutenant's Woman*, is another Rossetti poem that foreshadows or suggests the narrative of the lover across
the sea, a tale similar to the imagined story that Fowles's Sarah Woodruff
adopts, describing herself to others as an abandoned lover, the "woman"
of a French Lieutenant who resides elsewhere. In the poem "If," published
in 1866, Christina Rossetti's character yearns for her lover, and, with great
sadness, envisions her own death, asking the birds to tell him, wherever
he may be, that she is dying.

If

If he would come today, today, today
Oh what a day today would be;
But now he's away, miles and miles away
From me across the sea.

O little bird flying, flying, flying
To your nest in the warm west,
Tell him as you pass that I am dying,
As you pass home to your nest.

I have a sister, I have a brother,
A faithful hound, a tame white dove;
But I had another, once I had another,
And I miss him my love, my love.

In this weary world it is so cold, so cold
While I sit here all alone
I would not like to wait and to grow old
But just to be dead and gone.

Make me fair when I lie dead on my bed,
Fair where I am lying;
Perhaps he may come and look upon me dead
He for whom I am dying.

Dig my grave for two with a stone to hoe it.
And on the stone write my name:
If he never come I shall never know it
But sleep on all the same.[34]

In his illustration for this poem, engraver Frederick Sandys drew a monumental woman seated at the sea cliffs. Caught in reverie, contemplating an absent lover, she presses a strand of her long golden hair to her lips. The tone of the work is melancholy, the artist interested in psychology and in the drama of a central and dominant figure in a moment of extreme emotion and focused introspection. In drawing such as this, art historian Simon Cooke points out that Sandys saw "romance not as fulfillment, but as frustration."[35] The woman's pose, her choice to chew on the strand of hair and to tug on the blades of grass, all suggest her weary longing. Draped as she is in layers of clothing, the woman is large and strong and mindful. She seems aware of the world's defining barriers, penned as she is in a landscape where long fences divide the territory and where jagged and darkened cliffs lead down to the sea.

Over and above Christiana Rossetti, other women of the Pre-

Frederick Sandys: Untitled wood engraving (1886). In this illustration for Christina Rossetti's poem "If," which begins, "If he would come today," the woman's
pose, her choice to chew on the strand of hair and to tug on the blades of grass,
suggest her longing and her disappointment. Draped in layers of clothing,
Sandys' woman is large and strong and mindful. Like Sarah before she evolves,
the woman seems aware of the world's defining barriers, penned as she is in a
landscape where long fences divide the territory and where jagged and darkened
cliffs lead down to the sea (The Victorian Web).

Raphaelite Sisterhood were making their claims along with the males. Jan Morris's book *The Pre-Raphaelite Circle* catalogues some of them. There is Joanna Boyce Wells, one of the foremost women painters of her generation, who exhibited work at the Royal Academy in 1856, who wrote that "Genius is in truth nothing but a strong desire for knowledge and the spirit of industry is its truest mark."[36] There is Evelyn de Morgan, an extremely shy woman who fought family opposition to pursue an art career. She studied at the Slade, traveled to Italy, and aligned herself with the Pre-Raphaelites, painting large canvases with allegorical and Symbolist themes.[37] Then, too, in the next generation, Lucy Madox Brown-Rossetti, the daughter of Ford Madox Brown and the wife of William Rossetti was, by all accounts, a passionate woman, "a strange mixture with a violent temper and a strong brain, [who] took an intellectual interest in political affairs and the arts."[38] While her debut exhibit occurred in 1869, her experiences in childbirth—five children in eight years—caused her to cut short her career; and, yet, an invalid much of her life, she maintained her intellectual energy, taking up writing and completing a biography of Mary Shelley in 1886.[39] Also noteworthy is May Morris, the younger daughter of William and Jane Morris, who, like her mother, had an interest in textiles and fine embroidery. She became a leading textile artist in the Arts and Crafts movement and founded the Women's Guild of Art. She loved the dramatic works of Ibsen and participated in the pioneering production of *A Doll's House* with her friend Eleanor Marx. She taught school, edited her father's *Collected Works* in twenty-four volumes, and promoted conservation and welfare.[40]

Clearly, Fowles may have been prompted to consider Sarah's situation in terms of such women, in terms of female innovators who saw genius as a strong desire for knowledge and a ready energy. Perhaps, in the end, the aesthetic continuum and the tonal variety of the New Woman's understanding might be suggested in two specific artistic visions. One is the painter Marianne Stokes, who traveled to Hungary and who captured the beauty of the feminine, its lyrical and spiritual being in such works as *Melisande* (1895).[41] In this work, the female gaze is inward, complicated. The woman, seated on a rock by a stream, studies the water, allowing her rich gown to trail in the stream. Stokes advances a vision of the self-contained and quiet woman, but a doomed woman nonetheless. She presents the moment when Melisande, having abandoned her crown which rests in the water in the lefthand corner of the picture, listens to the stream.

124

Soon, according to the operatic legend, she will meet Goland, marry him and, in time, come to fall in love with his brother, Pelleas. In this idyllic woodland space, however, the trees rooted behind her like some prefigured destiny, Melisande does not know her fate. She is a pensive young woman, a dreaming Symbolist figure who wears a costume covered with mysterious, hieroglyphic designs. Stokes offers her as tragic soul, as printed text of the feminine in transition, as fairy-tale figure meditating, as woman constructing self.

And last, to turn from Stokes's tragic vision, it seems appropriate to glance at the work of Eleanor Fortescue-Brickdale, a pioneering painter who, with humor and gentle satire, often took a sardonic look at relationships. In her first exhibited work, the painting titled *The Pale Complexion of True Love* (1898), she chooses a comedic theme.[42] She borrows her title from Shakespeare's *As You Like it*, Act 3, Scene IV, from a speech given by the elderly shepherd, Corin, who makes reference to the younger man, Silvius, and his unrequited love for the shepherdess, Phebe: "If you will see a pageant truly play'd / Between the pale complexion of true love / And the red glow of scorn and proud disdain, / Go hence a little and I shall conduct you." In the painting Fortescue-Brickdale's courtier bends to kiss the lady's skirt, honoring her; but the lady is in no mood for flattery from an obsequious gentleman. Her back stiff, her white wimple flared in cockerel-like alarm, she holds her hands up in mock disdain, fiddles with her jeweled necklace, and glances down at him as if to wish him gone.

These, then, are some of the women in the Rossetti circle and beyond, women connected to the Pre-Raphaelite Sisterhood who created art and poetry and who, as we now have discovered, continued to gaze back. They are, however, absent from the Pinter-Reisz film. A new screen adaptation of *The French Lieutenant's Woman* might, as it comes to closure, make

---

Opposite: Marianne Stokes: *Melisande* (1895). In this work, the female gaze is inward, complicated. Melisande, seated on a rock by a stream, studies the water, her rich gown trailing in the stream. Here Stokes advances a vision of the self-contained and quiet, but doomed woman, doomed at the moment when she has abandoned her crown which rests in the water, in the left hand corner of the picture. In the painting's idyllic space, the trees rooted behind her like some prefigured destiny, Melisande does not know her tragic fate. She is a pensive girl, almost a dreaming Symbolist figure, wearing a garment covered with mysterious, hieroglyphic designs. Stokes offers her as an image of the feminine in transition, as a fairy-tale figure meditating, as a woman constructing self (Wallraff-Richartz Museum, Köln, Germany).

Eleanor Fortescue Brickdale: *The Pale Complexion of True Love* **(1898). In her own satirical and sardonic way, the artist Brickdale paints a courtier bending down to kiss the hem of a lady's skirt, honoring her. The lady, however, is in no mood for flattery from an obsequious gentleman. Her back stiff, her white wimple flared in cockerel-like alarm, she holds her hands up in mock disdain, fiddles with her jeweled necklace, and glances down at him as if to wish him gone (private collection; photograph © Whitford & Hughes, London, UK/Bridgeman Images).**

generous space for them, for Fowles himself must have intuited that the Tudor House was a space that empowered women. While the Pinter-Reisz screenplay offers us a meta-cinematic structure, a Hollywood couple moving through the pain of loss and betrayal, finding a relationship through the narrative defined in a Victorian filmscript and then breaking with it, the Fowles novel allows Sarah Woodruff much more. Because Sarah chooses to live in a house where she is admitted to the daily conversation of genius, both male and female, the art and poetry created by Sarah's newfound female companions should make their claim among the other, better known, Pre-Raphaelite images in a new film version of *The French Lieutenant's Woman*; for these women offer us the intellectual and artistic signals of a new world, of a New Woman. Their Sisterhood does, in fact, help us to understand what might have happened to Sarah as she situated herself with genius and eccentricity, with stunners and strumpets, with Wonderland and Tragedy, even as Charles, unmoored, walked toward "the unplumb'd, salt, estranging sea."[43]

Notes

1. John Fowles, *Harper's Magazine* July 1968, p. 88.

2. John Fowles, *The French Lieutenant's Woman* (New York: Little, Brown, 1969), p. 10.

3. Roland Barthes, *Camera Lucida* (New York: Hill and Wang, 1980), p. 27.

4. Harold Pinter, screenplay for *The French Lieutenant's Woman* (Boston: Little, Brown, 1981), p. 13.

5. Fowles, *The French Lieutenant's Woman*, p. 176.

6. *Ibid.*, p. 461.

7. *Ibid.*, p. 456.

8. *Ibid.*, p. 450.

9. Brenda Allen, "*The French Lieutenant's Woman* on Film," in *John Fowles*, ed. James Acheson (New York: Palgrave Macmillan, 2013), p. 122.

10. Allen, "*The French Lieutenant's Woman* on Film," pp. 123–24.

11. Pinter, screenplay for *The French Lieutenant's Woman*, p. 124.

12. *Ibid.*, p. 98.

13. T.S. Eliot, *The Four Quartets*, in *The Collected Poems and Plays of T.S. Eliot* (New York: Harcourt Brace, 1971), p. 117.

14. Pinter, screenplay for *The French Lieutenant's Woman*, p. 99.

15. *Ibid.*, pp. 102–03.

16. *Ibid.*, p. 103, p. 100.

17. Tucker quoted in William Stephenson, *Fowles's* The French Lieutenant's Woman (London: Continuum, 2007), p. 100.

18. Fowles, *The French Lieutenant's Woman*, p. 452.

19. Eileen Warburton, *John Fowles* (New York: Viking, 2004), p. 295.

20. Diane Roe, *The Rossettis in Wonderland* (London: Haus Press, 2011), p. viii.

21. *Ibid.*, p. ix.

22. *Ibid.*, pp. ix–x.

23. *Ibid.*, p. x.

24. Fowles, *The French Lieutenant's Woman*, p. 441.

25. Alfred Tennyson, *Selected Poems* (London: Penguin, 2008), p. 10.

26. Jan Marsh, *The Pre-Raphaelite Circle* (London: National Portrait Gallery, 2005), p. 70.

27. *Ibid.*, p. 87.

28. *Ibid.*, p. 87.

29. Fowles, *The French Lieutenant's Woman*, p. 447.

30. *Ibid.*, p. 448.

31. *Ibid.*, p. 450.

32. *Ibid.*, p. 456.

33. Christina Rossetti, *The Complete Poems* (London: Penguin, 2005), p. 796.

34. *Ibid.*, p. 572.

35. Simon Cooke, "Frederick Sandys and Periodical Illustration," The Victorian Web, n.p.

36. Marsh, *The Pre-Raphaelite* Circle, pp. 68–69.

37. *Ibid.*, p. 112.

38. *Ibid.*, pp. 115–16.

39. *Ibid.*, p. 115.

40. *Ibid.*, pp. 118–19; Marianne Stokes, *Melisande*, 1895, Wallraf-Richartz Museum.

41. Jan Marsh and Gerrish Nunn, *Pre-Raphaelite Women Artists* (New York: Thames and Hudson, 1999), pp. 147–48; Eleanor Fortescue-Brickdale, *The Pale Complexion of True Love*, 1898, Athenaeum.

42. *Ibid.*, p. 152.

43. Fowles, *The French Lieutenant's Woman*, p. 467.

Rhizome and Romance:
The Ebony Tower on Video
DIANNE VIPOND

> *I like the marvelous only when it is strictly enveloped in reality....*—Henri Alain-Fournier, in a letter of 1911

This statement by Henri Alain-Fournier served as an inspirational axiom for John Fowles during the many years he spent writing *The Magus*.[1] Not only is this dichotomy between what may be interpreted as realism and romance an accurate description of Fowles's signature style, it reflects significant aspects of both the form and content of his 1974 collection of short fiction, *The Ebony Tower*, and it characterizes the central dramatic tension of the 80-minute long adaptation of the title novella "The Ebony Tower" for Granada Television's Great Performances in 1984. Arguably one of the most important writers of the second half of the twentieth century, Fowles set himself new aesthetic challenges with the writing of each of his novels. His shorter fiction is no exception and quite clearly reveals a hallmark of his method—the welding of innovative narrative technique to literary tradition within a metafictional context, a theme at the forefront of "The Ebony Tower."

The Ebony Tower is a hybrid text consisting of the novella "The Ebony Tower"; background information provided by the author in "A Personal Note"; Fowles's translation of Marie de France's Celtic romance "Eliduc"; and three short stories: "Poor Koko," "The Enigma," and "The Cloud." The title itself, *The Ebony Tower*, provides a point of departure for examining how Fowles explores the theme of the relationship of the real to the ideal as he employs attributes from both realism and romance to structure his narratives. The idea of an ebony tower evokes the proverbial "ivory tower" in which academic critics are said to reside, and thus helps to create a ten-

129

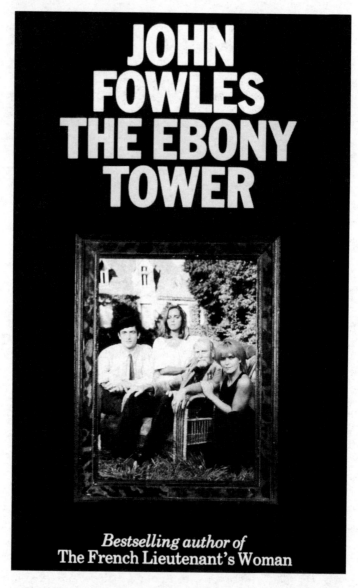

This paperback book cover shows the main characters in the television adaptation *The Ebony Tower*, in which English painter and critic David Williams (Richard Rees) visits a famous representational artist Henry Breasley (Laurence Olivier) in France, where he lives in a latter-day enchanted forest with two assistants, Diana (Greta Scacchi) and Anne (Toyah Wilcox) (© 1974, John Fowles, courtesy HarperCollins Publishers, Ltd.).

sional energy that will fuel one of several conflicts that drive the narrative, namely, that between artist and critic.

Henry Breasley (Laurence Olivier) is a celebrated artist living with two young women, producing representational art images and mentoring Diana (Greta Scacchi), a young, former art student known as "the Mouse," described by Breasley as his muse. David Williams (Richard Rees) is also a respected artist but a producer of non-representational, abstract art. Williams is a complacently married Londoner, an art instructor, and a man of words. As the narrative begins, he arrives to interview Breasley at his studio in the French forest where he lives, in self-imposed exile from England. Breasley's other female companion is Anne, known as "the Freak" (Toya Willcox), who is a punkish-looking rebel-counterpart to Diana. Intense discussions about art and life take place over dinner, during a picnic, and intermittently among David, Henry, Diana, and Anne. David and Diana find themselves attracted to one another and David, evidently prepared to leave his wife for her, proposes that they go to bed and leave together the next day. Diana declines both proposals, choosing instead to remain with Breasley, leaving David, unsettled, to reunite with his wife at the end of the story.

No less popular than critically acclaimed, Fowles's fiction is infused with qualities from both realism and romance, which may, in part, account for his wide readership. His work speaks to a yearning deep within the human psyche—the desire to inhabit an idealized but credible alternative world. In Chapter 13 of *The French Lieutenant's Woman*, Fowles writes: "[novelists] *wish to create worlds as real as, but other than the world that is.*"[2] His experience of reading Henri Alain-Fournier's *Le Grand Meaulnes*, a novel he credits with having a profound emotional impact on his work, is likely a source for his theory of the novel and perhaps for the fictional celebrated painter Breasley's first name, Henry[3]

Published in 1974, just about the mid-point of Fowles's literary career, *The Ebony Tower* serves as something of a plateau from which to view both his earlier work and that which followed. Written "as a break" from composing his lengthy, semi-autobiographical novel *Daniel Martin*, *The Ebony Tower* was followed in 1977 by *Daniel Martin* and by the revised version of *The Magus*, both indubitably quest novels, the former a postmodern meditation on realism, the latter firmly anchored in the romance tradition.[4] Clearly, realism and romance were on Fowles's mind as he was writing *The Ebony Tower*. The working title for this collection of short fiction was *Variations*, referring to variations on "certain themes" and "methods of narrative presentation" he had employed in his earlier fiction, underscoring the self-consciousness of his oeuvre while also indicating that *The Ebony Tower* is an important touchstone, a far more significant text within his body of work than has been the general critical consensus.[5]

A short but highly revealing text in *The Ebony Tower* is "A Personal Note," a five-page preface to "Eliduc" that provides the reader with valuable information for interpreting the stories. By interjecting this paratext that is one part literary history, one part literary theory, and one part literary criticism between the "The Ebony Tower" and "Eliduc" to explain their relationship in some detail, Fowles foregrounds the aesthetic dimensions of the narratives in his collection and encourages his readers to read them critically. What Diana says about Henry Breasley in "The Ebony Tower" could apply equally well to John Fowles: "He's always so much more aware of what he's doing than you think."[6] This description of Breasley was considered significant enough to have been reworked by John Mortimer in the film adaptation as "Oh, Henry. You know *exactly* what you did"—a line delivered by Anne rather than Diana, but to the same effect.[7] "A Personal Note" makes such self-consciousness explicit by alerting the reader to the self-reflexivity of the texts of these postmodern metafictional romances that derive their energy and effectiveness from their relationship to realism. Patricia Waugh recognizes the inherent interdependence of fiction and reality, of realism and romance with her definition of metafiction as "fictional writing which self-consciously and systematically draws attention to its status as an artefact in order to pose questions about the relationship between fiction and reality."[8]

Also in "A Personal Note," Fowles describes the relationship of *The Ebony Tower* to his earlier novels and explains the provenance and significance of "Eliduc" not only to his fiction but to the development of the novel in general; he sees the Celtic romance as "seminal in the history of fiction."[9] The Celtic romance is a quest narrative, usually associated with courtly love and often set in an enchanted forest, where a knight errant engages in a variety of adventures and undergoes several tests of skill and character as he searches for a buried treasure whose form may be concrete (e.g., wealth) or abstract (e.g., wisdom). In *Don Quixote*, a book that parodies the chivalric romance and is frequently regarded as the first modern novel, Miguel de Cervantes employs the metafictional device of the discovery of a hidden text. The hidden text reveals secrets to a few select initiates, secrets that contain "the essential knowledge of the universe, the answers to the Great Questions."[10] Analogously, *The Ebony Tower* may be regarded as something on the order of a buried treasure or hidden book, a volume of seemingly unremarkable short stories "buried" between the publication of two major novels, *The French Lieutenant's Woman* and *Daniel Martin*, but nevertheless holding secrets to the Fowlesian fictional universe. Fowles, like Cervantes, appropriates the structure and conventions of the romance to use for his own parodic, metafictional purposes in *The Ebony Tower* as he experiments with a variety of sub-genres from literature and popular fiction: the *Künstlerroman* ("The Ebony Tower"), crime fiction or the thriller ("Poor Koko"), detective fiction ("The Enigma"), and what might be called an existential mystery ("The Cloud"). His translation of Marie de France's "Eliduc," an authentic early romance, operates as a reminder of how the novel, or *roman*, originated and serves as a reference point for the romantic elements within the collection. John Mortimer's adaptation of "The Ebony Tower" finds a cinematic way to incorporate these intertextual elements into the film adaptation with a scene in which Diana is shown reading to Henry in bed—from "Eliduc."

The Ebony Tower may also be read as a prototype for what Gilles Deleuze and Félix Guattari describe as a rhizome, the dimensions of which are more horizontal and diagonal than vertical or linear. A literary rhizome, like the subterranean stem from which Deleuze and Guattari derive their metaphor, consists of variations, fragments, multiplicities, plateaus, and middles or betweens rather than beginnings or ends. It is a non-hierarchical assemblage, a new kind of book. No stranger to new kinds of books, Fowles's oeuvre may be regarded as a recursive, rhizomatic assemblage, with *The Ebony Tower* its epitome. Its multiplicity is registered through its generic diversity: a novella and three short stories as well as a translation and a personal note from the writer, encompassing fiction, translation, and non-fiction.

The Ebony Tower is literally the middle work within Fowles's oeuvre, making it prototypically rhizomic. This position affords it the perspective to operate as a microcosmic version of Fowles's larger fictional universe. It offers both commentary on its predecessors and anticipates those works that come after it. As such, it resembles a plateau, another concept related to the rhizome: multiplicities connected to multiplicities to form or extend a rhizome.[11] This description also applies to literature in general, indicating the inherently rhizomic nature of intertextuality.

Intertextuality provides the primary means of mapping the dynamic of a literary rhizome, a technique Fowles exploits to an extreme degree in his short fiction. Deleuze and Guattari also refer to all books and literature as assemblages: "As an assemblage, a book has only itself, in connection with other assemblages."[12] This suggests an intrinsic relationship between intertextuality and "assemblage" or "rhizome" such that intertextuality may be said to provide the infrastructure for the rhizomic assemblage that is literary history, creating an identity between the two concepts. Because *The Ebony Tower* consists of self-contained texts, it provides the ideal generic landscape from which to explore and exploit intertextuality—it is an intertext by virtue of its basic structure, thus microcosmically emulating literature at large. Inter/intratextuality contributes to several dialogical relationships relevant to *The Ebony Tower*: (1) among the texts within the volume as a self-contained collection, (2) among the texts of *The Ebony Tower* and Fowles's other work, (3) among the texts of *The Ebony Tower* and literary works by other authors, (4) among the adaptation, the collection, and the novella, and (5) among the adaptation of "The Ebony Tower" and other cinematic productions.

A dramatic example of the first and third dialogical relationships occurs when a weasel is run over by David as he leaves Coëtminais in "The Ebony Tower," then reappears transmogrified in "Eliduc," where the dead weasel is revived by its mate. Thus, both explicitly and implicitly, the more realistic twentieth-century novella is linked with the medieval romance. What makes this example particularly interesting is that the historically earlier "Eliduc" is placed *after* the novella in Fowles's collection, so that the reader's introduction to the intertextual element, the weasel, is by way of the contemporary story rather than the earlier Celtic tale. In this way, Fowles displaces the usual chronological order with a more rhizomic organization that suggests reciprocity and non-hierarchical relationship rather than derivation and influence. Furthermore, rhizomic also aptly describes the relationship between the originary text of "The Ebony Tower" and its video adaptation as *The Ebony Tower*. The weasel episode is the very passage that Diana reads to Henry in bed, thus incorporating into the film a magical moment from the Celtic romance. There is, in addition, a brief, auditory allusion to "Eliduc" at the fish market when one of the locals can be heard saying, "weasel dead"; the remark seems out of context, its relevance surely lost on most spectators, but it is just as surely a rhyzomic outgrowth in the film. As Peter Brooker considers the intertextual relationships between fictions and their adaptations generally, he notes: "[t]he moment of reading or viewing … can and frequently will reverse the chronology of source text and its adaptation, putting the second before the first" which then will "resituate and transform the supposedly fixed and authentic original."[13]

Intertextuality is a key aspect of both novella and film, and probably the most important example of it is that meant to establish and account for Breasley's greatness as an artist. The novella devotes a page to describing Breasley's masterpiece, "the huge *Moon-hunt*, perhaps the best known of the Coëtminais *oevre*, a painting David was going to discuss at some length and that he badly wanted to study at leisure again."[14] The painting is described in the story as a risky parody of Paolo Uccello's *The Hunt in the Forest* or, as Fowles refers to it, *Night Hunt*;

> the memory of the Ashmolean Uccello somehow deepened and buttressed the painting before which David sat. It gave an essential tension, in fact: behind the mysteriousness and the ambiguity (no hounds, no horses, no prey … nocturnal figures among trees, but the title was needed), behind the modernity of so many of the surface elements there stood both a homage and a kind of thumbed nose to a very old tradition."[15]

In this passage, Fowles provides the reader with a succinct description of the parodic elements that inhere in metafiction. A reader can imagine the fictional painting, but an art designer for the film adaptation would have

Paolo Uccello, *The Hunt in the Forest* (about 1470). In Fowles's "The Ebony Tower" this Italian Renaissance painting is referred to as *Night Hunt*, which has inspired Breasley's representational masterpiece, *Moon-hunt* (© Ashmolean Museum, University of Oxford).

had to produce something visible that would impress viewers along with David. As *Night Hunt* is the most prominently displayed art work in Oxford's Ashmolean Museum, Breasley's *Moon-hunt* is said to have similar "pride of place" in the room where David waits upon his arrival. In that scene as well as several others, the camera tracks in toward or otherwise focuses on the large painting to further underscore its significance. *Moon-hunt's* depiction of a dark wood with silvery, moonlit trees and human figures among them is mysterious, indeed, but also modern—and inter-textual in that the "tension" between past and present is between art works in the mind of the spectator. Fowles's invocation of the Renaissance paint-ing is meant to help readers imagine Breasley's work of art in a way that is literally inter-textual.

Another kind of intertextuality is between "The Ebony Tower" and Fowles's *The Magus*, which Anne, the Freak, is said in the novella to be reading. The film adaptation incorporates this intertext but doesn't make it clearly evident. The story names Fowles's earlier novel, which David guesses is a book about astrology: "she would be into all that nonsense."[16] With this intertextual reference, Fowles is able to satirize readers who associated his early novel with the occult rather than discerning its deeper, more complex human themes; the reference also points to David's poor judgment, and alerts the reader to the many parallel relationships between "The Ebony Tower" and *The Magus*. In the film adaptation, Anne can be seen several times reading a bulky paperback with Fowles's name just dis-cernible, and in the last instance the cover is identifiably the 1977 Triad/ Panther reprint of *The Magus: A Revised Version*. Evidently, the filmmakers were using the Fowles novel as part of the *mise en scène*, intending an intertextual, even metatextual significance, but the book is seen so briefly that most spectators would not be able to read the author's name or rec-ognize the cover illustration. Thus the final cut of the film fails to take full advantage of this opportunity for intertextual play.

The adaptation further exploits intertextuality through allusions to other films. When Anne asks David if he wants "to see a picture," she raises her elbow to reveal a tattoo of an eye just above her armpit, a gesture reminiscent of many similar, highly stylized, usually over-dramatized moments in the film adaptation of *The Magus*. And Breasley repeatedly refers to David as "old cock," a British expression roughly equivalent to old friend or old fellow that echoes Jay Gatsby, the archetypal idealist, addressing the more realistic Nick Carraway as "old sport" in not only the novel but both film adaptations.[17] This implicit allusion to Gatsby serves as a reminder of the unbreachable distance between the real and the ideal.

Intertextuality of another type occurs when Fowles does not simply refer to "Eliduc" but actually incorporates it into his anthology of short fiction. Because it is his own English translation, the tale becomes a hybrid text, the product of a collaboration between Marie de France, who "grafted her own knowledge of the world on the old material," the *matière de Bretagne*, and John Fowles who interpreted and translated her "rhyming octosyllabic couplets" into English prose and included it among a collection of his own late twentieth-century short fiction.[18] His comment about how Marie utilized "the old material" but made it her own in "Eliduc" reveals something of Fowles's own artistic method, of Henry Breasley's aesthetics in "The Ebony Tower" as seen in his use of Uccello's *Night Hunt* in his *Moonhunt* painting, and operates equally well as a description of the story's adaptation for British television.

Drawing upon the tradition of the chivalric romance, Fowles places not only each of his protagonists in the role of the knight errant—engaged in his or her own personal quest—but also manipulates the reader into a similar position, pursuing a quest that becomes an ongoing search for meaning within the enchanting forest of *The Ebony Tower*. Such an exploration proves enigmatic, resists closure, and yields complexity, complication, and contradiction as each story thwarts any attempt at a unified, definitive interpretation. As I have argued elsewhere, "[i]n *The Ebony Tower*, Fowles translates the poststructuralist thought of a variety of continental philosophers into narrative, into fictions that ... through the metaphor of the ebony tower suggest that human knowledge is necessarily partial and that meaning is a process of interpretation, a context-dependent construction subject to endless revision."[19] Fowles seamlessly blends postmodernist literary techniques with the romance element in the stories, ultimately causing *The Ebony Tower* to emerge as one of his most complex and enigmatic but endlessly engaging works of fiction—a work deserving of an adaptation capable of capturing the depths of the original.

A reciprocal relationship exists between the two ebony towers that comprise Fowles's collection of short fiction: one, the volume in its entirety consisting of six diverse texts and, two, the novella that lends its title to the collection. Thus a rhizomic and intertextual quality underscores the importance of the relationships among the various texts of the *The Ebony*

Tower. Both Fowles's literary text and its television adaptation are hybrid forms characterized by multiplicity, another clear point of conjunction. The rhizomic nature of *The Ebony Tower* seems particularly compatible with adaptation, which, according to Robert Stam, "forms part of a flattened out and newly egalitarian spectrum of cultural productions. Within a comprehensively textualized world of images and simulations, adaptation becomes just another text, forming part of a broad discursive continuum."[20] The narrative media of literature and film are further related through another shared characteristic, intertextuality, which has had a profound impact on reconceptualizing adaptation studies and has effectively dismissed the persistent discourse of fidelity. In *Literature through Film*, Stam describes adaptation as "a turn in an ongoing dialogical process," one that is inherently intertextual and finally transtextual.[21] Every adaptation is necessarily a re-reading, a re-interpretation, a re-presentation of the original literary hypotext. As this process proliferates, the two towers—the anthology and the novella—produce a third, the adaptation. Art gives rise to art and initiates an ongoing dialogue among its various incarnations that leads to productive cross-fertilization and a generative hybridity resulting from its fundamental intertextuality.

The original working title for this volume of essays was *Fowles on Film*, referring not only to the many adaptations of Fowles's literary texts but also recognizing and suggesting his interest in film and his awareness of the profound impact it has had upon twentieth and twenty-first century mindscapes, including his own. In his 1969 essay "Notes on an Unfinished Novel," he writes that he has seen approximately two and a half thousand films, averaging about two a week, excluding television, since the age of six; he asks, "How can so frequently repeated an experience not have indelibly stamped itself on the *mode* of imagination?"[22] For Fowles, one of the key differences between the novel and film is that the former is a linguistic medium that relies upon the reader's imagination for completion, to transform abstract signs into concrete images, whereas film is primarily a visual medium that provides each viewer with the same visual representation. And while deciphering visual codes requires the audience's interpretive skill, film does not make as many demands on the imagination because the medium provides readymade images. Fowles recalls recording his dreams by noting their "purely cinematic effects: panning shots, close shots, tracking, jump shots, and the rest."[23] Of all of Fowles's fiction, *Daniel Martin* exhibits the most self-consciously cinematic technique. And although Fowles has described the novel as "a homage to Lukács," it is as much a homage to the art of cinema.[24] Hollywood is a major setting, and Dan is a screenwriter, Jenny an actress. There are countless references to the film industry, many of which operate as brief disquisitions on the art of cinema, but most importantly, the true tribute consists in the appropriation and utilization of cinematic techniques in the novel. This is most readily evident in the manipulation of point of view, through descriptive passages written with camera angles in mind, and overt arrogation of methodology and terminology such as that which occurs in the final lines of the chapter titled "Petard": "Then she turned and left the room." On the next line: "Cut."[25] Realism is a preoccupation of both Lukács and the art of cinema. According to Brian McFarlane, the novel and film pay more attention to "representational realism in their detail than the other literary forms."[26] In *Daniel Martin*, Fowles recognizes the necessarily delicate balance between realism and its counterpart romance that both novelist and filmmaker must negotiate as they practice their respective arts.

In his 1981 essay "The Filming of *The French Lieutenant's Woman*," Fowles suggests that the evolution of the novel is partly a result of efforts to communicate "all those aspects of life and modes of feeling that can *never* be represented visually."[27] He points out that the first showing of the very first film in 1895 coincides with "the birth of psychoanalysis," the publication of Freud's *Studies in Hysteria* that same year; nevertheless, Fowles intimates that the novel is more inner-directed than film.[28] Despite his stature as a novelist, Fowles admits to his fascination with film technique and writes: "for ... cinema conceived and executed by artists as an art ... I have always had the greatest liking and respect." Comparing the novel to film, he notes: "The two ways of telling stories are much nearer sisters than anything else ... the shared need to narrate, to create new worlds of character and atmosphere ... brings us incomparably closer together than any other pairs of artists in different arts."[29] Yet, it is precisely the different methods of narration each employs that so differentiate these two narrative arts.[30]

Despite his abiding interest in and high regard for film, Fowles was not pleased with the film adaptations of *The Collector* and *The Magus*; in fact, he thought *The Magus* was one of the worst films of the sixties.[31] On the other hand, he was not unhappy with the cinematic translations of either *The French Lieutenant's Woman* or "The Ebony Tower." Harold Pinter's ideas for handling the paratextual and metafictional dimensions of the novel were effective largely because they were original. By refusing to be chained to the source text by the notion of fidelity and by discarding conventional methods of adaptation, Pinter was able to be true to the spirit of Fowles's novel and contribute to a film that stands as a work of art in its own right.

Although Fowles would have preferred to see a comparable feature film made of "The Ebony Tower," he was interested in having Sir Laurence Olivier play Breasley and John Mortimer write the screenplay, but these possibilities seemed to be predicated on a Granada Television produc-tion.[32] Olivier insisted that any "blue" language be removed from his lines, and he wanted more of a final scene than the original narrative provided for his character. In both cases, he was accommodated. And despite Fowles's impatience with the second requirement, the way Mortimer han-dled the scene helped to clarify and articulate a key theme—passionate engagement with life as the wellspring of authentic art. Traditionally, moments of epiphany are handled in film with silence, a strategy that does not always successfully communicate what a character has learned. In the adaptation, David's epiphanies are couched in silence: his slow, deliberate, preoccupied walk to the car when Diana fails to meet him in the village as arranged and the shot of David in the arrivals lounge at Orly—lost in thought, mentally in another world (Coëtminais)—before distractedly focusing on his wife, Beth, when she greets him, a scene that dramatically juxtaposes the real world of marriage and airports with the memory of an idealized *domaine perdu*. In both novella and film, conclusions are left for the audience to draw, but the fact that the status quo ante is restored at the end suggests that none of the characters has experienced personal growth.

Negotiations continued with Granada and contracts were forthcom-ing in March of 1983. Robert Knights would direct and Greta Scacchi would play Diana, with Roger Rees as David and Toyah Willcox as Anne. Fowles thought Mortimer's script was "middling—in places muddling—good" and notes that to please Olivier, he changed some of the relation-ships.[33] After viewing the rough cut of *The Ebony Tower* in November, Fowles wrote in his journal that it "is better than I hoped." He mentions "good performances from the girls" and is satisfied that Olivier's health problems did not interfere with his performance. But he had two com-plaints: he wanted "more lingering shots, in places, longer perspectives" and he didn't feel "David's defeat" was pronounced enough at the end of the film—likely a reference to the silent epiphanies noted above.[34] There are quite a few "lingering shots" in the film, as it is. Usually, they are suggestively erotic and focus on naked female bodies as objects of desire, as in the shots of the Mouse and the Freak sunbathing by the house and at the picnic, or swimming in the nude. And although it is tempting to see them in terms of what Laura Mulvey would describe as a voyeuristic "male gaze," they are balanced by an almost equal number of shots that linger over David's clothed and unclothed body in a variety of settings, which effectively cancels out the maleness of the gaze and redirects the audience's attention to the sensual dimension of the film in general.[35] A case could certainly be made for the narrative as a meditation on desire, with this kind of camera work reinforcing such a reading. Fowles's other regret was with the paucity of long perspectives. Such shots would have suggested focus and distance, and in the context of *The Ebony Tower* an otherworldliness, which instead was largely achieved through musical passages of a rather eerie tonality.[36] More long shots might have produced the desired effect less obtrusively, as did the play of shadow and light in scenes such as the walk through the forest to the picnic area by the lake. In this sequence, the already ethereal quality of Coëtminais is heightened by haunting notes of birdsong and the dappled light of the forest; it culminates in a cinematic replication of Édouard Manet's *Le Déjeuner sur l'herbe*, in which life is seen to imitate art.

Although the novel genre has inspired more cinematic adaptations than any other literary form, Brian McFarlane points out that "[t]he novella, pitched somewhere between novel and short story, is probably the filmmaker's obvious material: not long enough to need laborious pruning, not so short as to require much new invention."[37] Such compatibility of forms may partially account for the successful adaptation of "The Ebony Tower." Other factors related to the particular medium of its adaptation, television, also contributed to its success. Unlike the director-*auteur* in cinema, in the television world, "[t]he screenwriter [is] regarded as the originator of the drama," which results in writing and words being more highly valued than other aesthetic elements within the medium.[38] Such an attitude fosters respect for the original text and supports faithfulness to it without requiring absolute fidelity. The conditions of early television production are responsible for establishing many of the conventions of television adaptations that persist to this day: "sedate camerawork; an emphasis on words and on detailed *mise-en scène*; and careful exploitation of the possibilities of seriality."[39] This last aspect—serialization—allows for the inclusion of more of the original narrative, with screen time to develop such details as mood and atmosphere; develops character relationships and conflict at a more leisurely pace; and encourages the viewers' mental processing of themes and motifs at the same time that it builds interest and suspense. Historically, the social mission of early television broadcasting in England was to "educate, inform, and entertain," a charge that could be fulfilled efficiently and effectively by bringing classic and contemporary literature to the small screen.[40]

For Granada Television, 1981 was a watershed year with *Brideshead Revisited* setting new standards for classic novel adaptations, largely realized in the renowned heritage films of Merchant and Ivory that were yet to be made.[41] Their distinguishing properties coalesced into conventions of classic novel adaptations during the eighties including "high production values; 'authentic,' detailed costumes and sets; 'great British actors'; light classical music; slow pace; steady, often symmetrical framing; an interest in landscapes, buildings, and interiors as well as characters; strong, gradually developed protagonists accompanied by entertaining cameo roles; and intelligent, 'faithful' dialogue."[42] Many of these characteristics were already present in Granada's adaptation of "The Ebony Tower" in 1984. Naturally, one of the major differences between a series such as *Brideshead Revisited* and made-for-television films such as *The Ebony Tower* is length, which can have a significant impact on pacing and character development. For Fowles, "[t]he arbitrary limits imposed on film length are ... one principal reason ... the cinema remains at its best a major art, and television, except in very rare hands ... still dangerously close to a recording device."[43] For him, the shorter film length was a positive trait for *The Ebony Tower*. And the fact that Granada had produced *Brideshead Revisited* and *The Jewel in the Crown* was evidence not only of the company's high production values but also of the exceptional quality of their literary adaptations, all of which clearly contributed to the success of *The Ebony Tower*.

Those most responsible for bringing "The Ebony Tower" to the screen clearly possessed a comprehensive understanding of the novella's most salient themes and pervasive allusions, and they were able to incorporate many of them into their adaptation while highlighting the central issues of art, the artist, and aesthetics. As largely a visual medium, one of the film adaptation's major strengths is its ability to foreground the primary focus of "The Ebony Tower": art. And with the visual art of painting serving as Fowles's metaphor for art in general, the visual medium of film is a particularly compatible one for communicating his theme; the form is an excellent match for the content. The adaptation exploits this coincidence through details of the *mise-en-scène* such as the paintings of all sizes and provenance that dominate the interior of Breasley's home, or the often tableaux-like arrangement of characters in various scenes reminiscent of paintings, including tea on the lawn, the high angle shot of Breasley and Diana talking on the bench in the garden below David's window, and the picnic scene echoing *Le Déjeuner sur l'herbe*. A highly dramatic example and one of the most remarkable scenes in the film occurs when Anne runs from the house to the studio to check on Diana for David, only to find that she is "busy … working with Henry."[44] Anne's flagrantly artificial red hair that has dominated portrait-like shots of her throughout the film becomes a focal point in this sequence. As the camera tracks her while she runs, distance and movement combine to blur the foreground as her hair blends with the red flowers in the landscape to become a painting both in and of motion, highly evocative of Claude Monet's *Poppies, Near Argenteuil*.[45] This scene emphasizes film's particular ability to represent art as it simultaneously celebrates the distinctive features of its own artistry. Not surprisingly in a narrative about art, the main characters are artists: a renowned painter, Henry Breasley; a critic, art teacher and artist in his own right, David Williams; and former art students, Diana, the Mouse, and Anne, the Freak. Such a cast of characters provides ample opportunity for discussion of all things artistic, thus operating as a metafictional medium for bringing issues of reality and fictionality, of realism and romance to the reader's and viewer's attention while underscoring the aesthetic dimensions of the narrative.[46] Although the adaptation contains a magnitude of rich references to art, the artist, and aesthetics, three key scenes will provide a sense of how each is depicted.

The opening scene introduces the main theme of art as it portrays David stopped by the roadside in the lush countryside of Brittany sketching a landscape. The first shot is a close-up of a hand (later disclosed to be David's) using a ruler to paint drably colored, horizontal and vertical lines on a piece of paper. Because the camera angle is initially subjective, the audience sees only what David sees, his own drawing. As David looks up, the next rather surprising shot is of a vista of majestic trees in their natural setting against a skyline—all revealed to be the subject matter of his artistic efforts. With great economy, the film establishes the difference between reality and artifice, between realism and non-representational art as it also introduces something about David's aesthetics and his character with its portrayal of his precise, methodical movements as he draws trees as abstract vertical lines. It also foreshadows Henry's later characterization of David's painting as geometry by focusing on his use of the ruler as he paints. The next few frames show David, as the contemporary knight errant, driving down the winding road through the forest in his quest to reach *Manoir Coëtminais*, where he is to interview Henry Breasley.[47] When he arrives at the entrance to the driveway, the gate is locked, forcing him to walk the remainder of the way to the house. Thus, telescopically, the film communicates the spirit of the epigraph taken from Chrétien de Troyes's *Yvain* with which Fowles begins his novella, a passage in French that mentions a difficult journey through a forest which is fraught with many dangers before the right path is found. In this way, the chivalric romance is collapsed into David's quest, one that results in personal and artistic insights that are suggested rather than definitively portrayed, a significant aspect of the narrative in both media.

Later in the narrative, an argument over dinner about art and aesthetics provides a clue as to how ambiguity and suggestion work and why indirectness is important in the overall context of *The Ebony Tower* by providing one possible explanation of the title. During his first night at Coëtminais, David encounters one of the dangers of his "perilous journey," an argument with Henry about the relative merits of abstract versus representational art. Henry says that abstract expressionism is "the biggest betrayal in the history of art" and calls it "the ebony tower."[48] Diana translates this for David as Henry's way of saying "abstract art ... avoids human responsibility" and explains that the ebony tower is "[Henry's] place for dumping all the paintings that are obscure because he thinks the painter is scared of being clear."[49] A great irony of this conversation is that both Henry and David have the utmost respect for Georges Braque; Henry treasures a Braque still life that hangs over his bed, and David would like to see himself "following in the footsteps of ... Braque"—an admission that appears to have precipitated the quarrel.[50]

As noted earlier, the ebony tower recalls the ivory tower, and together they create an energy that sustains them in a dynamic relationship with each other, a tension that remains deliberately unresolved at the end of the narrative. The unresolved tension between the ebony tower as the real and the ivory tower as the romantic ideal generates energy that signals a

mystery at the center of all of Fowles's novels, one that is partially characterized by an ideal that is used to seduce the reader/viewer and protagonist but which, finally, points the way to the real. The two towers seem
to exist in a relationship similar to the one Fowles describes in the 1968
preface to *The Aristos*, as the relationship between the Few and the Many,
which he sees as running through each individual rather than existing as
opposing social forces.[51] Similarly, *The Ebony Tower* suggests that the unresolved tension between the real and the ideal is part of the human condition—to be anchored in reality but inevitably yearning for more—for
the ideal. Such an interpretation reinforces the description of *The Ebony
Tower* as a meditation on desire and its often attendant disappointment,
the subject of Henry's newest painting *Kermesse*.

An alternative explanation for the lack of resolution in *The Ebony
Tower* would align the ivory tower with modernism and the ebony tower
with postmodernism. The ivory tower inhabited by the modern artist
would ultimately allow for a unified thematic explanation of the story
based on the analysis and resulting synthesis of the major elements of the
narratives, whereas a postmodernist "reading" would take into account
their obscurity and lack of resolution, even contradiction. If any meanings
were to be hazarded, they would necessarily be provisional and plural. In
this way, *The Ebony Tower* may be interpreted as a prototypically postmodern work of art, one that simultaneously represents and articulates
the aesthetic principles upon which it has been constructed at the same
time that it honors and parodies that which preceded it. With this in mind,
David's ambiguous behavior toward Diana, depending upon how it is
being viewed, may be interpreted as either a moral victory or an artistic
defeat—or as both—and Breasley may be perceived as acting either out
of selfishness or selflessness, *that is*, authentic selfhood. Such irresolution
or contradiction is the manifestation of Henry's definition of the ebony
tower, and, rather counter-intuitively, reveals how such narratives are actually closer to realism, perhaps more appropriately called metarealism,
because they differ significantly from the traditional realism that relies
firmly on mimesis to construct their illusions.[52] The art of Henry Breasley
as well as that of John Fowles is predicated upon the aesthetic tenets David
detects in Breasley's *Moon-Hunt*, explicitly stated in the novella: "behind
the modernity of so many of the surface elements there stood both a homage and a kind of thumbed nose to a very old tradition," a reference to the
parody that is so often interwoven into postmodern, metafictional acknowl-

edgment of a predecessor, as in the use of "Eliduc" in both the book and the film.[53] A journal entry from the period when Fowles was translating "Eliduc" states: "What interests me is the childish absurdity of the thing. The super-ego just being made a fool of."[54] This may suggest some of his motivation for including the story and echoing it in "The Ebony Tower" where Henry has created his own little idealized world at Coëtminais in defiance of social disapprobation and the demands of the superego. Fowles perceives a basic conflict between individual desire and social expectations that often results in freedom being compromised. In this case, Henry, unlike David, asserts his freedom.

A related scene that focuses on the artist as a key theme is the one Mortimer wrote to satisfy Olivier's desire for a final scene of substance. It makes "the man versus the artist controversy" explicit, a topic that continues to be a subject of debate. Henry insists that man and artist are one, David that they are separate entities. David tells Henry what he thinks of him as both man and artist, thus reinforcing his earlier, disapproving comment related to Henry's wish to marry Diana: "Being a genius doesn't give you the right to ruin someone else's life."[55] At Coëtminais, David comes face to face with the amorality of art. Henry counters David's accusations by telling him to see the National Gallery painting *Saint George and the Dragon*, by Uccello, to clarify his perception of Henry's relationship with Diana. Olivier's Henry describes the painting in this way: "There he is, the Knight in shining armour, charging away at the poor old dragon and the princess ... and you know what? The princess has got the dragon on a lead—her pet, her tame companion. They've been perfectly happy together, don't you see, for a long time. Go and look at it, and ask yourself, didn't St. George make a tiny little bit of a twerp of himself?" The audience is left with a final image to contemplate when the painting appears under the credits at the end of the film. Although it was not preserved in the final version of the film, in the screenplay there is an allusion to "Eliduc" as well as to *Saint George and the Dragon* when Henry issues David an empty invitation: "Why not stay? The Knight and the dragon and the princess ... all living together. How's that for a happy ending?"[56] Although Henry seems to have the last word, it is the illusory world-making quality of art represented by the painting that is being valorized here as one of the most significant venues for interpreting human experience: the play of the real with the ideal, of the dream with reality. Once more, as with the original story, *The Ebony Tower* refuses to provide any

Paolo Uccello, *Saint George and the Dragon* (about 1470). In the video *The Ebony Tower* the formidable artist Breasley offers a feminist interpretation of this painting as an instance of masculine presumption, as Saint George insists on rescuing a damsel who is not in distress, who has her pet dragon on a leash (National Gallery, London).

facile conclusion; finally, it is left to the viewer/reader to parse their relationship.

Ultimately, raising complex questions about the human condition is of greater importance than a carefully orchestrated answer to any of them. Each of The Ebony Towers—the volume of short fiction, the novella, and the film adaptation of the novella—asks such questions in the terms of its particular medium. And while each can certainly stand alone as a work of art, in conversation they are generative. Perhaps someday an ambitious filmmaker will take on the task of adapting Fowles's entire collection of short fiction either as a film or as a serial—a project unheard of in 1983 but not without precedent in the 21st century.[57] Such a work would add to the ongoing, recursive, transtextual conversation already underway among the various "towers."

147

Notes

1. Alain-Fournier, John Fowles, Afterword, *Le Grand Meaulnes*, trans. Lowell Bair as *The Wanderer or the End of Youth* (New York: New American Library), p. 223. John Fowles tells readers that he kept this quotation on the wall before him as a benchmark for his own writing as he taught himself to write during the decade-long composition of *The Magus* (emphasis in the original).

2. John Fowles, *The French Lieutenant's Woman* (Boston: Little, Brown, 1969), p. 96.

3. John Fowles, "A Personal Note," in *The Ebony Tower* (New York: Little, Brown, 1974), p. 118. Fowles further suggests, on p. 121, that Henry may have been named for Henry II, to whom Marie de France, the author of "Eliduc," may have been related. Henry II was known for his not particularly courteous manners.

4. "An Interview with John Fowles," *Conversations with John Fowles*, ed. Dianne L. Vipond (Jackson: University Press of Mississippi, 1999), p. 117. In Barnum's 1984 interview with John Fowles, he explains how he came to write *The Ebony Tower* as a break from composing the 629-page *Daniel Martin*; that "The Ebony Tower" was his first experience writing a *nouvelle*; how he was experimenting with how much he could leave out of each story; and how the texts in the collection came to be ordered.

5. Fowles, "A Personal Note," p. 117.

6. John Fowles, "The Ebony Tower," in *The Ebony Tower*, p. 68.

7. John Mortimer, screenwriter, *The Ebony Tower*, Granada Television, 1984.

8. Patricia Waugh, *Metafiction* (New York: Methuen, 1984), p. 2.

9. Fowles, "A Personal Note," p. 117.

10. Carroll B. Johnson, "Phantom Pre-texts and Fictional Authors: Sidi Hamid Benengeli, *Don Quijote* and the Metafictional Conventions of Chivalric Romances," *Cervantes: Bulletin of the Cervantes Society of America* 27.1 (2007): 182.

11. Gilles Deleuze and Félix Guattari, *A Thousand Plateaus*, trans. Brian Massumi (Minneapolis: University of Minnesota Press, 1987), p. 22.

12. Deleuze and Guattari, *A Thousand* Plateaus, p. 4.

13. Peter Brooker, "Postmodern Adaptation: Pastiche, Intertextuality and Refunctioning," *The Cambridge Companion to Literature on Screen*, ed. Deborah Cartmell and Imelda Whelehan (Cambridge: Cambridge University Press, 2007), p. 114.

14. Fowles, "The Ebony Tower," p. 18.

15. *Ibid.*, p. 18.

16. *Ibid.*, p. 61.

17. F. Scott Fitzgerald, *The Great Gatsby*, in *Three Novels* (New York: Scribner's, 1953), p. 38, for example. The most recent film adaptation is directed by Baz Luhrmann (Warner Bros., 2013).

18. Fowles, "The Ebony Tower," pp. 120–21.

19. Dianne Vipond, "The Ebony Tower and the Search for Meaning," in *John Fowles*, ed. James Acheson (Basingstoke: Palgrave Macmillan, 2011), pp. 197–98.

20. Robert Stam, *Literature and Film* (Oxford: Blackwell, 2005), pp. 9–10.

21. Robert Stam, *Literature through Film* (Oxford: Blackwell, 2005), p. 4.

22. John Fowles, "Notes on an Unfinished Novel," in *Wormholes*, ed. Jan Relf (New York: Henry Holt, 1998), p. 21 (emphasis in the original).

23. *Ibid.*, p. 21.

24. Tony Graham, et al., "John Fowles: An Exclusive Interview," *Socialist Challenge* December 1977, p. 17.

25. John Fowles, *Daniel Martin* (New York: Little, Brown, 1977), p. 125.

26. Brian McFarlane, "Reading Film and Literature," *The Cambridge Companion to Literature on Screen*, ed. Deborah Cartmell and Imelda Whelehan (Cambridge: Cambridge University Press, 2007), p. 20. McFarlane goes on to define *mise en scène* as "actors

in collaboration with their physical surroundings as manifested to the viewer through camera angle, distance and movement, and lighting," on p. 22.

27. John Fowles, "The Filming of *The French Lieutenant's Woman*," in *Wormholes*, ed. Jan Relf (New York: Henry Holt, 1998), p. 37 (emphasis in the original).

28. *Ibid.*, p. 37.

29. *Ibid.*, p. 40.

30. McFarlane, "Reading Film and Literature," p. 30.

31. Carlin Romano, "A Conversation with John Fowles," *Boulevard* 2 (Spring 1987): 144. Woody Allen would agree with him, as reported by David Streitfeld in "A Writer Blocked" for the *Washington Post* 6 May 1996, p. D1.

32. John Fowles, *The Journals: Volume 2*, ed. Charles Drazin (New York: Alfred A. Knopf, 2006), p. 270.

33. *Ibid.*, p. 273.

34. *Ibid.*, 281.

35. Laura Mulvey, "Visual Pleasure and Narrative Cinema," *Screen* 16.3 (1975): 11. The essay established the term *gaze* in cinema studies.

36. The music for the film was composed by Richard Rodney Bennett and conducted by Marcus Dods.

37. McFarlane, "Reading Film and Literature," p. 26.

38. Sarah Cardwell, "Literature on the Small Screen: Television Adaptations," *The Cambridge Companion to Literature on Screen*, ed. Deborah Cartmell and Imelda Whelehan (Cambridge: Cambridge University Press, 2007), p. 185.

39. *Ibid.*, p. 187.

40. *Ibid.*, pp. 187–88.

41. *Brideshead Revisited*, dir. by Charles Sturridge and Michael Lindsay-Hogg, Granada Television, 1981.

42. Cardwell, "Literature on the Small Screen," p. 189.

43. Fowles, "Filming," p. 39.

44. Fowles, "The Ebony Tower," p. 147.

45. Claude Monet, *Poppies, Near Argenteuil*, 1873.

46. Fowles's *The Collector* (1963) anticipates some of the ways in which aesthetic themes are handled in "The Ebony Tower."

47. Fowles, "The Ebony Tower," p. 26. The self-consciousness, i.e., the metatheatricality of the film is indicated by Breasley's comment about the name of the house: "Coëtminais? Forest of the Monks. We enjoy the forest and forget the vows of chastity"; the passage suggests an intertextual reference in its veiled allusion to the ending of "Eliduc."

48. Fowles, "The Ebony Tower," p. 56.

49. *Ibid.*, p. 64.

50. *Ibid.*, pp. 46–47, 60. Along with Pablo Picasso, Georges Braque is considered one of the founders of Cubism, an artistic movement that is clearly a precursor of abstract expressionist art.

51. John Fowles, "Preface to a New Edition," *The Aristos*, 2d ed. (New York: Little, Brown, 1970), pp. 9–10.

52. A *Metarealism* is a term used by Lawrence Durrell in his ideally metafictional novel sequence *The Avignon Quintet* to refer to the self-consciousness of his style—a style partaking of magic realism, metaphysics, and metafiction to generate a productive hybridity.

53. Fowles, "The Ebony Tower," p. 18.

54. Fowles, *Journals*, p. 145.

55. Fowles, "The Ebony Tower," p. 114.

56. John Mortimer, *The Ebony Tower*, Granada Television, 1984.

57. See the 2012 film adaptation of David Mitchell's novel *Cloud Atlas*, written, produced, and directed by Lana Wachowski, Tom Tykwer, and Andy Wachowski.

The Magus as Thriller: David Fincher's Film The Game

JAMES AUBREY

Who would have guessed that John Fowles's long, encyclopedic, philosophical novel *The Magus* could be made into a movie thriller?[1] After all, *The Magus* has no car chases, no gunplay, no life-or-death emergencies. *The Game*, however, includes all of those in its creatively updated, genuinely exciting version of Fowles's novel.

"Thriller" is indeed the label used by Janet Maslin to describe *The Game* in her review for *The New York Times*, and the word *thriller* is likewise prominent on the front of the DVD case for the 1998 video release of the 1997 film directed by David Fincher, starring Michael Douglas, Sean Penn, and Deborah Kara Unger.[2] The thriller genre is often associated with Hitchcock films because they typically place the spectator in a state of thrilling suspense, often over who will obtain some "MacGuffin," as Hitchcock liked to call the object or goal that characters are pursuing.[3] In Fincher's previous film, *Seven*, the object of pursuit was a serial killer, and a pattern of clues involved the seven deadly sins. In *The Game*, however, as in *The Magus*, there is no MacGuffin. The goal of the protagonist is to find out who is ultimately responsible for a program of self-improvement—again, an unlikely object of pursuit for a thriller. But another aspect of a thriller is what culture critic Belinda Luscombe calls "a ballooning sense of trepidation," a phrase that aptly describes the growing feelings of paranoia experienced by the Michael Douglas character in *The Game*, as others seem to be taking over his everyday life, and then to be threatening it. What is curiosity in *The Magus* becomes fear in *The Game*, as screenwriters John Brancato and Michael Ferris sensationalize the experiential surprises of *The Magus* by placing their protagonist in physical danger, often at night, often in rough-looking parts of the city that are very different from his accustomed world of privilege—and more likely to generate a sense of trepidation in American filmgoers than would an exotic Greek island, the setting of the Fowles novel.

But is the movie based on the book? In 1997, while *The Game* was still playing in movie theaters, I received a phone call from a bookseller in California named Bob Goosman, whose business includes buying and selling materials related to John Fowles. "Have you seen *The Game*?" he asked me. I hadn't. "Go, and tell me it's not a ripoff of *The Magus*." I did, and it is, undoubtedly, derived from the Fowles novel, without acknowledgment, but it didn't deserve the label "ripoff," as if it were an inferior product of lazy theft. *The Game* is a brilliant work of creative adaptation. Its relationship to *The Magus* is like the similarly unacknowledged relationship of the film *Clueless* to Jane Austen's *Emma*: a cleverly updated parallel text that is as fine a film as the original is a fine novel.[4] A parallel text is not an identical text, of course, and in many ways the differences between *The Game* and *The Magus* account for why *The Game* was so much more successful with its audience than was the more faithful film adaptation of *The Magus* in 1968.[5] Differences not withstanding, a more generous production of *The Game* would have acknowledged that its screenplay owed a debt to John Fowles.

First, about the similarities. The underlying parallel is structural: in both *The Magus* and *The Game* an unhappy male undergoes staged experiences designed by a benefactor to encourage his protégé to change his personal life, which has been following an unsatisfying routine when the story begins. After a series of shocking and painful ordeals, the protagonist turns detective in order to find out the reality behind the manipulations, only to discover that they are ongoing. The story in both *The Magus* and *The Game* ends inconclusively, with an ambiguous scene between male and female lead characters, who must decide whether to forgive each other and leave the games behind for more self-managed, creative lives together. The open endings of both stories invite readers of the novel and spectators of the film to decide what will happen next.

The most telling evidence of borrowing from *The Magus* is the naming of characters in *The Game*. In both works the protagonist is named Nicholas. In *The Magus* the benefactor who sets events in motion is named Conchis; in *The Game*, he is named Conrad, sometimes called Connie. If Brancato and Ferris had wanted to disguise their script's resemblance to

Fowles's novel, they could easily have selected names for their main characters that did not so clearly resemble those of *The Magus*; so I am guessing that the screenwriters intended a subtle homage to their source.

Other similarities include the extravagant lengths to which the benefactor's agents go to set up seemingly mysterious interventions into the protégé's life, including in both stories a doll associated with death and an attractive female who pretends also to be an unwilling participant in the game-playing, then later reveals herself to be part of the conspiracy to play him. In both stories the Nicholas character comes close to committing suicide. In both stories, Nicholas is drugged before undergoing what is staged to seem a near-death experience, followed by a waking up in a strange place, stripped of his previous identity and thus potentially a changed man but distracted by a wish to punish those who have manipulated him. There are, of course, many differences between the novel and the film, as there must be in any adaptation across media. Besides *The Game*'s new time and place, 1990s San Francisco, Nicholas Van Orton is 48 years old, wealthy, and privileged—unlike *The Magus*' recent university graduate and novice teacher, Nicholas Urfe. The romantic sub-plot also is different: at the end of the novel the mysterious female, Julie, has disappeared, and Nicholas is brought together for a possible reconciliation with his former girlfriend, Alison. In the film, however, Nicholas merely restores amicable relations with his ex-wife; the possibility of a romantic future lies with Christine, the mysterious woman of the games. It is this combination of borrowed similarities and invented differences that help to make *The Game* such a compelling thriller.

The clever idea of marketing the experiences of *The Game* as a consumer service available to anyone who will pay to play, rather than leaving the selection of candidates to chance, may have been inspired by Fowles. The original working title for *The Magus* was *The Godgame*, in which the main character's unhappy life seems to be scripted, as if determined by some mysterious, godlike power that one grants to others and to circumstances, instead of assuming personal responsibility for one's actions. In his introduction to the revised version of *The Magus*, in 1977, Fowles announced that he still liked the novel's "alternative title, whose rejection I still sometimes regret: *The Godgame*."[6] This feeling of regret probably expresses Fowles's longing to be philosophical, a characteristic that led him in 1964, against the advice of others, to insist on publishing a book-length collection of his thoughts and reflections, *The Aristos*.[7] To Fowles, the word *godgame* would have signaled the novel's philosophical agenda, aligned with the then-current Existentialist belief that life should not be led as if one lives in a game being played by God, with humans as mere game pieces and their behavior essentially determined from "above." In a 1998 interview Fowles stated, "The one thing I wanted to be clear about in *The Magus* is that there is no god"; when the novel was first published in 1965, however, he may have felt less strongly about foregrounding this anti-religious agenda, for he did change the title from *The Godgame* to *The Magus* before publication.[8] The title *The Magus* had its own problems. The Latin word *magus*, for magician" or "sorcerer," also can mean "wise man" (plural *magi*), "but that wasn't clear to most readers until they had discovered the 1965 epigraph describing the Tarot card for The Magician; and that explanation of the title seemed to promise magic or, at least, psychic mystery. So the title *The Magus* might have suited the climate of the 1960s, but for the 1990s it would not do for a thriller. The title *The Game*, on the other hand, did not carry any supernatural baggage or Latinate obscurity, so it made a perfect title for the 1997 film, which did not wish to retain the novel's philosophical agenda. Indeed, *The Game* changes the idea that game-playing leads to responsible self-awareness, to the idea that life is a game and should be played for enjoyment. If there are philosophical implications to *The Game*, they are that watching the film is a similar kind of game playing, engaged in for pleasure. Indeed, the expensive form of entertainment offered by Consumer Recreation Services (CRS) resembles a movie production, as one character points out to the protagonist late in the story. So, much as Fowles invites his readers to become magicians themselves with his meta-fiction, Fincher invites his audiences to play the game as they watch his meta-cinema. The decision to call the film *The Game* was genius.

On the level of immediate responses, as thriller, *The Game* works well because the premise is realistic. In *The Magus* one must suspend disbelief in an eccentric millionaire who is staging events to teach visiting schoolteachers to live better lives. In *The Game*, however, the project is set up as a service provided by a company whose extremely high fees allow it to provide the expensive resources to stage the exciting interventions into the lives of otherwise bored customers. Conrad Van Orton (played by Sean Penn) has been through their program and decides to purchase CRS's delivery of life-changing experiences as an expensive birthday present for his brother, Nicholas (played by Michael Douglas), a bored investment banker. In *The Magus* the name of the millionaire, Conchis, is evidently meant to suggest consciousness, but that significance calls attention to the artificiality of the whole set-up. Nicholas Urfe wonders "Why me?" and so do readers. For *The Game*, changing the novel's god-like game designer to a service company makes the set-up seem plausible, particularly to an American audience steeped in capitalism, who might readily accept that a rich investment banker might be bored with his life and that a business might exist to serve the needs of such a person for whom money is no object.

The Nicholas characters in both works are self-centered and not particularly likeable. In the novel, Fowles devotes 63 pages to generating audience identification with Nicholas Urfe's character before the mysteries begin. In opening scenes of the film, Nicholas Van Orton is shown to be unhappy, treating clients and employees with anger or disrespect, and he seems to be lonely in the evenings, with only the television news for companionship. In order to help spectators identify with Nicholas of *The Game*, during an automobile ride he remembers his father's suicide, shown in a flashback to his childhood, in the style of an 8mm home movie from the 1950s. However, the most effective rhetorical device is a montage of scenes in which Nicholas is required by CRS to go through an annoying battery of tests and to complete numerous forms, examinations, and interviews. He is told by his advisor, Jim Feingold (played by James Rebhorn), that he will be participating in a game specifically tailored for him, "like an experiential Book-of-the-Month Club." Nicholas' reluctance and irritation are overcome by his curiosity and his having promised his brother to give CRS a try. These scenes humanize his character and encourage the audience to identify with him in spite of his position of extreme privilege, so spectators feel as surprised as Nicholas does when CRS calls to tell him that his application has been rejected. That is, of course, merely the first of many deceptive manipulations.

Nicholas' first experience courtesy of CRS is to arrive home one night and find a life-sized clown doll with a CRS key in its mouth, lying on his driveway at the location where Nicholas' father had killed himself when Nicholas was a child, by jumping off the roof of their mansion, shown earlier in the flashback. Nicholas takes the doll inside, unaware that there is a video camera in the clown's right eye that is communicating with Daniel Schorr (played by himself), a widely recognizable anchor of the *CBS Evening News* in the 1990s. Suddenly during the newscast, Schorr begins to address Nicholas by name and to taunt him for not knowing how Schorr can see his movements. Schorr gives Nicholas an emergency number but warns him not to ask about the object of the game. Nicholas is unsettled by the experience, so there is irony as he sets his alarm system to "home secure" as he goes to bed. The audience feels unsettled as well, not knowing what to believe is "real" if CRS can manipulate the national news media. A disturbing doll has a similar role in *The Magus* when Nicholas Urfe is walking through the woods to Conchis' villa and encounters two objects hanging from a tree, one a human skull and the other a doll: "Its neck was in a noose. It was hanging in both senses. About eighteen inches high, clumsily carved in wood and painted black, with a smiling mouth and eyes naively whitened in. Round its ankles were its only 'clothes'—two wisps of white rag." Fowles's narrator goes on to advise the reader that "the doll was Julie, and ... that she was evil, she was black, under the white innocence she wore."[9] This providing of an interpretation makes the doll in *The Magus* seem less mysterious and less disturbing than the one intro-duced in *The Game*. For the film, Brancato and Ferris just present the doll, whose uncanny appearance signals the strangeness of the game and whose location indicates, without comment, that CRS knows that Nich-olas' unhappy life could be related to his childhood memory of his father's suicide. Thus, with this first mysterious event, *The Game* compresses and dramatizes a sequence of mysterious events and deepens the character of Nicholas, psychologically, by connecting it to flashback visuals instead of many pages of backstory.

Thirty-five minutes into the film, Nicholas meets Christine (played by Deborah Kara Unger), who becomes his companion for most of the ensuing adventures. Nicholas encounters her when she is paid to spill a drink on him at an expensive restaurant, where she is a waitress. When she is consequently fired, another waiter leaves Nicholas a note stating, "Don't let her get away." Nicholas takes the bait and pursues her onto the street, where a stranger collapses in front of them. They take him to a supposed hospital, where they become trapped in an elevator when the power is cut. When the two manage to climb out through the ceiling, they find themselves on a different floor, at night, in the headquarters of CRS. Chased by security guards, they escape by jumping from the building into garbage dumpsters, but then they are chased by the police and a menacing dog. After another escape, Nicholas goes home, only to find that his living room has been painted with day-glo graffiti such as "Don't cry" and "Go ask Alice," reinforced by a sound system playing Jefferson Airplane's "White Rabbit." Wondering if Christine also is getting tormented, Nicholas tracks her to an apartment, where he begins to suspect that she is in on the game and only pretending to help him. When he dismantles a camera in her smoke detector, he provokes a raid on the apartment by a SWAT team from vans labeled Cable Repair Services (CRS) shooting what seem to be real bullets. Nicholas escapes in a taxi from California Royal Sedans (CRS, again), but its driver jumps out and sends Nicholas and the cab into San Francisco Bay, where Nicholas barely escapes drowning. Just when he believes that he has found safety from the people who are chasing him, in a remote cabin with Christine, she drugs his coffee and tells him, "My name is not Christine." As he loses consciousness, the screen fades to black. Christine's declaration of complicity echoes a similarly devastating line in *The Magus*, spoken by Julie just before Nicholas is forcibly injected with a drug that causes him to lose consciousness: "My name isn't Julie."[10] Nicholas Urfe wakes up a captive and is put on trial, during which he undergoes a symbolic death and subsequently wakes up on mainland Greece, literally and symbolically surrounded by a ruin.[11] In *The Game* Nicholas Van Orton wakes up in Mexico, lying in a coffin that is covered but not nailed shut. Devastated and broke, and symbolically without identification, he struggles for days to get back to San Francisco.

As in *The Magus*, Nicholas in *The Game* is determined to find out who has been manipulating him. In the novel the pace slows down as Nicholas plays detective, but in *The Game* Nicholas quickly finds the actor who initially interviewed him, kidnaps him with a handgun, and forces him to take them both to CRS headquarters, where they find everyone Nicholas has encountered in the story thus far, assembled in a large room. When Nicholas confronts Christine, gunfire erupts and Nicholas is chased to the roof of the building, where he shoots one of his pursuers—who turns out to be his brother. Devastated again, thinking that he has killed Conrad and not realizing that the game is still in play, Nicholas throws himself off the roof of the building—only to land on a giant, inflated cushion that has been placed there to catch him when he jumped or, if necessary, was pushed, to end the adventures. After the fall, recovered but still bewildered, Nicholas is congratulated by his brother, still wearing fake blood from the supposed shooting, for having completed the program. The assembled actors join in celebrating a re-birthday, and Nicholas offers to co-sign the CRS invoice for services rendered, thus terminating the game with a huge monetary payment; this finality is unlike the situation in the novel, where the game is a metaphorical state of mind—and may be ongoing.

Like *The Magus*, however, the final scene of *The Game* ends on an indeterminate note. In the novel, Julie and her twin sister have disappeared, but Nicholas and his previous girlfriend, Alison, meet in London's Regent's Park, where Nicholas suspects that they are still being watched. In a move that is meant to shock her—and any watchers—Nicholas slaps Alison in the face, presumably for having participated in the various deceptions he has experienced. Whether she leaves or stays with Nicholas at the end is left up to the reader to decide. In *The Game* both female characters are conflated into "Christine," the waitress, and the film ends with her and Nicholas meeting outside the CRS building on a dark, rainy street while the others celebrate inside. She explains that she is on her way to catch a plane to Australia to participate in another game. When Nicholas expresses an interest in getting together with her when she returns, she reminds him that he doesn't know anything about her, not even her real name, which she says is Claire, from Oklahoma. Then, with a sheepish grin, she corrects herself: "No, Colorado. I've been doing this way too long!" As she gets into the taxi, she proposes that Nicholas might come along to the airport, where they could have coffee together. She has made flirtatious remarks before, so this seems clearly to be an invitation for him to consider a romantic relationship. Nicholas looks at her, pondering his options. The last shot of the film is from a high angle, about 100 feet away, as Nicholas continues to stand outside the taxicab, not having accepted or rejected her invitation, as "White Rabbit" begins to play again on the sound track, this time suggesting that Nicholas must decide whether to follow the mystery woman down another rabbit-hole for a more adventurous and probably happier life.

This device of inviting audiences to "choose your own" ending, adventure, etc., became a postmodernist commonplace in the late twentieth century. John Fowles has been credited with having pioneered the idea in his 1969 novel *The French Lieutenant's Woman*, with its invitation to the reader to choose between two endings, but he had been experimenting with the idea four years earlier with the indeterminate ending of *The Magus*.[12] In 1997, with its similar situation and unresolved question at the end, *The Game* deletes the unmotivated slap but preserves the spirit and improves the sense of Fowles's original indeterminate ending.

The idea that we limit ourselves if we imagine life to be a game manipulated by a god underlies *The Magus*. The novel aspires to teach a moral, perhaps embedded in the literary quotation from T.S. Eliot:

> We shall not cease from exploration
> And the end of all our exploring
> Will be to arrive where we started
> And know the place for the first time.[13]

The Magus is about attaining this new awareness. In one of his last interviews Fowles stated, simply, "I want to teach morally."[14] *The Game* has no such ambitions. Although one of its characters refers Nicholas to the biblical verse at John 1:25: "I once was blind, but now I see"; any new awareness that Nicholas attains will improve the happiness of his personal life, not make him a better person, let alone a religious one. The publicity poster for the film shows Michael Douglas' face with the top of his head turning into pieces of a jigsaw puzzle, suggesting that the title of *The Game* refers to mental pleasures of playing games such as chess or racquetball— both shown in the film—and to the satisfaction of finding out the truth behind Consumer Recreation Services. Despite the biblical reference, *The Game* is less about acquiring self-knowledge than *The Magus*, and more about learning to play.

There is one aspect of both the novel and the film adaptation that oddly undercuts the spirit of play, and that is the representation of ethnic difference. Both works traffic in negative stereotypes. In *The Magus* the only black character is Joe, a mute servant to Conchis who has sex with Julie in a pornographic film that is used to manipulate Nicholas into feeling outrage and wanting to punish her. Joe's skin color is being used to heighten the supposed treachery of Julie's behavior, which Nicholas—and readers—might have found less offensive if Joe had been white (as his character is in the 1968 film adaptation). There is a similar ethnically-charged dimension to *The Game*, where many scenes take place in San Francisco's Chinatown and many bystanders look Asian. The actors playing the staff at the Hotel Nikko have Japanese names, and their characters are involved in stealing Nicholas' credit card and setting up his supposed room with drugs and pornography. When Nicholas and Christine must jump from a building into dumpsters below, they are watched with amusement by the Asian-looking workers on break from a nearby restaurant. And when Nicholas recognizes a signed photo of the actor who recruited him, he takes it off the wall of another Chinese restaurant and leaves the owner shouting after him, "Hey! Where you taking my picture?" Film reviewer

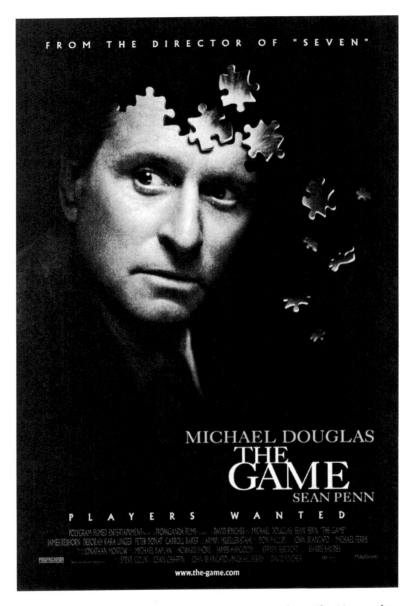

This promotional poster for *The Game* (1997), based on *The Magus*, shows Nicholas Van Orton (Michael Douglas) as the character whose unhappy life seems to be disintegrating as he participates in a mystifying, experiential program offered by Consumer Recreation Services. The poster tag line, "PLAYERS WANTED," invites spectators to feel like participants in meta-cinema (Photofest).

Sheryl Rau is blunt: "*The Game*'s representation of urban hell is filled with Asian immigrants and smacks of racism."[15] I would not argue that this aspect of the film is borrowed from the book but, rather, that both works reflect some similar, disturbing attitudes about ethnic differences prevalent in both British and American societies.

So, after all, what kind of adaptation is *The Game*, besides unacknowledged? It is, for one, an "indigenization," which transfers an original work across time and place, for *The Game* updates and Americanizes the British novel, moving it from England and Greece to the United States and Mexico, from some time in the 1950s or '60s to sometime in the 1990s. Unlike the 1965 novel or its 1968 film adaptation, *The Game* adheres to an aesthetic canon of realism, not fantasy. It aims primarily to entertain rather than to instruct. It is a "loose" adaptation that does not try to be "faithful" to the original. Because it does not acknowledge its original, *The Game* is not what Linda Hutcheon in *Theory of Adaptation* would call "palimpsestuous," that is, the audience is not aware while watching *The Game* that *The Magus* preceded it; so spectators are not affected by prior knowledge of an original, do not feel what Hutcheon describes as the "enriching paternalistic doubleness" as they discern the layers of a palimpsest.[16] Nor is *The Game* "ripped off," a phrase Hutcheon specifically objects to for its implications that an adaptation is inherently "second rate"; for all adaptations are derived from another work and are not to be judged negatively for that fact alone.[17] As Hutcheon also points out, adaptations are like translations, and the intent of an adaptor, like that of a translator from one language to another, has been well described by Walter Benjamin as "'derivative, ultimate, ideational.'"[18] *The Game* is all three, derived from an original, ultimately limited as to its structure, and promoting the same idea—here, that experiential learning can awaken the learner to a richer life, with or without new awareness of one's responsibilities for the choices involved. However, *The Game* is ultimately not like *The Magus*, where a richer life is supposed to be one of examined, serious, individualized social responsibility. In *The Game* a richer life is similarly sociable, but found in pursuit of social stimulation, of recreation rather than responsibility—in play.

Notes

1. John Fowles, *The Magus: A Revised Version* (Boston: Little, Brown, 1977).
2. *The Game*, directed by David Fincher, Polygram, 1997.

3. François Truffaut, *Hitchcock*, 2d ed. (New York: Simon & Schuster, 1983), p. 138.

4. *Clueless*, directed by Amy Heckerling, Paramount, 1995; Jane Austen, *Emma* (Peterborough, Ontario: Broadview, 2004).

5. *The Magus*, directed by Guy Green (Twentieth Century–Fox, 1968). For a discussion of this film, see "Cinematic Godgames," this collection.

6. John Fowles, foreword to *The Magus: A Revised Version* (Boston: Little, Brown, 1977), p. 10.

7. John Fowles, *The Aristos* (Boston: Little, Brown, 1964).

8. *The Return of the Magus*, dir. Mike Pearce (Athens: Inkas Productions, 1999–2000).

9. Fowles, *The Magus*, p. 459.

10. *Ibid.*, p. 488.

11. *The Magus*, dir. Guy Green, Twentieth Century–Fox, 1968.

12. John Fowles, *The French Lieutenant's Woman* (Boston: Little, Brown, 1969); *The Magus* (Boston: Little, Brown, 1965). The choice in *The French Lieutenant's Woman* is set up in Chapter 55, p. 406; the options are the ending of Chapter 60, on p. 460, or the ending of Chapter 61, on p. 467.

13. T.S. Eliot, misquoted in Fowles, *The Magus*, 69. The original reads "to arrive where we started" instead of "to return to where we began," in T.S. Eliot, *The Complete Poems and Plays* (New York: Harcourt Brace, 1971), p. 145.

14. *Return of the Magus*.

15. Sheryl Rau, "Michael Douglas Gets It in *The Game*," *CU-Denver Advocate* 24 September 1997, p. 9.

16. Linda Hutcheon, *A Theory of Adaptation* (New York: Routledge, 2006), p. 120.

17. *Ibid.*, p. 169.

18. Walter Benjamin, quoted in Hutcheon, *A Theory of Adaptation*, p. 88.

Postmodern Documentary: *The Return of the Magus* on Video

CRAIG SVONKIN

Nostalgia is an often derided aesthetic, but one that permeates *The Return of the Magus*, a documentary that John Fowles helped to make in 1998 for Greek television, in English with Greek subtitles.[1] The film uses a visit to Greece by Fowles as a structuring device: the camera follows him to and around the island of Spetses, where from 1951 to 1953 he had been a teacher at a private boys' school much like the Lord Byron School of his novel *The Magus*.[2] Fowles is filmed first at home in the United Kingdom, in Lyme Regis, having his portrait painted, then arriving by boat to Spetses. He visits the Villa Jasemina, the model for Conchis' Villa Bourani in the novel, and discusses Greek history with Philippos Demertzis, a descendent of Laskurina Bouboulina, heroine of the 1821 Greek War of Independence. With the Parthenon as a backdrop, Fowles discusses Greek light, politics, and the British theft of Greek antiquities with philosopher and poet Nikos Dimou. He discusses *The Magus* with Professor Kirki Kefalea of the University of Athens, screenwriter of the documentary. He watches an actor read from a Greek translation of the novel. Intermittently throughout, in voice-over, the youthful-sounding, British-sounding Mark Heally reads passages as Fowles reenacts scenes from *The Magus*, standing in for his fictional protagonist, Nicholas Urfe. At the end of the 54-minute film, back in England, the painter finishes his portrait of Fowles, dated 1998. Given all of these disparate elements, *The Return of the Magus* might appear to be a strange, messy and seemingly haphazard mix of documentary genres: part superficial introduction to Greek history through talking head shots with historical experts and descendants of historical figures, even a historical recreation of a naval battle; part travelogue for English speakers

162

Dr. Kirki Kefalea talks with John Fowles in 1998, during the making of *Return of the Magus*, a documentary for Greek television. They are shooting on the Aegean island of Spetses, at the Villa Jasemina, model for the house of Maurice Conchis in Fowles's 1965 novel *The Magus* (private collection).

using Fowles as their intermediary, with mini-lessons about Greek history, art, and culture; part commemoration of Fowles's 1998 nostalgic return trip to Spetses, with the elderly Fowles at 72 showing his age and the effects of a stroke, walking in his own youthful footsteps as he revisits the sites he first knew 47 years before when he came to Greece and fell in love with his future wife, Elizabeth, and with Greece itself; and part introduction to Fowles's novel *The Magus*.

While *The Return of the Magus* may seem fascinating but somewhat incoherent, given its rapid jumps from one type of documentary scene to another, what offers a loose unity to this diverse, mixed-form work are a number of overarching themes, including nostalgia, mortality, and the impact of the past on the present. For one, Fowles's love of Greece is evident throughout the film. As Fowles wrote in an introduction to The Modern Library edition of *The Magus* in 1998, the same year the documentary was filmed, "[W]hat I hope readers of *The Magus* will realize is my deep love, half cultural and physical, half intense and very present, for all Greece itself, then and now. I can't really be Greek, but I wish I were."[3] *The Return of the Magus* also includes many shots of Fowles looking contemplatively at Greek scenery, his face full of nostalgia, love, and pathos. These filmed moments, occurring as they do more than any other type of shot, become something of a filmic leitmotif. With Fowles's face evocative of his and our knowledge of the imminence of death, *The Return of the Magus* also is a film about time, loss, and mortality. The documentary thus becomes something of a modern Greek gothic production, haunted by ghosts of Fowles's past, of his lost youth. Given that Fowles had suffered a stroke ten years earlier, and that his wife had died of cancer in 1990, it is perhaps unsurprising that issues of nostalgia and loss come to dominate *The Return of the Magus*.[4] In an interview for *The Paris Review* conducted shortly after his stroke, Fowles explained that he felt that "time is running out," that he was "much more aware of death."[5] The sense of mortality and tone of nostalgia that permeate *The Return of the Magus* mark it as a late work in Fowles's career.

The Return of the Magus evidences a complexity that brings together two seemingly incompatible aesthetics; on the one hand, many scenes seem gothic, uncanny, and haunted, but on the other these scenes are juxtaposed with scenes of intense beauty and wonder. There are many shots in the film of Fowles looking beatifically as we share in his appreciation of the beauty of the Greek island of Spetses. Fowles obviously worships Greece, but it is a Greece that he has created from his memories and fictions as much as it is the real Greece. For Fowles, Greece is a half-remembered, half-created space, a heterocosm. As James Aubrey has stated about the 1977 revision of *The Magus*, "it is easy to imagine that Fowles derived … pleasure from revisiting—as he was revising—one of his favorite 'other worlds' of the imagination."[6] Early in *The Return of the Magus*, we see Fowles looking out over the harbor of Spetses from a balcony, while on the sound track we hear a voice-over adapted loosely from *The Magus*: "I had fallen in love with the idea of Greece long before I saw the reality. I loved someone, but what she was not to know was that I had been deceiving her with another woman during the latter part of September. The woman was Greece [itself]." At this point the film cuts to a beautiful Greek woman on the waterfront, apparently a personification of Greece, who turns in close-up to look up seductively at the elderly Fowles. These sorts of moments occur again and again in the documentary, moments of the surreal or the hyperreal, moments meant to indicate Fowles's love for the beauty of Greece but moments that also seem to indicate a move to interiority, to dreaming and memory. These moments also indicate the uncanny gothic aesthetic of Fowles's relationship to Greece, a space that haunts Fowles, given his lost youth and his sense of mortality, lately reinforced by the death of his wife, Elizabeth, whom he had first met and fallen in love with on Spetses.

The double aesthetic of beauty and the uncanny in *The Return of the Magus* becomes evident in Fowles's response to Kirki Kefalea's question to him about when he first started writing *The Magus*: "It [Greece, Spetses] haunted me. In that case there was a ghost element. It did haunt me for years. And then when I first began I was under the influence of a famous novel by Henry James, *The Turn of the Screw*, where there is clearly a ghost, and it is supernatural." I would argue that Fowles's reading of *The Turn of the Screw* is a misreading, for James's novella is cleverly ambiguous as to whether there are actual ghosts present or not. But Fowles's is an interesting misreading, for it reveals, I believe, his own anxieties about his own ghost stories. *The Magus* is something of a rational Gothic novel in the mode of Ann Radcliffe, where the seemingly uncanny and unexplainable mysteries turn out to be mostly explainable, as are the elaborate exercises created by the powerful and wealthy Conchis. However, when Fowles began writing *The Magus*, it had, in its incipient form, "a clear supernatural element," not surprising given that he remembers initially attempting "something along the lines of Henry James's masterpiece, *The Turn of the Screw*."[7] In the foreword to his revised version of *The Magus*, Fowles explains that he was attempting to instill in his own story something ineffable, beyond language—something akin to "the capacity of [Alain-Fournier's] *Le Grand Meaulnes* [...] to provide an experience beyond the literary."[8] Spetses had inspired him with its "uncanny" pine forest silences, with its "curious sense of timelessness and of incipient myth," to desire to try to write "words defeated before the inexpressible."[9] But Fowles eventually turned away from the ineffable and uncanny toward the real as he wrote *The Magus*; he "gradually ... realized I have to be real, I have to be a realist."[10]

Interestingly, in making *The Return of the Magus*, the largely explained gothic of *The Magus* is transformed back, atavistically, into something mysterious again, something more overtly uncanny. A number of gothic moments occur in the documentary, elements that indicate the phantoms haunting Fowles. Early in the film, Fowles is photographed entering the grounds of the Anargyrios and Korgialenios School of Spetses, the Greek private school where he taught as a young man. As Fowles is depicted walking around the school, the sounds of disembodied bells and children's voices can be heard, before the film cuts to an old black and white photo, a symbol of the past and of historical authenticity. This scene plays like a scene from a ghost story, as if Fowles's memories were mystically taking form, materializing out of the past. But the documentary doesn't just imply that Fowles's memories and past are ghosts that haunt him. As Fowles explores the school, the filmmakers employ some ghostly special effects. First, a classroom is shown, with nobody in it. Slowly Fowles appears, seemingly out of thin air, as if he is a ghost of the past visiting the future, or perhaps vice versa. But the filmmakers don't leave the effect at that; they reverse it in a scene that comes two minutes later, as Fowles slowly disappears, like Lewis Carroll's Cheshire Cat, leaving behind only the image of the school. Whether these effects were created in camera or in post-production, they must have required consultation with Fowles prior to filming, so he would have been a party to the creation of the feeling of the uncanny. They nicely capture what Fowles experienced as the haunt-edness of Spetses, its mythic spirit, which he felt when away from its inhab-ited corner, where the island was "truly haunted, though by subtler—and more beautiful—ghosts than I have created."[11] The documentary special effects throw back *The Return of the Magus* to that incipient form of *The Magus*, when the story still had the "clear supernatural element" Fowles saw in *The Turn of the Screw*.[12]

Perhaps in returning the documentary to its fantastic roots, moving it away from the merely uncanny toward the liminal space of the fantastic, Fowles and the filmmakers were attempting to achieve a similar sort of Jamesian gothic balancing act between the uncanny and the marvelous. Tzvetan Todorov has defined the fantastic as a space between believing that "devils, sylphides, or vampires" are the result of "an illusion of the senses, of a product of the imagination" and believing that they are "an integral part of reality." He explains that the "fantastic occupies the dura-tion of this uncertainty. Once we choose one answer or the other, we leave the fantastic for a neighboring genre, either the uncanny or the marvelous. The fantastic is the hesitation experienced by a person who knows only the laws of nature, confronting an apparently supernatural event."[13] It is possible that in attempting to reclaim the fantastic in *The Return of the Magus*, Fowles and his fellow film makers are creating a metaphorical gothic or uncanny aesthetic. The metaphor could be for that which cannot be grasped, for that which "[m]ost young people know they don't know; and the not knowing in this ephemeral, uncertain world is generally the nearest we shall ever get to the truth. In one sense this is a monument to nescience, not knowing."[14] Another possible way to interpret the reintegration of these uncanny tropes into *The Return of the Magus* is that their ghostliness represents Fowles's deceased wife, Elizabeth, whose absence haunts Fowles and the documentary. The fact that there are some fleeting old black and white photos of Elizabeth shown, but that she is never directly named or overtly discussed, makes her ghostly evocations all the more powerful.

One might ask how much of *The Return of the Magus* is Fowles's work. I would argue that while there were other co-creators involved, we are justified to read the documentary as a late work by Fowles, and an interesting one at that. Kirki Kefalea is listed in the credits as the sole writer of the documentary, but it is clear that Fowles was a significant co-contributor, a collaborator in the writing of the piece, as his words, interests, and aesthetic tendencies permeate the television film. Kefalea has acknowledged the central role Fowles played in the conceiving, writing, and making of *The Return of the Magus*:

> This idea [to make a documentary in Greece about *The Magus*] came to [Fowles] already when I first visited his home in Lyme Regis, in October 1991. After that, we had together long discussions about the Spetses project, and how John could go back to the island, meet Botassis family and make the documentary film. For him this was a great chance to revive the whole "Greek experience" of 1951–1952, which has marked his writing career, as he used to say in our conversations.[15]

One of the strangest elements in the documentary, and one that bears the postmodernist literary fingerprints of Fowles, is the uncanny temporal play that occurs in many scenes when the elderly John Fowles reenacts moments that are either from his younger life or from *The Magus*, or a conflation of the two. The elderly Fowles's voice in the documentary sounds raspy, but the voice of Mark Heally sounds very different, British accented but young and vigorous as he reads. The lines are taken from *The Magus* but not clearly identified as coming from any particular source. These moments are temporally and narratologically destabilizing, as we, the audience, cannot know without a great deal of foreknowledge where these lines originated. As the elderly Fowles strolls through the Greek scenery, we find ourselves wondering: What is he thinking? Is he meant in any particular scene to represent his younger self, or the young Nicholas Urfe? Or his elderly, British, authorial self, returning to the scene of his early literary and intellectual inspiration, revisiting the sites that inspired him to write his highly personal novel *The Magus*?

When asked whose idea it was to use John Fowles as the actor in the re-creation of moments from *The Magus*, screenwriter Kefalea responded that showing "scenes from *The Magus* using John to act the part of Nicholas was John's idea." Thus Fowles deserves credit for the most destabilizing and postmodernist element of the documentary, namely the choice to blur fact and fiction by filming John Fowles revisiting the influential Greek sites of his youth as an elderly man, and having him act out scenes from the life of his fictional protagonist and youthful alter ego, Nicholas Urfe. During the scene most clearly taken from *The Magus*, the scene of Nicholas stranded on the island of Monemvasia with a loaded pistol left there by Conchis, the use of the elderly Fowles to play his youthful literary alter-ego and creation, Nicholas, while a young British man performs the voice-over, reading the younger Fowles's words, creates a complex disjunction of age and character, of time and memory, and thus an uncanny temporal confusion, rife with nostalgia for Fowles's youth and an exploration of the blurring between past and present, fiction and memoir. I would argue that the complex aesthetic mixing of nostalgia and postmodern metatextuality in *The Return of the Magus* expresses the same aesthetic as *The French Lieutenant's Woman*. Although uncredited, Fowles seems to have had considerable creative control, so it would not be inaccurate to read *The Return of the Magus* as John Fowles's last postmodernist work. Perhaps, given his unhappiness with the 1968 screen adaptation of *The Magus*, one might even consider *The Return of the Magus* to be Fowles's revision of that film, equivalent to his 1977 revision of the novel.[16]

Considering that *The Return of the Magus* was made when Fowles was seventy-two, it shouldn't be surprising that nostalgia is a primary emotional note of the film. But nostalgia and issues of time and loss are central to the novel *The Magus* itself, with its elaborate temporal mind games that the mysterious Greek millionaire Conchis plays with Fowles's alter ego, Nicholas. Issues of time and loss also play out in Fowles's other literary works, including *The French Lieutenant's Woman*. Linda Hutcheon, in *A Poetics of Postmodernism*, calls works like Fowles's 1969 *The French Lieutenant's Woman* "historiographic metafiction," meaning by this term those novels that are both "intensely self-reflexive and yet paradoxically also lay claim to historical events and personages."[17] *The Return of the Magus* seems to fit this description, given how it touches briefly on the Greek Revolution, Greek culture, and Greek historical figures, but also, and perhaps primarily, because it offers the viewer a very personal, self-reflexive look at Greece filtered through the eyes, memories, experiences, fiction, and thoughts of John Fowles.

In *The Return of the Magus* Fowles comments directly on history as opposed to fiction as a form, arguing that novelists are liars: "[W]e have to invent. Therefore we should not obey real history." Throughout the documentary, Fowles demonstrates interest in Greek history but, as a novelist, more interest in his own memories, his own experience of Greece, his own personal, subjective history. For example, in the section of the documentary subtitled "Lessons in History," we are introduced to black and white photos of a Greek villa interspersed with live shots of the Villa Jasemina, but disorientingly with no explanation of the origin or meaning of the photos. A man who appears to be a young Fowles is shown in some of the photos with a young woman, also unidentified. Is this Fowles's future wife, Elizabeth? Who is who in these shots? It is difficult to tell, as the filmmakers have chosen not to make things perfectly clear for the viewer. We are eventually shown the elderly Fowles sitting at a window, looking out. He explains that his current sitting position was a favorite sitting position of Eleftherios Venizelos, who we are told was one of the greatest statesmen of Greece. But then Fowles states, "I've always loved this place." With such shifts the documentary sometimes confuses viewers, perhaps purposefully, and mixes the historical and the personal in order to make the historical reflect on and reveal Fowles, himself.

Historiographic metafictional texts such as *The Return of the Magus* move back and forth between the two orders of language or narrative use that the French linguist Émile Benveniste discusses in his *Problems in General Linguistics*: *histoire*, or historical utterances which attempt to describe past events without any reference to the speaker; and *discours*, which assumes "a speaker and a hearer, and in the speaker, the intention of influencing the hearer in some way," as well as being the very sort of language through which a speaker "constitutes himself as a *subject*."[18] In *discours*, "the subject makes use of the act of speech and discourse in order to 'represent himself' to himself as he wishes to see himself, and as he calls upon the 'other' to observe him."[19] Paul Cobley explains *discours* as corresponding "to the kind of 'meta' level where the narrator of a novel such as *The French Lieutenant's Woman* enters the action and relates his knowledge of a ceramic pot; *histoire* consists of presenting the laying out of objects on a table by a character, for example, without mentioning that one is narrating, and possibly creating a situation whereby 'the events seem to narrate themselves.'"[20]

Whereas *The Magus* makes more use of *histoire* narrative than *discours* narrative, *The French Lieutenant's Woman* moves back and forth between *histoire* and *discours*, creating a postmodern work that seems to fit Hutcheon's genre of historiographic metafiction, *The Return of the Magus* may be the most postmodern of all, combining and blurring as it does the historical and the self-reflexive. In its emphasis on *histoire*, it seems that *The French Lieutenant's Woman* served as a pre-text for *The Return of the Magus* as much as did *The Magus*, at least when it comes to the narrative and thematic structure of the works. *The Return of the Magus* shares *The French Lieutenant's Woman*'s metatextual tendencies, foregrounding the author or narrator's *discours* role, with the elderly Fowles's perspective, opinions, memories, and emotions central to the documentary.

The Return of the Magus intermittently evokes that famous moment in Chapter Thirteen of *The French Lieutenant's Woman* when the author-narrator comes out of hiding from behind his curtain of fabricated generic realism, intruding on and commenting on the action, thereby transforming the mimetic into the overtly metatextual. The author-narrator states: "I do not know. This story that I am telling is all imagination. These characters I create never existed outside my mind. If I have pretended until now to know my characters' minds and innermost thoughts, it is because I am writing in (just as I have assumed some of the vocabulary and 'voice' of) a convention universally accepted at the time of my story: that the novelist stands next to God."[21] When Fowles's narrator, or perhaps it is Fowles himself, speaks directly about his writing process and what it means to be an author, he is revealing what a realist author ordinarily attempts to suppress in the hope that his or her reader will ignore it, namely the knowledge that there is a linguistic "I," an author or narrator speaking to you, the reader. Fowles unsuppresses the very textuality and constructedness of the text, and the moment is a postmodern electric shock for the unprepared reader.

Similarly shocking metatextual moments abound in *The Return of the Magus*, with one of the most striking being the moment when the elderly Fowles recreates the scene where Nicholas is stranded on Monemvasia by Conchis, with a revolver as temptation to suicide. This recreated scene from the novel begins with shots of scenery and the voice of Mark Healy reading from the novel. The images seem to indicate a first-person perspective, one that might correlate to the first-person narration of the novel by Fowles' alter-ego, Nicholas. Then, we are shown a man's hands taking a revolver out of a black box, and the man is revealed to be the elderly Fowles, acting out what the young voice is reading from *The Magus*. At this point, the narrative point-of-view is bifurcated and confused, for the camera has turned Fowles into a third-person protagonist, but the voice over by Mark Healy remains first-person. We can figure out from the context that the elderly Fowles is reenacting a scene written by the young Fowles, but the age difference between the sight of the elderly Fowles and the sound of the young voice-over artist is disconcerting. The scene then cuts to a shot of Fowles speaking directly into the camera with the Mediterranean behind him: "I was always clear with one thing in *The Magus*. And that was that there is ... no God as people would like to imagine. And the last thing that the psychologist Conchis who was manipulating me proposed was to leave me at this marvelous site, which I first saw in 1952, and leave me a gun." This dialogue throws us into a postmodern vertigo of confused and blurring subjectivities. We are witnessing a fascinating confusion and blending of Fowles and his character that makes us, too, think about mortality and the imminence of death, of fiction and memory. The authorial "I" at the beginning of the direct-to-camera speech ("I was always clear with one thing in *The Magus*") transforms into Fowles's character within a few lines ("Conchis who was manipulating me"). If one were to ask what is going on in this scene, and who is speaking, it would not be easy to answer. Is Fowles speaking here as Nicholas? If so, why does his statement begin with "I was always clear with one thing in *The Magus*"? Is Fowles purposefully blurring the lines between fiction and autobiography? Or is he, perhaps, admitting that his character is just a double for himself? Whatever our interpretation, the very next scene complicates our understanding further, for after the screen goes blank, out of the blackness appears a Greek actor, Costas Cazakos, reading from a Greek translation of *The Magus*, with Fowles now seated in an audience, listening to this actor reading lines from his novel. We now have a multiplicity of Fowleses, with the growing number of actors and reenactors complicating any hope of a fixing a Fowles subject.

We next see and hear Fowles speaking to a Greek audience at a reading, stating: "I'm here in Greece to make a television program in which I shall declare my very deep love for this country." This statement is a powerful moment of postmodern meta-commentary, for Fowles is describing and predicting the very moment we are watching but, interestingly, is doing so before that moment has been made into a watchable film. Fowles and his fellow filmmakers thus include discussion of the process of creation inside the product of creation, again in a manner similar to the author-narrator in *The French Lieutenant's Woman* commenting on his creation of the very characters we have just been reading about. In this way, *The Return of the Magus* deconstructs the pretense that is foundational for most documentaries and most fiction—the pretense of the real, the pretense of narrative necessity, the pretense that the documentary we are watching or the novel we are reading is an inevitable past or "reality," rather than what it actually is, namely, one of many possible authorial or directorial works that might well have come out very differently. Just a few moments later in the documentary, Fowles breaks the magician's code and, paradoxically, ironically explains one of his realist author tricks: "All of us who are writers, novelists, poets, must try and find some way to represent the past as if it is the present." What Fowles is doing here by reminding the reader that he is an author and this is his bag of tricks is reminiscent of a postmodern illusionist, of a charlatan or a magus so sure of his skills that he describes the way his trick works as he performs it anyway. I believe that the impact of Fowles drawing the audience's attention to the textuality and constructedness of his text in *The Return of the Magus* is nothing like Brecht's alienation effect; instead, Fowles's metatextuality is postmodernist in the sense described by John Barth: "Postmodernism consists somehow of being able to tie your necktie in a perfect full-Windsor knot while telling somebody what the stages are in tying a necktie—and at the same time discoursing on the history of men's neckwear from the court of Louis XIV to the present and still not screwing up the knot."[22]

What Fowles achieves in *The Return of the Magus* is similar to, but an inversion or a complication of what Fowles or Fowles's narrator describes in chapter thirteen of *The French Lieutenant's Woman*, namely, a blurring of the biographical and the fictional, of the present and the past: "So perhaps I am writing a transposed autobiography; perhaps I now live in one of the houses I have brought into the fiction; perhaps Charles is myself disguised. Perhaps it is only a game ... or perhaps I am trying to pass off a concealed book of essays on you."[23] The Fowles of *The French Lieutenant's Woman* could very well be the Fowles of *The Return of the Magus*, except that in the documentary, rather than the fictional character being a mask for the real Fowles, it seems that the real Fowles becomes the character so that the character can then become the "real" Fowles. It does indeed feel to the viewer of *The Return of the Magus* that he is playing a complex John Fowles in Wonderland game, one where the rules are uncertain and the players keep switching roles, but one where Greece is a space of wonder.

Parallels among *The Return of the Magus, The French Lieutenant's Woman*, and *The Magus* are fascinating here. In *The French Lieutenant's Woman*, Fowles plays games with his readers, manipulating, confusing, and teasing them. In *The Magus*, it is Conchis who plays elaborate mind games with Fowles's alter-ego, Nicholas.[24] Conchis creates a "meta-theatre" for Nicholas, pointing out, "We are all actors here, my friend. None of us is what we really are. We all lie some of the time, and some of us all the time."[25] And in *The Return of the Magus*, it seems that it is Fowles and his fellow filmmakers who are playing mind games with us, the viewers. While "the metatheater of Conchis" in *The Magus* may very well be "analogous to the metafiction that Fowles is writing," I would argue that that is even more the case in *The Return of the Magus*.[26] So, the documentary recapitulates and then transforms the book(s) without making it clear that it is doing just that, thus blurring the distance between Fowles's life and his novel while repeating elements from both. We can see this blurring when we attempt to pin down just what exactly is being depicted in *The Return of the Magus*. Should the documentary be read as a look back at *The Magus*? As a play with or response to other Fowles works, including *The French Lieutenant's Woman*? As a look at the spaces, real-life events, and memories that influenced the writing of *The Magus*? As a contemplation of Fowles's 30–40 years of subsequent life, thoughts, and experiences since writing *The Magus*? As a temporally confusing adaptation/reenactment of *The Magus*? Or as some complex combination of all of these?

Linda Hutcheon explains that historiographic metafiction is postmodern in its challenge to generic conventions—challenging either by smashing heterogeneous genres together or by working "within conventions in order to subvert them."[27] *The Return of the Magus* does both—it brings together heterogeneous documentary genres, as I've previously explained, and it also subverts and confuses the conventions of documentary, particularly through the confusions that are created with voice-over narration coming from unidentified sources, a practice which purposefully confuses the exact referent and intent of many of the scenes being depicted. James Aubrey has commented on just this point about the genre complexity or confusion in *The Return of the Magus*: "Such reenacted scenes might be categorized as motion-picture illustrations of the novel, or they might be considered some kind of biographical visualizations of Fowles's creative process, or they might even be regarded as a new, extremely faithful adaptation of the novel."[28] I would add to Aubrey's thoughtful list some other possible interpretations, including that these reenactment scenes can be read as filmic palimpsests, with the elderly Fowles writing, through these performative acts, over his writing over his own memories, embodying them, fictionalizing them, and commenting on them. Thus Fowles has created a complex new postmodern, palimpsestous memory artifact that combines his "real" past experiences in Greece, the fictional past of his novel, and his biographically present moment of nostalgia, mourning, and memory. Linda Hutcheon contends that "adaptation is a kind of extended palimpsest."[29] I would argue that *The Return of the Magus* offers the ideal example to demonstrate the palimpsestuous nature of adaptation. The fact that the scenes where the elderly Fowles reenacts scenes from his novel can be interpreted in such divergent ways is just one more indication of the wonderful postmodernism of *The Return of the Magus*, a film that offers historical instruction in brief snatches only to undermine or complicate them, to, as Hutcheon explains of the form, rethink history "as a human construct."[30]

While I find Linda Hutcheon's generic term *historiographic metafiction* to be a useful one for describing what is taking place in *The Return of the Magus*, I cannot agree entirely with her argument that the focus on the past that is central to historiographic metafiction is always "as far from 'nostalgia' as anyone could wish." Given Fowles's often melancholy and nostalgic documentary, I would disagree with Hutcheon's early opinion that metafictional, postmodern texts are entirely ironic, and thus in no way connote an "evasion of the present, [or] idealization of a (fantasy) past, or a recovery of that past as edenic."[31] Hutcheon herself seems to have rethought her initial belief that postmodernism and nostalgia cannot mix, and that nostalgia and irony are entirely oppositional.[32]

The documentary appears to conclude with a rejection of nostalgia in the form of a reading of Fowles's poem "Tora," a celebration of the now, the eternal present, the word-scroll that ends the film and explains the significance of this poem complicates Fowles's stated embrace of the present, as does the focus on the past through so much of the film. Over a montage of images of Fowles, ants, Greece, and a portrait of Fowles being painted (and what is a painting of a writer but a grasping after the eternal in a mortal, fleeting world?) the following note by Fowles appears:

> I wrote this poem on Easter Sunday on the terrace at Bourani beside a nest of black runner ants. TORA is the modern Greek word for "now" and the presence of what I wished to celebrate: The stupendous nowness of existence—its formidable recurringness. As always, this seemed intensely real at Bourani. Spetses, Spring 1998, John Fowles.

The complex ironies concerning time and mortality in the passage are worth tracing. First, Fowles's writing of the importance of the now, of the present, is juxtaposed with the fact that he wrote this poem on Easter Sunday. This irony would not be lost on Fowles, an avowed atheist who denies the existence of God in the documentary, only to join in a Greek Orthodox Holy Week religious procession, where he lights a candle, a symbol of memory and eternity. Ants may live in an eternal now, but they are also often used as visual symbols of decay and death. But people long for immortality, and cannot fathom the death of loved ones or themselves. Thus people create holidays such as Easter, a celebration of resurrection and immortality. An atheist writer and poet can desire immortality, even as he has rationally concluded that no such thing exists, at least not in the Christian sense, as I believe is indicated by Fowles's writing of a poem, his sitting for a portrait, his signing of a note to end a documentary, and his creation of a heterocosmic world including the naming or renaming of its elements—Spetses renamed Phraxos, the Anargyrios and Korgialenios School of Spetses remade into the Lord Byron School, and the Villa Jasemina transformed into the Villa Bourani. The desire for that which one believes one cannot have, so central to mourning, nostalgia, and heterocosmic fiction writing, is a very real, if at times ironic or dehiscent desire, and one central to *The Return of the Magus*.

I read the Fowles documentary text as fundamentally split—simultaneously ironic toward his past life and *The Magus*, its Ur-texts, and at the same time nostalgic toward an idealized past that can never be reclaimed. But *The Return of the Magus* is all about repetition, about Fowles's desire to return to his own past, to do it again. Sigmund Freud, in *Beyond the*

Pleasure Principle, discusses the aesthetic pleasure of childhood play, arguing that the pleasure is linked to the repetition of the play, and is gained through the child's imaginative mastery of situations not mastered in reality.[33] Freud thus implies that play serves a function similar to that of a child's dream or a writer's novel—it fulfills desires that are not attainable in real life, but only in the heterocosm created by the dreamer or writer. Freud views repetition as acceptable in a child but a potential sign of neurotic compulsion in an adult: "[T]here really does exist in the mind a compulsion to repeat which overrides the pleasure principle."[34] It thus seems that Freud might view as neurotics those adults who, like myself, gain pleasure in returning to holy childhood or adolescent sites, or in revisiting our past creative works and attempting to revise them. It is therefore interesting that in the foreword to his revised version of *The Magus*, Fowles wrote: "[*The Magus*] must always substantially remain a novel of adolescence written by a retarded adolescent. My only plea is that all artists have to range the full extent of their own lives freely. The rest of the world can censor and bury their private past. We cannot, and so we have to remain partly green till the day we die." Fowles goes on to explain that the world may complain about the fact, but that for most writers "the much younger self still rules the supposedly 'mature' and middle-aged artist."[35] Nostalgia thus isn't just a weakness or escape for Fowles, it is an artistic necessity. This necessity is played out to full effect in *The Return of the Magus*, which offers Fowles an opportunity to return to, comment on, gaze at, adapt, reenact, and recapitulate both his own past and that of his fictional creation.

Freud's binary between a healthy childhood desire for repetition and an unhealthy adult compulsion to wallow in a repetition of childhood fantasies and memories is, I believe, an artificial binary. The adult's pleasure in nostalgia seems a variation of the child's, for while children generally have a greater desire for repetition than adults, even adults desire that form of repetition that we would normally call nostalgia. I agree with Svetlana Boym's definition of nostalgia as the "longing for a home that no longer exists or has never existed," and her claim that such nostalgia is a "sentiment of loss and displacement, but it is also a romance with one's own fantasy."[36] Fowles, in the recreations of scenes from *The Magus* in *The Return of the Magus*, got to participate in a filmic romance with his own heterocosmic fantasy, as Kirki Kefalea's email comment indicates: "We had to remake many times the scenes with John, especially in Mon-

emvasia, but it was very amusing! He also enjoyed all this project, especially the scenes where John was the actor-protagonist of his own novel!"[37]
Boym explains that "[a] cinematic image of nostalgia is a double exposure,
or superimposition of two images—of home and abroad, past and present,
dream and everyday life. The moment we try to force it into a single image,
it breaks the frame or burns the surface."[38] Nostalgia, Boym states, is not
just a longing for a place, but for a time: "At first glance, nostalgia is a longing for a place, but actually it is a yearning for a different time—the time
of our childhood, the slower rhythms of our dreams. In a broader sense,
nostalgia is a rebellion against the modern idea of time, the time of history and progress. The nostalgic desires to obliterate history and turn it
into private or collective mythology, to revisit time like space, refusing
to surrender to the irreversibility of time that plagues the human condition."[39] Boym's description fits Fowles's attitude, except for his complex
celebration of newness in his poem "Tora"—but even that celebration of
the now seems more a rejection of capitalist, progressive, Western time
for an embrace of a Homeric or mythic sense of time—a sense of time
where the now remains eternal, immortal. It is interesting to note that
with *The Return of the Magus*, the loop of temporal and fictional play links
the elderly to the young Fowles, the fictional Nicholas to the real John. In
taking what was a real youthful experience, which became a piece of fiction, and re-embodying that fictional alternative reality with the real, now
elderly John Fowles, he brings the loop to its end, which is its mythic
beginning.

The pleasure of making *The Return of the Magus* must for Fowles
have been connected to the aesthetics of "nostalgia" and, thus, fundamentally divided against itself. The nostalgic past is half-remembered and
half-imagined, and the desire to enter that youthful space as an elderly
man threatens to destroy the myths and illusions of youth. The pleasure
of the nostalgic metatext is the pleasure of negotiating that threat by walking a narrow tightrope, bringing together one's longing for a fantasy past
that never was and thus cannot be reclaimed, and one's re-creating the
remembered image or experience.

The Return of the Magus is just such a tightrope. In its attempt to unify
a jumble of diverse aesthetic, thematic, and generic elements, in its complex metatextuality, its overt intertextuality, and in its attempt to create
an emotional, nostalgic, postmodern heterocosm, a world *"as real as, but
other than the world that is,"* the film surprises the viewer with a beautiful,

thought-provoking, and frustrating cinematic tapestry—a tapestry that offers a glimpse of the late creative work of John Fowles.

Notes

1. *The Return of the Magus*, dir. Mark Pearce, screenplay Kirki Kefalea, Inkas Film and T.V. Productions, 1999–2000.

2. James Aubrey, *John Fowles* (Westport, CT: Greenwood Press, 1991), pp. 16–19.

3. John Fowles, revised foreword to *The Magus: A Revised Version*, Modern Library (New York: Random House, 1998), p. xi.

4. Eileen Warburton, *John Fowles* (New York: Viking Penguin, 2004), pp. 427, 442.

5. James R. Baker, "John Fowles: The Art of Fiction CIX," *The Paris Review* 111 (Summer 1989), p. 196.

6. John Fowles, Foreword to *The Magus* (Boston: Little, Brown, 1977), p. 5.

7. *Ibid.*, p. 5.

8. *Ibid.*, p. 6.

9. *Ibid.*, p. 9.

10. *Return of the Magus*.

11. Fowles, Foreword to *The Magus*, p. 8.

12. *Ibid.*, p. 12.

13. Tzvetan Todorov, *The Fantastic*, trans. Richard Howard (Ithaca: Cornell University Press, 1975), p. 25.

14. Fowles, revised Foreword to *The Magus*, p. xi.

15. Kirki Kefalea, correspondence with James Aubrey, 30 Nov. 2014.

16. *The Magus*, directed by Guy Green (Twentieth Century–Fox, 1968).

17. Linda Hutcheon, *Poetics of Postmodernism* (New York: Routledge, 1998), p. 5.

18. Émile Benveniste, *Problems in General Linguistics*, trans. Mary Elizabeth Meek (Coral Gables: University of Miami Press, 1971), p. 67.

19. Benveniste, *Problems in General Linguistics*, 67.

20. Paul Cobley, *Narrative*, 2d ed. (New York: Routledge, 2014), p. 158; embedded quotation from Benveniste, *Problems in General* Linguistics, p. 208.

21. John Fowles, *The French Lieutenant's Woman* (Boston: Little, Brown, 1969), p. 95. The author declares himself to be the narrator in Chapter 61, when he enters the story as a Victorian character and re-starts the plot by re-setting his watch, pp. 462–63.

22. Quoted in Carolyn Alessio, "Postmodernism as Predigital? Novelist John Barth Embraces the Net," *Chicago Tribune* 27 October 2000, n.p.; Fowles, *The French Lieutenant's Woman*, p. 57.

23. Fowles, *The French Lieutenant's Woman*, p. 95.

24. Fowles, Foreword to *The Magus*, p. 413.

25. *Ibid.*, p. 411.

26. Aubrey, *John Fowles*, p. 99.

27. Hutcheon, *Poetics of Postmodernism* (New York: Routledge, 1988), p. 5.

28. James Aubrey, correspondence with Craig Svonkin, 2 Dec. 2014.

29. Linda Hutcheon, *A Theory of Adaptation* (New York: Routledge, 2006), p. 33.

30. Hutcheon, *Poetics*, p. 16.

31. *Ibid.*, p. 39.

32. Linda Hutcheon, "Irony, Nostalgia, and the Postmodern," *Methods for the Study of Literature as Cultural Memory*, ed. Raymond Vervliet and Annemarie Estor (Atlanta: Rodopi, 2000), pp. 189–207.

33. Sigmund Freud, *The Freud Reader*, ed. Peter Gay (New York: W.W. Norton, 1989), p. 601.

34. *Ibid.*, p. 605.

35. Fowles, Foreword to *The Magus*, p. 10.

36. Svetlana Boym, *The Future of Nostalgia* (New York: Basic Books, 2001), p. xiii.

37. Kefalea, n.p.

38. Boym, *The Future of Nostalgia*, pp. xiii–xiv.

39. *Ibid.*, p. xv.

Works Cited

Alain-Fournier. *The Lost Domain [Le Grand Meulnes]*. Translated by Frank Davison. Afterword by John Fowles. New York: Oxford University Press, 1986. Print.
_____. *The Wanderer, or The End of Youth [Le Grand Meulnes]*. Translated by Lowell Bair. Afterword (revised) by John Fowles. New York: New American Library, 1971. Print.
Alessio, Carolyn. "Postmodernism as Predigital? Novelist John Barth Embraces the Net." *Chicago Tribune* 27 October 2000: n.p. Print.
Allen, Brenda. "*The French Lieutenant's Woman* on Film." In *John Fowles*. New Casebooks. Ed. James Acheson. New York: Palgrave Macmillan, 2013. 118–32. Print.
Allen, Woody. Letter to James Aubrey, 10 June 1988. Typescript.
Andrew, Dudley. "Adaptation." *Concepts in Film Theory*. New York: Oxford University Press, 1984. 96–106. Print.
Arnold, Eve. *Film Journal*. London: Bloomsbury, 2002. Print and photography.
Aubrey, James [R.]. Correspondence with Craig Svonkin, 2 Dec. 2014. Manuscript.
_____. Correspondence with Kirki Kefalea, 24 Nov. 2014. Email.
_____. Introduction. *John Fowles and Nature: Fourteen Perspectives on Landscape*. Cranbury, NJ: Associated University Presses, 1999. Print and photography.
_____. "John Fowles and Creative Non-fiction." In *John Fowles*. New Casebooks. Ed. James Acheson. London: Palgrave MacMillan, 2013. Print.
_____. *John Fowles: A Reference Companion*. Westport, CT: Greenwood Press, 1991. Print and photography.
_____. "The Pre-Raphaelite 'pack of satyrs' in John Fowles's *The French Lieutenant's Woman*." *Nineteenth Century Prose* 18.1 (Winter 1990/91): 32–36. Print.
_____. "Toward 'parity of existence': Blending Cultures in (and Out of) John Fowles's *The French Lieutenant's Woman*." *Anglistik* 13.1 (2002): 77–93. Print.
_____. "'Uncrucifying the self': John Fowles and the Motif of the Hanged Man." *Journal of Evolutionary Psychology* 13.3/4 (1992): 296–307 and 14.1/2 (1993): 109–18. Print.
Baker, James R. "John Fowles: The Art of Fiction CIX." *The Paris Review* 111 (Summer 1989): 43–63. Reprinted in Vipond, *Conversations*, 182–97. Print.
Barnum, Carol. "An Interview with John Fowles." *Conversations with John Fowles*. Literary Conversations Series. Ed. Dianne L. Vipond. Jackson: University Press of Mississippi, 1999. 102–18. Print.
Barthes, Roland. *Camera Lucida: Reflections on Photography*. New York: Hill and Wang, 1980. Print.
_____. "The Death of the Author." *Image-Music-Text*. Translated by Stephen Heath. 1977; reprinted New York: Hill and Wang, 1978. 142–48. Print.
Benveniste, Émile. *Problems in General Linguistics*. Translated by Mary Elizabeth Meek. Coral Gables: University of Miami Press, 1971. Print.
Bergen, Candice. *Knock Wood*. New York: Simon & Schuster, 1984. Print.
Berman, Marshall. *All That Is Solid Melts into Air: The Experience of Modernity*. London: Penguin, 1988. Print.

Works Cited

Bettelheim, Bruno. *The Uses of Enchantment: The Meaning and Importance of Fairy Tales.* New York: Alfred Knopf, 1976. Print.

"The Blue Beard." *The Classic Fairy Tales.* Ed. Iona and Peter Opie. London: Oxford University Press, 1974. Print.

Boym, Svetlana. *The Future of Nostalgia.* New York: Basic Books, 2001. Print.

Bradbury, Malcolm. *The After Dinner Game,* 2d ed. London: Arena, 1989.

_____. Screenplay for *The Enigma.* John Fowles Collection, Harry Ransom Center for the Humanities, Austin, TX. Series 1, Box 13, Folder 4. Script.

Brideshead Revisited. Directed by Charles Sturridge and Michael Lindsay-Hogg. Screenwriting by John Mortimer, Evelyn Waugh, and others. Performances by Jeremy Irons and Anthony Andrews. Granada Television, 1981. Video.

Brooker, Peter. "Postmodern Adaptation: Pastiche, Intertextuality and Re-functioning." *The Cambridge Companion to Literature on Screen.* Cambridge Companions Series. Edited by Deborah Cartmell and Imelda Whelehan. Cambridge: Cambridge University Press, 2007. 107–20. Print.

Brown, Craig. "Evading Authority. Review of John Fowles's 'The Enigma' BBC2." *Times Literary Supplement* 15 February 1980: n.p. Print.

Buchberger, Michelle. Correspondence with David Tringham, Mar. 2013. Email.

Caine, Michael. *What's It All About?* Turtle Bay Books. New York: Random House, 1992. Print.

Cardwell, Sarah. "Literature on the Small Screen: Television Adaptations." *The Cambridge Companion to Literature on Screen.* Cambridge Companions Series. Edited by Deborah Cartmell and Imelda Whelehan. Cambridge: Cambridge University Press, 2007. 181–95. Print.

Carroll, Lewis. Photograph of the Dante Gabriel Rossetti family. 1863. Print.

Cassirer, Ernst. *Mythical Thought.* Volume 2 of *The Philosophy of Symbolic Forms.* New Haven: Yale University Press, 1971. Print.

Clueless. Directed and written by Amy Heckerling. Performances by Alicia Silverstone and Paul Rudd. Paramount, 1995. Film.

Cobley, Paul. *Narrative,* 2d ed. New York: Routledge, 2014. Print.

The Collector. Directed by William Wyler. Performances by Terence Stamp and Samantha Eggar. Columbia Pictures, 1965. Film.

Cooke, Simon. "Frederick Sandys and Periodical Illustration." *The Victorian Web: Literature, History and Culture in the Age of Victoria.* Victorianweb.org 15 July 2013. Web. 16 Aug. 2014.

Daly, Mary. *Gyn/Ecology: The Metaethics of Radical Feminism.* Boston: Beacon Press, 1978. Print.

Deleuze, Gilles, and Félix Guattari. *A Thousand Plateaus: Capitalism and Schizophrenia.* Translated by Brian Massumi. Minneapolis: University of Minnesota Press, 1987. Print.

Dunn, Henry Treffry. *Rossetti Reading Proofs of Ballads and Sonnets* [with Theodore Watts-Duncan] *at 16 Cheyne Walk.* 1882. National Portrait Gallery. Painting.

The Ebony Tower. Directed by Robert Knights. Screenplay by John Mortimer. Performances by Laurence Olivier, Greta Scacchi, Richard Rees, Toyah Willcox. Granada Television, 1984. Video.

Eliot, T.S. *Four Quartets.* In *The Collected Poems and Plays of T.S. Eliot 1909–1950.* New York: Harcourt Brace, 1971. 115–45. Print.

The Enigma. Directed by Robert Knights. Screenplay by Malcolm Bradbury. *Playhouse,* February 1980. T3 Media, 1980. Video.

Fortscue-Brickdale, Eleanor. *The Pale Complexion of True Love.* 1898. Athenaeum. Image.

Fowles, Elizabeth. Correspondence with Denys and Monica Sharrocks. The John Fowles Collection. Harry Ransom Center for the Humanities, Austin, TX. Print.

Fowles, John. Afterword. *The Wanderer or The End of Youth [Le Grand Meulnes],* by

Alain- Fournier. Translated by Frank Davison. New York: New American Library, 1971. 208–23. Print.

_____. *The Aristos: A Self-portrait in Ideas*. Boston: Little, Brown, 1964. Print.

_____. *The Aristos: A Self-Portrait in Ideas*, rev. ed. Boston: Little, Brown, 1970. Print.

_____. *The Black Thumb*. Unpublished screenplay in the John Fowles Collection, Harry Ransom Center for the Humanities, Austin, TX. Series 1, Box 1, Folders 13–14. Typescript.

_____. *The Collector*. Boston: Little, Brown, 1963. Print.

_____. *Daniel Martin*. Boston: Little, Brown, 1977. Print.

_____. Diaries. The John Fowles Collection, Harry Ransom Center for the Humanities, Austin, TX. 9 vols. Manuscript.

_____. *The Ebony Tower*. Boston: Little, Brown, 1974. Print.

_____. "The Ebony Tower." In *The Ebony Tower*. Boston: Little, Brown, 1974. 1–114. Print.

_____. "The Enigma." In *The Ebony Tower*. Boston: Little, Brown, 1974. 189–247. Print.

_____. "Essay by John Fowles." In *Land*, by Fay Godwin. Boston: Little, Brown, 1985. ix–xx. Print.

_____. "The Filming of *The French Lieutenant's Woman*." Originally the untitled Foreword to *The French Lieutenant's Woman: A Screenplay*, by Harold Pinter. Reprinted with this title in *Wormholes: Essays and Occasional Writings*. Edited by Jan Relf. New York: Henry Holt, 1998. 34–42. Print.

_____. *The Final Chapter*. Unpublished short story in the John Fowles Collection, Harry Ransom Center for the Humanities, Austin, TX. Series 1, Box 19, Folder 14. Typescript.

_____. Foreword. *The Magus: A Revised Version*. Boston, Little, Brown, 1977. 5–10. Print.

_____. Foreword. Screenplay for *The French Lieutenant's Woman*, by Harold Pinter. Boston: Little, Brown, 1981. vii–xvi. Reprinted in *Wormholes*. Print.

_____. Foreword. *The Undercliff: A Naturalist's Sketchbook of the Devon to Dorset Coast*, by Elaine Franks. Boston: Little, Brown, 1989. 7–9. Print.

_____. *The French Lieutenant's Woman*. Boston: Little Brown, 1969. Print.

_____. *The God Game (The Magus)*. Screenplay dated 8 Aug. 1967 in the John Fowles Collection, Harry Ransom Center for the Humanities, Austin, TX. Typescript.

_____. "Hardy and the Hag." In *Thomas Hardy After Fifty Years*. Edited by Lance St. John Butler. London: Macmillan, 1977. Print.

_____. "I Write Therefore I Am." *Evergreen Review* (1964): 16–17, 89–91. Print.

_____. Introduction. *The Magus [A Revised Version]*. Modern Library. New York: Random House, 1998. ix–xi. Print.

_____. *The Journals: Volume One [1949–1965]*. Edited by Charles Drazin. London: Jonathan Cape, 2003. Print.

_____. *The Journals: Volume Two [1966–1990]*. Edited by Charles Drazin. London: Jonathan Cape, 2006. Print.

_____. *A Maggot*. New York: Little, Brown, 1985. Print.

_____. *The Magus*. Boston: Little, Brown, 1965. Print.

_____. *The Magus: The God Game*. Screenplay in the John Fowles Collection. Harry Ransom Center for the Humanities, Austin, TX. Typescript.

_____. *The Magus: A Revised Version*. Boston: Little, Brown, 1977. Print.

_____. *Mantissa*. Boston: Little, Brown, 1982. Print.

_____. "Notes on an Unfinished Novel." Reprinted in *Wormholes: Essays and Occasional Writings*. Edited by Jan Relf. New York: Henry Holt, 1998. 13–26. Print.

_____. "Notes on Writing a Novel." *Harper's* July 1968: 88–97. Revised 1969 and reprinted as "Notes on an Unfinished Novel" in *Wormholes: Essays and Occasional Writings*. Edited by Jan Relf. New York: Henry Holt, 1998. 13–26. Print.

_____. "On Being English, but Not British." *Texas Quarterly* 7.3 (1964): 154–62; reprinted in *Wormholes*, pp. 79–88. Print.

_____. "A Personal Note." In *The Ebony Tower*, pp. 117–22. Print.

Works Cited

_____. *Wormholes.* Edited by Jan Relf. New York: Henry Holt, 1998. Print.

Fowles, John, and Frank Horvat. *The Tree*. London: Aurum Press, 1979; reprinted New York: Ecco Press, 1983. Print and photography.

The French Lieutenant's Woman. Directed by Karel Reisz. Written by Harold Pinter. Performances by Jeremy Irons and Meryl Streep. Juniper Films. United Artists, 1981. Print.

Freud, Sigmund. *The Freud Reader*. Edited by Peter Gay. New York: W.W. Norton, 1989.

_____. *The Uncanny*. London: Penguin, 2003. Print.

The Game. Directed by David Fincher. Screenplay by John Brancato and Michael Ferris. Performances by Michael Douglas, Sean Penn, and Deborah Kara Unger. Polygram Filmed Entertainment, 1997. Film.

Graham, Tony, Hilary Arnold, Sappho Durrell, and John Thackera. "John Fowles: An Exclusive Interview." *Socialist Challenge* 15–31 December 1977: 17. Reprinted Vipond, *Conversations*, pp. 59–64. Print.

The Great Gatsby. Directed by Jack Clayton. Performances by Robert Redford and Mia Farrow. Paramount, 1974.

The Great Gatsby. Directed by Baz Luhrmann. Performances by Leonardo DiCaprio and Carey Mulligan. Warner Bros., 2013.

Hall, William. *Sir Michael Caine: The Biography*. London: John Blake, 2006. Print.

Herman, Ian. *A Talent for Trouble: The Life of Hollywood's Most Acclaimed Director, William Wyler*. New York: G.P. Putnam, 1995. Print.

Hutcheon, Linda. "Irony, Nostalgia, and the Postmodern." *Methods for the Study of Literature as Cultural Memory*. Edited by Raymond Vervliet and Annemarie Estor. Atlanta: Rodopi, 2000. 189–207. Print.

_____. *The Poetics of Postmodernism: History, Theory, Fiction*. New York: Routledge, 1988.

_____. *A Theory of Adaptation*. New York: Routledge, 2006. Print.

"John Fowles." *Counterpoint*. Edited by Roy Newquist. Chicago: Rand, McNally, 1964. 219. Print.

"John Fowles: The Literary Magus." Directed by John Cork, produced by Corkland as an extra feature to accompany *The Magus* on DVD, distributed by Twentieth Century–Fox Home Entertainment in 2006. This 23-minute documentary includes interviews with Eileen Warburton ("The Biographer"), Bob Goosman ("The Admirer"), Dianne Vipond ("The Professor"), Ray Roberts ("The Editor"), David Tringham ("The Collaborator"), and Anna Christy, daughter of Elizabeth Fowles by a previous marriage. Video.

Johnson, Carroll B. "Phantom Pre-texts and Fictional Authors: Sidi Hamid Benengeli, *Don Quijote* and the Metafictional Conventions of Chivalric Romances." *Cervantes: Bulletin of the Cervantes Society of America* 27.1 (2007): 179–99. Print.

Jung, C.G. *Symbols of Transformation: An Analysis of the Prelude to a Case of Schizophrenia*. Translated by R.F.C. Hull. Bollingen Series 20. Volume 5 in *The Collected Works of C.G. Jung*. New York: Pantheon, 1956.

Kefalea, Kirki. Correspondence with James Aubrey, 30 Nov. 2014. Email.

The Last Chapter. Directed by David Tringham. Screenplay by David Tringham. Performances by Denholm Elliott and Susan Penhaligon. Cassius Films. Fox-Rank, 1972; re-released by the British Film Institute, 2010, in a BFI Flipside, Dual Format Edition as a DVD extra accompanying *Private Road*. Film.

Madsen, Axel. *William Wyler: The Authorized Biography*. New York: Thomas Cromwell, 1973. Print.

The Magus. Directed by Guy Green. Written by John Fowles. Performances by Michael Caine, Candice Bergen, Anna Karina, and Anthony Quinn. Blazer Films. Twentieth Century–Fox, 1968. Film.

Manet, Édouard. *Le Déjeuner sur l'herbe*. Painting.

Marsh, Jan. *The Pre-Raphaelite Circle: National Portrait Gallery Insights*. London: National Portrait Gallery, 2005. Print.

_____, and Gerrish Nunn. *Pre-Raphaelite Women Artists*. New York: Thames and Hudson, 1999. Print.

Maslin, Janet. Review of *The Game*. *New York Times* 12 Sept. 1997: C1. Print.

McFarlane, Brian. "Reading Film and Literature." *The Cambridge Companion to Literature on Screen*. Cambridge Companions Series. Edited by Deborah Cartmell and Imelda Whelehan. Cambridge: Cambridge University Press, 2007. 15–28. Print.

Millais, John Everett. *The Bridge of Sighs*. 1858. Victoria and Albert Museum. Etching.

Monet, Claude. *Poppies, Near Argenteuil*. 1873. Painting.

Mulvey, Laura. "Visual Pleasure and Narrative Cinema." *Screen* 16.3 (1975): 6–18. Print.

Naremore, James. "Introduction: Film and the Reign of Adaptation." *Film Adaptation*. New Brunswick: Rutgers University Press, 2000. 1–16. Print.

Olshen, Barry N. *John Fowles*. New York: Frederick Ungar, 1978. Print.

Onega, Susana. *Form and Meaning in the Novels of John Fowles*. Ann Arbor: UMI Research Press, 1989. Print.

Parsons, John Robert Parsons. Photograph of Jane Burden Morris. 1865. Photography.

Pinter, Harold. Screenplay for *The French Lieutenant's Woman*. Boston: Little, Brown, 1981. Print.

Rau, Cheryl. Review of *The Game*. *CU-Denver Advocate* 24 Sept. 1997: 9. Print.

Reed, Rex. "Candice Bergen." *Travolta to Keaton*. New York: William Morrow, 1979. 134–38. Print.

Return of the Magus. Directed by Mark Pearce. Screenplay by Kirki Kefalea. Interviews with and performances by John Fowles. Athens: Inkas Productions, 1999–2000. Video.

Roe, Diane. *The Rossettis in Wonderland: A Victorian Family History*. London: Haus Press, 2011. Print.

Romano, Carlin. "A Conversation with John Fowles." *Boulevard* 2 (Spring 1987): 37–52. Reprinted in Vipond, *Conversations*, pp. 134–48. Print.

Rossetti, Dante Gabriel. *The Day Dream*. 1880. Victoria and Albert Museum. Painting.

_____. *Writing on the Sand*. 1858–59. British Museum. Painting.

Rossetti, Christina. *The Complete Poems*. London: Penguin, 2005. Print.

Salami, Mahmoud. *John Fowles's Fiction and the Poetics of Postmodernism*. Cranbury, NJ: Associated University Presses, 1992. Print.

Sandys, Frederick. *If He Would Come Today*. Illustration for poetry by Christina Rossetti in *The Argosy*, midsummer 1886. The Victorian Web. Wood engraving.

Scholes, Robert. *Fabulation and Metafiction*. Champaign: University of Illinois Press, 1979. Print.

Singh, Raman K. "An Encounter with John Fowles." *Journal of Modern Literature* 8 (1980): 181–202. Print.

Stam, Robert. *Literature Through Film: Realism, Magic, and the Art of Adaptation*. Oxford: Blackwell, 2005. Print.

_____, and Alessandra Raengo, eds. *Literature and Film: A Guide to the Theory and Practice of Film Adaptation*. Oxford: Blackwell, 2005. Print.

Stamp, Terence. *Double Feature*. London: Bloomsbury Press, 1989. Print.

Stephenson, William. *Fowles's The French Lieutenant's Woman*. London: Continuum, 2007. Print.

Stokes, Marianne. *Melisande*. 1895. Wallraf-Richartz Museum. Painting.

Streitfeld, David. "A Writer Blocked." *Washington Post* 6 May 1996: D1. Print.

Tarbox, Katherine. *The Art of John Fowles*. Athens: University of Georgia Press, 1988. Print.

Tennyson, Alfred. *Selected Poems*. Penguin Classics. London: Penguin, 2008. Print.

Todorov, Tzvetan. *The Fantastic: A Structural Approach to a Literary Genre*. Translated by Richard Howard. Ithaca: Cornell University Press, 1975.

Tringham, David. *The Last Chapter*. Screenplay adapted from "The Final Chapter," unpublished story by Fowles in the John Fowles Collection, Harry Ransom Center for the Humanities, Austin, TX. Series 2, Box 39, Folder 5. Produced as a short film by Cassius Film Productions, 1972, directed by Tringham, and re-released as a DVD extra accompanying *Private Road* as BFI Flipside 014. Typescript.

_____. Letter to Michelle Buchberger, 13 Mar. 2013. Print.

Truffaut, François. "Une certain tendance du cinéma français." *Cahiers du Cinéma*, 1954. Print.

_____. *Hitchcock*, 2d ed. New York: Simon & Schuster, 1984.

Uccello, Paolo. *Hunt in the Forest*. 1470. Ashmolean Museum, Oxford. Painting.

_____. *Saint George and the Dragon*. 1470. The National Gallery, London. Painting.

Vipond, Dianne L. *Conversations with John Fowles*. Jackson: University Press of Mississippi, 1999. Print.

_____. "*The Ebony Tower* and the Search for Meaning." In *John Fowles*. Ed. James Acheson. New Casebooks. Basingstoke: Palgrave Macmillan, 2013. 132–45. Print.

Waite, A.E. *The Pictorial Key to the Tarot: With 78 Plates, Illustrating the Greater and Lesser Arcana, from Designs by Pamela Colman Smith*. 1911; reprinted Mineola, NY: Dover, 2005. Print.

Warburton, Edna Eileen Hand. *John Fowles and the Dead Woman: The Theme of Carnal Knowledge and the Technique of Source Inversion in John Fowles's Fiction*. University of Pennsylvania doctoral dissertation, 1980. 172–218. Print.

_____. *John Fowles: A Life in Two Worlds*. New York: Viking Penguin, 2004. Print.

Waugh, Patricia. *Metafiction: The Theory and Practice of Self-Conscious Fiction*. New Accents. New York: Methuen, 1984. Print.

Whistler, James McNeill. *Symphony in White, No. 1: The White Girl*. 1862. National Gallery, Washington, DC. Painting.

Woodcock, Bruce. *Male Mythologies: John Fowles and Masculinity*. Totowa, NJ: Barnes & Noble, 1984. Print.

Yallop, Richard. "The Reluctant Guru." *The Guardian* 9 June 1977: n.p. Print.

Zinoman, Jason. *Shock Value: How a Few Eccentric Outsiders Gave Us Nightmares, Conquered Hollywood, and Invented Modern Horror*. New York: Penguin, 2011. Print.

About the Contributors

James **Aubrey** is a professor of English at Metropolitan State University of Denver. His publications include several articles on John Fowles, as well as *John Fowles: A Reference Companion* (Greenwood, 1991) and *John Fowles and Nature: Fourteen Perspectives on Landscape* (Associated University Presses, 1999). His research interests include the literature and cinema of India.

Michelle **Buchberger** is an assistant professor of English at Miami University, Ohio. She earned a Ph.D. in English literature from Brunel University, London, and has worked in education since 1989, teaching in secondary and post-secondary institutions in the U.S. and the U.K. Her research interests include John Fowles and contemporary British fiction but have recently broadened to include interdisciplinarity and the creative process.

Carol **Samson** is on the faculty of the University Writing Program at the University of Denver. A short story writer and a playwright, she published stories in *Open Windows* and *Black Ocean Press* journals, and she wrote the play *After Tea*, based on the writer's diaries of Virginia Woolf, which was performed at the International Virginia Woolf Conference in 2008.

Craig **Svonkin** is an associate professor of English at Metropolitan State University of Denver, where he teaches literature and cinema studies, and serves as executive director of the Pacific Ancient and Modern Language Association. His scholarly interests include postmodern poetics and children's literature, particularly the novels of L. Frank Baum and J. K. Rowling.

Dianne **Vipond** is a professor of English at California State University, Long Beach, where she teaches twentieth-century British and American literature and has been involved in the preparation of secondary school English teachers. Her research focuses on the work of John Fowles and Lawrence Durrell.

Eileen **Warburton** is the author of *John Fowles: A Life in Two Worlds* (Viking, 2004). For 30 years a friend to Fowles and his family, she based the book on his unedited diaries, collected letters, private papers, public documents, and hundreds of hours of interviews with the author and his closest associates. She has been a programming administrator for numerous cultural heritage agencies and is the author of four books on regional history or historic preservation.

Index

Page numbers in **bold italics** indicate pages with illustrations.

Index

Index